# HINAYANA BUDDHISM

# Hinayana Buddhism

M Srivastava

MD Publications Pvt Ltd
New Delhi
www.mdppl.com

*Published by* :

**MD Publications Pvt Ltd**
"MD House", 11, Darya Ganj,
New Delhi - 110 002
Phone : +91-11- 45355555
E-mail : contact@mdppl.com
Website: www.mdppl.com

**ISBN : 978-81-7533-352-9**

Published and Printed by Mr. Pranav Gupta on behalf of **MD Publications Pvt Ltd** at Repro India Limited.

# PREFACE

Hinayana is a Sanskrit and Pali term literally meaning: "the low vehicle", "the inferior vehicle", or "the deficient vehicle". The term originated within Mahayana Buddhism, to refer to the older pre-existing schools of Buddhism. A more recent term Nikaya Buddhism has been coined by scholars to represent early pre-sectarian Buddhist Schools. Hinayana is sometimes said to be referring solely to the Early Buddhist Schools, and not to the current Theravada school, while sometimes it is held to be also cognate with the modern Theravada tradition. The legitimacy of using the term Hinayana to refer to the early Buddhist schools is disputed while use of "Hinayana" to refer to the contemporary Theravada is seen as pejorative. The term appeared around the 1st or 2nd century CE.

Known as the Theravada School, or the School of the Elders (Sthaviravada) also pejoratively referred to as the Hinayana (Lesser Vehicle) by Mahayana adherents, who claim that Hinayana emphasizes personal liberation/salvation in contrast to the collective liberation of the Mahayana (Greater Vehicle). The Theravada or Hinayana school is based on the teachings of its founder, the Historical Buddha. Known also as Gautama Buddha or Prince Siddhartha, the Historical Buddha lived in India from around 560 to 480 BC. For comparative purposes, his contemporaries were Confucius and Lao-tzu (the founder, the "old boy" of Chinese Taoism) - slightly later in the West comes Plato (427 - 347 BC).

The term Hinayana (smaller Vehicle) appeared only much later, around the first century CE, when teachings of a different nature appeared which were called Mahayana (greater Vehicle). In India, non-Mahayana or Hinayana sects developed independent from the form of Buddhism existing in Sri Lanka. Today, there is no Hinayana tradition in existence anywhere, although Theravada could be called the tradition most like Hinayana. The ultimate goal of the Theravadin and other non-Mahayana practice is to attain the state of an Arhat, as Buddhahood is considered practically unachievable for nearly everyone within this aeon.

Hinayana "Lesser Vehicle" and dates back to around 500 BCE, making it one of the oldest forms of Buddhism still in existence. It can still be found in Sri Lanka and some areas of Southeast Asia. Hinayana Buddhism focuses on monasticism and the struggle to achieve a saintly life. It is because it is focused on this, rather than on attaining complete enlightenment and Buddhood it is called the "Lesser Vehicle." Hinayana Buddhism follows the basic principles of the Pali canon and is often likened to primitive Buddhism. It focuses on the four Noble Truths and the Eightfold Path that places it closer to the original teachings of Buddha instead of Mahayana that has always strived to reinterpret Buddha's esoteric doctrine and make it universally acceptable.

Hinayana (Huinayanas) professes to follow the basic principles of the Pali canon and, by this standard, may be identified with primitive Buddhism. Certainly its emphasis on the four Noble Truths and the Eightfold Path places it nearer to the original teachings of Gautama than Mahayana whose express purpose was to reinterpret the Buddha's esoteric doctrine in order to make it universally acceptable.

I am very grateful to Mr. Pranav Gupta, Director of MD Publications Pvt Ltd, New Delhi, for his kind cooperation and support for this book.

**M Srivastava**

# CONTENTS

# 1

# Hinayana Buddhism
## An Introduction

Hinayana is a Sanskrit and Pali term literally meaning: "the low vehicle", "the inferior vehicle", or "the deficient vehicle". According to the MacMillan Library Reference *Encyclopedia of Buddhism*, it is a polemical term coined by Mahayana Buddhists to denigrate their opponents. The term appeared around the 1st or 2nd century CE. Its use in scholarly publications is controversial. There are differing views on the use and meaning of the term, both among scholars and within Buddhism.

The legitimacy of using the term Hinayana to refer to the early Buddhist schools is disputed while use of Hinayana to refer to the contemporary Theravada is seen as pejorative. In the Chinese, Korean, Vietnamese and Japanese languages, the term means small vehicle (meaning "small", meaning "vehicle"), and in the Tibetan language (theg chung) the word means "small" or "lesser" vehicle. The word Hinayana is formed of hîna: "low", "inferior", "deficient", "defective", and yana: "vehicle", where "vehicle" means "a way of going to enlightenment".

Hinayana is used by Mahayanists as a name to refer variously to one or more doctrines, traditions, practitioners or thoughts that are generally concerned with the achievement of Nirvana as an Arahant or a *Pratyeka-Buddha,* as opposed to the achievement of liberation as a *Samyaksambuddha,* wherein the *Samyaksambuddha* (according to Mahayana lore) is deemed to operate from a basis of vowing to effect the spiritual liberation of all beings and creatures from the suffering of *samsara* (not just himself or a small number of others). Hinayana is sometimes said to be corresponding solely to the Early Buddhist Schools, and not to the current Theravada school, while sometimes it is held to be also cognate with the modern Theravada tradition. Many hold that the term was coined to be purposely pejorative, while others do not.

- Hinayana as *doctrine* would (from a Mahayana perspective) include the Sutras taught by Buddha that admonish the practitioner to follow the *Sravaka* path or strive for *Paccekabuddha*-hood. In such teachings there is no emphasis on pledging to emancipate the totality of sentient beings from the pain and bondage of *samsara* - the focus is more on practice for individual liberation. However, the Buddha did not teach in this manner according to the Pali Canon. In the Pali Canon the Buddha never admonishes his disciples to strive to become a *Paccekabuddha,* and *sravaka* just translates as follower or disciple: *any* disciple of Buddha would be a *savaka*. There is thus no mention of a '*Savaka* path' as '*savaka*' refers to all disciples, not to a limited class of disciples.
- Hinayana as a tradition in general would include those schools who solely follow the sutras of the Pali Canon or the Agamas (being, Pre-sectarian Buddhism and the Early Buddhist Schools). Some recent Mahayanist scholars have also used the name Nikaya Buddhism to refer to these schools. Some of these schools actively rejected the Mahayana sutras during the time of the rise of the Mahayana, around 2,000 years ago.
- Hinayana as practitioner would be an individual of any school (including Mahayana) who practices to eliminate suffering according to basic Buddhist teachings; if successful, he is called an Arahant. (Similarly, a follower of a *bodhisattva* path in any school would be Mahayana in this sense.) As a follower of what Mahayana terms "Hinayana", he or she will not strive to become a

Buddha, nor will he or she take the Mahayana *Bodhisattva*-vow of pledging to come back into *samsara* countless times in the future in order to liberate all other sentient beings from suffering. Also, the '*Pratyeka-Buddha*' is regarded by Mahayana as being Hinayanist. Mahayana only considers the ideal of a *Samyaksambuddha* 'Great'; the other enlightened ideals are considered by Mahayana orthodoxy to be (depending on the translation) either 'inferior', 'degrading', 'base' or 'low'.

Within Buddhism the differing interpretations of Hinayana have consequences that are sometimes quite far-reaching. It is primarily the interpretation of Hinayana as a tradition that has led to the most concern, especially as many people have seen the term as a slur against Pre-sectarian Buddhism, Theravada and the other Early Buddhist schools (the Nikaya Buddhism–schools). These schools solely follow the sutras that are included in the Pali Canon, and which are aimed at helping to achieve the extinction of suffering, as attained by the Arahants.

Jonathan Silk has argued that the term "Hinayana" was used to refer to whomever one wanted to criticize on any given occasion, and did not refer to any definite grouping of Buddhists. In the Vajrayana practice tradition of Buddhism the Hinayana is seen as one of the three major yanas (or 'vehicles') of Buddhism, alongside the Mahayana and Vajrayana. According to this view, there were three 'turnings of the wheel of dharma'.

In the first turning, Sakyamuni Buddha taught the dharma as the Four Noble Truths at Varanasi which led to the Hinayana schools, of which only the Theravada remain today (although they object to the term 'Hinayana'). In the second turning, the 'Perfection of Wisdom' sutras were taught at Vulture's Peak and led to the Mahayana schools. The teachings which constituted the third turning of the wheel of dharma were taught at Shravasti and expounded that all beings have Buddha Nature. This third turning is described as having led to the Vajrayana.

## ORIGINS OF HINAYANA: VEHICLES AND PATHS

It appears that the distinction between vehicles and paths arises in early Mahayana sutras, such as the *Lotus Sutra,* where it is stated that there is one path - the path to Nirvana - but there are different vehicles. The vehicles are described (by Mahayana) as representing the fruit of the two types of Buddha found in the Pali Canon, plus the path of the Arahants. For instance, in Chapter three of the *Lotus Sutra,* there is a parable of a father promising three carts to lure sons out of a burning building, where the goat-cart represents the *Sravaka*-vehicle; the deer-cart, *Pratyeka-Buddha*-hood; and the bullock-cart, *Samyaksambuddha*-hood.

According to early Mahayana (as found in the Lotus sutra), it is the *vehicles* that are taught as a method for journeying on the path to enlightenment. It is here that we can see the basis for term being used to indicate differences of doctrine. The Lotus Sutra declares that the bullock-cart is "supremely restful", implying that the goat-cart and the deer-cart are inferior to the bullock-cart. This is where we begin to see the terminological origins for the term *Hinayana*: The *Sravakayana* and the *Pratyeka-Buddhayana* as vehicles inferior to the superior bullock-cart of the *Mahayana.*

The Dharmakshema Mahaparinirvana Sutra also speaks of the inferior nature of the Hinayana when compared to the higher level of the Mahayana. In that sutra the Buddha states:

"Noble son, there are also two groups of people within this great congregation: those who seek the Inferior Way (*Hinayana*) and those who seek the Great Way (*Mahayana*). In past days I turned the lesser Wheel of the Dharma for the sravakas, but now here in Kuœinagara I turn the great Wheel of the Dharma for *Bodhisattvas*."

The term first appeared in the Mahayana Prajñaparamita literature. Possibly the earliest instance appears in the *Perfection of Wisdom in 8,000 Lines* (*Astasahasrika Prajñaparamita Sûtra*), believed by scholars to have been composed some time between the 1st century BCE and the 1st century CE. Chapter

11 ("Mara's Deeds") depicts a conversation between Buddha and the *Bodhisattva* Subhuti, where in Buddha admonishes those *Bodhisattvas* who disavow this sutra in favor of certain unnamed Buddhist sutras.

In the following passage, the term *Hinayana* is translated as "inferior vehicle" (emphasis added). "Subhuti, do these Bodhisattvas appear to be very intelligent who, having obtained and met with the irreversible, the great vehicle, and then again abandon this, turn away from this, and prefer an inferior vehicle [...] this is seen as being done to these Bodhisattvas by Mara."

## SUBSTITUTE TERMS FOR HINAYANA

Mahayana Buddhists sometimes refer to all forms of non-Mahayana Buddhism, past and present, including the Theravada school, as members of the Hinayana grouping. This term, which literally means "the inferior vehicle", tends to relate to those Buddhists who were deemed by Mahayanists to have rather narrow aspirations instead of vowing (as the Mahayanists ideally did) to strive for the liberation both of themselves and all other sentient beings from *samsara*, the "Hinayanists" were viewed as being excessively concerned with their own individual release into Nirvana.

The term, "Hinayana", is now widely regarded as derogatory and inaccurate (at least in reference to the Theravada, but also to the other, already non-existent, schools). In the Mahayana tradition, the label Hinayana is attributed to the Buddha himself (e.g. in the *Lotus Sutra*). As it is a polemical term and represents a specifically Mahayana point of view, other terms have been suggested to describe the Buddhist schools which chose not to adopt the Mahayana sutras.

Among the terms that have been used as substitutes for "Hinayana" are the following:

- Early Buddhism – It refers to the variations within Buddhism (both Pre-sectarian Buddhism as the Early Buddhist schools) that were current before the Mahayana movement emerged.

- Early Buddhist schools -This term properly covers all the schools that existed before the emergence of the Mahayana. The arising of the Mahayana school of Buddhism (1st / 2nd century CE) went together with the adoption of new (previously not-existing) sutras, and introduced new (or emphasized old but not very central) philosophies such as the *Bodhisattva* and having the intention of liberating all sentient beings. Since this constituted a serious break with the previous traditions and customs that the earlier schools had in common, the Mahayana is seen as a 'reformist' or revolutionary movement, and not included in any lists of the early schools. Thus, there is a large correlation between the earlier schools and the label 'Hinayana'. Also the Mahayana itself never groups itself with the previously existing schools. Some of the later 'early schools' might have arisen (meaning: split off) from another, older, early school, and might have come into existence at about the same time as the Mahayana. However, these schools kept to the larger framework and attitude of the earlier schools.
- Eighteen Schools (or Twenty Schools) -This term is historically oriented, based on the lists of the various Early Buddhist schools. However, the list itself is numerically inexact since the exact number and the names of the schools differ between the various lists. These were the schools that the emerging Mahayana-movement was familiar with because they were existing at that time. Subsequently, these eighteen schools split up further into a larger number, and the Hinayana label could have also been applied to those later split-offs. Also, the Mahayana writer Bhavya (Bhavaviveka) says in the Tarkajvala that Mahayana is included in the eighteen schools.
- Southern Buddhism -This frequently used geographical designation is appropriately applied to the Theravada, whose centers in Sri Lanka and Southeast Asia are located south of the centers of Mahayana (China, Tibet, and Japan). In its early period, however, there was significant overlap between the geographical regions of Mahayana and the early schools.

- Pali Buddhism -This term only applies to the Theravada, whose scriptures (the Pali canon) are in the Pali language. The other "Hinayana" schools wrote either in Sanskrit, in other Prakrits (notably Gandharî) or in Buddhist Hybrid Sanskrit, a mixed language with both Sanskrit and Prakrit elements.
- Sravakayana Buddhism -This term, referring to the "œravakas" meaning disciples, followers or hearers. They who followed the Buddha and sought solely to eliminate suffering, thus culminating in Arahantship. This term originates (like the term Hinayana) from within Mahayana Buddhism, and thus faces some of the same objections as "Hinayana", though it is less obviously derogatory. *Savakayana* is a bit different in that it does not refer to any actual school but purely to a tendency or intention to be found in the individual; one might be a member of a Mahayana school, but be personally following a *Sravakayana* path. Furthermore, it contrasts with "*Bodhisattvayana*".
- Nikaya Buddhism -This recently invented term was intended to cover the same ground as Hinayana, referring to the nikayas or "schools" into which Buddhism was split by the beginning of the Common Era. It may be interpreted as "Buddhism as taught in the Nikayas", the five primary divisions of the Tipitaka. However, this term is only used among the Theravada - other schools used the term Agamas -so "Nikaya Buddhism" is a misnomer when applied to non-Theravada early schools such as the Sarvastivada and Sammitiya.
- Theravada -This term properly refers to only one school among many non-Mahayana schools that once existed, many of which espoused philosophical notions contrary to those of the Theravadins. It would be altogether inaccurate to refer to such Buddhists as the Sarvastivadins as Theravadins. Some scholars, such as Dr. Walpola Rahula, have pointed out that there was small contact between early Mahayanists and Theravadins, and have suggested that the term "Hinayana" was never intended to include the Theravada. Judging by the content of

Mahayana polemic, it seems certain that other sects of northern India were the primary targets of the "Hinayana" critique.

- Conservative Buddhism
- Mainstream Buddhism- This term might be considered derogatory by Mahayanists, as it seems to suggest they are fringe (when in fact they are the majority)
- Sectarian Buddhism
- Non-Mahayana Buddhism

## HINAYANA AS A PEJORATIVE

There remains an open and active debate regarding the issue of whether Hinayana was coined to be pejorative or merely classificatory. The arguments for the term as being pejorative largely depends upon the etymological roots of the prefix 'Hîna': Hîna- is defined as such: "inferior, less, low, base, mean, incomplete, deficient, wanting and so on." Since the meaning of 'hina' covers both a pejorative and non-pejorative meaning, it is difficult to come to a definite conclusion. The term could have been chosen because it provided both meanings.

Those who assert the idea of Hinayana as a pejorative logically also are among those who subscribe the idea of an early (historical) Mahayana schism, and who believe that there was a history of polemics between the early Mahayana and other early Buddhist schools. An argument used by those who consider Hinayana to be pejorative is based on the fact that if the term was to mean only 'Small or Lesser vehicle', then the term chosen would have been, "Culla" or in Sanskrit "Ksulla-ksudra" giving us Ksudrayana - though 'ksudra' has also had a history of being used in a somewhat pejorative manner.

Those who assert that the term was coined in a merely classificatory manner (denying the historical Mahayana schism and a history of polemics) believe that the usage of 'hîna-' as a prefix represents those "inferior": inferior because they do not lead to the attainment of full Buddhahood (*Samyaksambuddha*). We can find Mahayana Sutras and traditions which repeatedly admonish the trainee *Bodhisattva* not to criticise any of the Buddhist schools.

The mere fact that there is such a strong admonishment against criticising the Hinayana indicates that it was either a common attitude, or that there was a degree of defensiveness within Mahayana regarding this issue. By the 3rd Century CE, in the ethics chapter of Asanga's *Bodhisattvabhumi*, we find an explicit injunction not to criticise or reject the Hinayana texts or traditions, where Trainee *Bodhisattva*s are instructed not to "disparage the Hinayana, or over-encourage others to learn Mahayana".

Candragomin wrote a very influential twenty verse summary of Asanga's Ethics, written or summarised as a set of vows to be taken by a trainee Bodhisattve. The 15th Verse (derived from Asanga's chapter on ethics) cites "rejecting the *Sravakayana*" as a root downfall. Candragomin's vows were adopted by the Indo-Tibetan Mahayana tradition via Atisha, and are still used today by the Gelugpa and Kagyupa schools.

**QUOTES FROM MAHAYANA SUTRAS**

In the early centuries CE, the Mahayana tradition was making efforts not to criticize or condemn the Hinayana vehicles:

Lotus Sutra (Ch.14): A bodhisattva [...] does not hold other Buddhists in contempt, not even those who follow the Hinayana path, nor does he cause them to have doubts or regrets by criticizing their way of practice or making discouraging remarks.

However, the Buddha also emphasises that the *Bodhisattva* should only preach the Mahayana in response to queries, not the Hinayana:

"If there are objections or queries, one is not to answer them by resort to the Dharma of the Lesser Vehicle [Hinayana], but one is to explain only in terms of the Greater Vehicle [Mahayana], causing persons to gain knowledge of all modes".

The 18,000 verse perfection of wisdom sutra (an early Madhyamaka Mahayana sutra) indicates a progression of training and an all-embracing approach: *Bodhisattvas* should practice all paths - whatever is a path of a *sravaka,* a *pratyeka* or a Buddha - and should know all paths in the opening verses of the *Vimalakirti Sutra*: Reverence to all Buddhas, *Bodhisattvas, Aryasravakas,* and *Pratyeka-Buddhas,* in the past, the present, and the future, and [...] Of bhikshus there were eight thousand, all arhats. They were free from impurities and afflictions, and all had attained self-mastery. Their minds were entirely liberated by perfect knowledge [...]

However, it should be noted that the form given in the recently published Sanskrit edition of the *Vimalakirti Sutra* is different. It merely has *namah sarva-Buddha-bodhisattvebhyah,* with no reference to anybody else. The salutation, as given above, derives from the Tibetan translation. Furthermore, it is not found in any of the three Chinese translations.

## HINAYANA AND THERAVADA

Most western scholars regard the Theravada school to be one of the Hinayana schools referred to in Mahayana literature, or regard Hinayana as a synonym for Theravada. These scholars understand the term to refer to schools of Buddhism that did not accept the teachings of the Mahayana Sutras as authentic teachings of the Buddha. At the same time, scholars have objected to the prejorative connotation of the term Hinayana and some scholars do not use it for any school.

Some Theravada Buddhists have opposed the identification of Theravada with Hinayana. As Walpola Rahula noted in his *Gems of Buddhist Wisdom*:

We must not confuse Hinayana with Theravada because the terms are not synonymous. Theravada Buddhism went to Sri Lanka during the 3rd Century B.C. when there was no Mahayana at all. Hinayana sects developed in India and had an existence independent from the form of Buddhism existing in Sri Lanka. Today there is no Hinayana sect in existence anywhere in the world. Therefore, in 1950 the World Fellowship of Buddhists inaugurated in Colombo unanimously decided that the term Hînayana should be dropped when referring to Buddhism existing today in Sri Lanka, Thailand, Burma, Cambodia, Laos, etc. This is the brief history of Theravada, Mahayana and Hinayana.

The argument that the Theravada should not be considered a "Hinayana" school from the Mahayana perspective is based on a different understanding of the concept "Hinayana". The proponents of this view argue that unlike the now-extinct Sarvastivada School, the primary object of Mahayana criticism, the Theravada school does not claim the existence of independent dharmas; in this it maintains the attitude of early Buddhism. Some contemporary Theravadin figures have thus indicated a sympathetic stance toward the Mahayana philosophy found in the Heart Sutra and the Fundamental Stanzas on the Middle Way.

The Mahayanists were bothered by the substantialist thought of the Sarvastivadins and Sautrantikas, and in emphasizing the doctrine of emptiness; Kalupahana holds that they endeavored to preserve the early teaching. The Theravadins too refuted the Sarvastivadins and Sautrantikas (and other schools) on the grounds that their theories were in conflict with the non-substantialism of the canon. The Theravada arguments are preserved in the Kathavatthu.

The Monier-Williams Sanskrit-English Dictionary gives a translation of 'Hinayana' as: Proper Noun: "simpler or lesser vehicle. Name of the earliest system of Buddhist doctrine."

Hîna is defined in the same dictionary as follows:

- Left behind, excluded or shut out from, lower or weaker than, inferior to (abl.) Mn. MBh. &c.
- Left out, wanting, omitted MBh.
- Defeated or worsted (in a lawsuit) Yajñ.
- Deficient, defective, faulty, insufficient, short, incomplete, poor, little, low, vile, bad, base, mean sBr. &c. &c
- Bereft or deprived of, free from, devoid or destitute of, without (instr., abl., loc., acc., or comp)

- *Pranair hînah* 'bereft of breath or life'
- Mantrad or mantrato hË%, 'devoid of sacred knowledge') Mundup. Katysr. Mn. MBh. &c
- Lost or strayed from (a caravan) Pan. i, 4, 23 Kaœ.
- Brought low, broken down in circumstances srS.
- M. a faulty or defective witness (of five kinds, viz. anya-vadin, kriya-dvecin, nôpasthayin, nir-uttara, ahûsa-prapalâyin) Yajñ. Sch.
- Subtraction (vyavakalana) MW.
- Mesua Ferrea L.
- (A), f. a female mouse (wr. for dîna) L.
- (Am), n. deficiency, want, absence (vela-hîne 'before the right time', unseasonably') VarB[S. Yajñ.

## PALI TEXT SOCIETY DICTIONARY

According to Pali Text Society's *Pali-English Dictionary* (1921-25), the word 'hîna is defined thus:

Hîna:

1. inferior, low; poor, miserable; vile, base, abject, contemptible, despicable
2. deprived of, wanting, lacking

## THE CONTEMPORARY AGE

In Buddhist terminology, the word "mappo" (in Japanese) is used to describe periods of turmoil and upheaval in society and personal life. It specifically refers to the decline of Buddhism after Sakyamuni. As Buddhism became more and more embroiled and entangled in worldly matters, there developed competing factions and interpretations. Mappo, which means the last age of the Dharma, symbolizes the lack of spiritual depth and vitality in Buddhism, as well as the world at large, despite the abundance of religious activity. As existential concept, mappo portrays our inner spiritual condition which is reflected in the outer world.

The essential meaning of this concept is that religion and the age becomes corrupt because the people within it have not maintained high spiritual values and goals. In terms of such an essential and existential definition, the reality of mappo in our time is evidenced in the absurdity, the ambiguity, the alienation, the anxiety, and the aloneness that plagues modern society. The absurdity of our mappo world is reflected in the immorality of war and of racism, both of which have paraded as being morally right. Absurdity is expressed in the easy resort to violence as a means to solve problems. It is reflected in politicians calling for peace but not cultivating the means and methods to achieve peace.

It is observable in the wide range of deceptions practiced all through society and particularly so in government. As social thinker Jacques Ellul has stated, "everything is under suspicion." Contemporary awareness of absurdity and ambiguity and of our mappo condition is expressed in the aimlessness of youth; in the difficulty they have in discovering clear values on which to base their lives. Patriotism has been degraded and exploited. History no longer appears to give direction. In a world technologically linked by commerce and communication, ideals have been used as cover-ups for exploitation.

The problem of values and ethics relative to issues of abortion or ecology highlight the ambiguities of modern life. The resulting sense of powerlessness and inner oppression in both the West and the East has stimulated many religious movements and quasi-religious movements, all of which have as their aim the provision of meaning and personal significance. Alienation, another powerful hallmark of mappo, has been eloquently expressed between social and economic classes, between generations, between sexes and races. This feature of alienation is probably the most clear and understood of the many features of our age. However, the deepest alienation, and the most powerful, is that from one's true self. This is the agonizing sense of alienation that is the result of failing to penetrate and appreciate the mystery and depth of one's own existence.

Our age attempts to prevent such insight through the blandishment of lures of material success. Such lures give a false sense of meaning based on the externals of possessions and distract our attention from the realities of ourselves, robbing our lives of a sense of inner worth. Despair becomes our companion and for the overwhelming majority of us, our age can easily be described as an age of anxiety, personal and social. We have lived each day under the constant threat of warfare of the most ultimate sort. Indeed, we have lived in such constant apprehension through decades of social division and threats of violence. Generations of racism, together with technological advances, have created an underclass which threatens the stability of society through violence or the varied consequences of economic deprivation and poverty.

These conditions cause us either to feel guilty about our own economic well-being or to become anxious about our security in society. We are constantly confronted with the loss of personal meaning in a mass society. Aloneness even in the midst of company becomes a common experience for hosts of people. There appears hollowness in life. Deep relations and commitments are often avoided, though we yearn for them. Apathy is widespread. Closure into a small intimate group is frequently chosen as a way of dealing with our loneliness, but even that proves a detour on the existential path of coming to terms with the reality of us.

All of us have had some familiarity with these traits. We all experience these marks of mappo: alienation, anxiety and aloneness at some point in our existence as we raise questions concerning the viability and integrity of our own lives. The ambiguity of our age is anguishingly visible as we look at the problem of religion which, though it flourishes, gives rise to the question as to whether it is part of the cause, rather than the cure, for the troubles of contemporary men and women. What is the problem of religion today? There are many ways to look at it. It is an intellectual problem. It is a social problem. It is a spiritual problem.

It is another basic indicator, along with alienation, anxiety, and absurdity, of our times as mappo. The intellectual problem of religion has deep roots in the development of western culture. In a variety of ways, the intellectual grounds of religious belief, the unity of faith and reason from which Greek philosophy and the Judeo-Christian tradition rose, have been eroded. There have been a variety of forces which have led to the secularization of life and the undermining of the meaning of religion. Five hundred years ago, while Pure Land Buddhism spread among the people of all classes in Japan, Copernicus and Galileo reoriented western man from a geocentric perspective to a heliocentric.

Man was no longer the center of the universe, and perhaps no longer the focus of God's concern as scripture had taught. Western man's world view thus had to change. Luther, the great Protestant reformer, dramatized and further contributed to the fragmentation of the western spiritual community. From Luther onward, the authority of the Pope never totally recovered from his challenge. Religion became a more individual and private or subjective affair. Next, Rousseau and the Romantics challenged the exaltation of civilization and rationality. The happy savage became the ideal. This view further undermined the spiritual disciplines of the West.

In the 19$^{th}$ century, Darwin dealt a strong blow to the sense of the sacredness of man, the individual created in the image of God, by confronting that image with scientifically demonstrable evidence of the theories of evolution and natural selection. Marx with his social theories showed religion as an exploitive force in the hands of the ruling class. Materialistic determinism replaced the will of God. And in this same chaotic age of new theories challenging old ideals, Freud showed that our hopes and dreams, our beliefs and faiths are all illusions resulting from our relations to our fathers. Religion, now viewed from the Freudian perspective, was a form of neurosis.

In the 20$^{th}$ century with Einstein, everything became relative to time, place, and perspective. In one brief century, one long lifespan, all the traditional supports for faith were weakened and washed away. The successive wars and struggles left individuals with little to hold on to as a basis for their lives, except the struggle somehow to survive and be happy for themselves alone. Yet they we survive in a world of interdependence and interrelatedness, our lives affected by and affecting the lives of others whose faces we may never see, names we may never know. Whatever our view of religion, and regardless of the contemporary erosion of its traditional supports, we are every day confronting the spiritual reality of issues and problems which are shaping our existential reality and the destiny of mankind.

Our dilemma is, how can we retain our humanity against the many assaults on our spirits coming from modern society? Spiritual reality runs in a deep fragile vein within our consciousness and has hidden roots still deeper in our subconscious. Nevertheless, the secularization and technological developments of our age have led to the dehumanization and depersonalization we also sense in the depth of our beings. Religious faith itself appears to many people to be obsolete. However, Harvey Cox, a Christian theologian surveying his own experiences in these terms has commented:

"..... ritual and religion are not going to wither away, and that the real issue now is whether they will be used for man's liberation or to keep him in bondage."

Cox also points out that, in regard to ritual, which is the expression of spiritual awareness and the experiential dimension of religion:

"Man never 'outgrows' rituals, although he certainly uses them for vastly different purposes and relates to them in ever-changing ways."

I myself believe that it is possible to view the variety of religious movements in these last decades of the 20th century as the vehicle of man's search for a new self which can transcend the emptiness of existence felt as a result of the conflicting forces of our mappo era. Robert Assagioli, a psychotherapist, notes in this connection:

"One major reason why the Self is coming back into currency is the tremendous search for self identity. Formerly an individual took himself so to speak for granted. He accepted himself as he was, or, more frequently, he identified himself with the group to which he belonged – family, tribe, clan, class, or nation or, if he was religious, with some great Being or God. But in our time, which may well be a time of total crisis, all these identifications fall away and the individual is thrown back on himself. This baffles him, he does not know who he is and this is the chief reason for the widespread 'existential anguish'.

In the effort to get beyond them to find the true self, youth particularly have resorted to a variety of means from the use of drugs to a return to religion and the occult. They have tried to experience a 'cosmic consciousness.' Assagioli notes:

"For these people, the awareness, first of the personal self and then of the Transpersonal Self as living realities, provide a needed structure that permits a steady gradual ascent. From such awareness also comes an understanding of the nature of spontaneous or induced experiences, leading to their assimilation into other parts of the personality."

From this standpoint, true Self-awareness can serve to direct and integrate human energies for positive, constructive human ends. If the contemporary spiritual protest represents in its deepest dimensions the apprehension of cosmic self-awareness, it may contribute to a deepening spiritual understanding by contemporary men and women, despite the variety of their belief and methods. Existential anguish may well be the condition for breakthrough to a fresh apprehension of spiritual reality and its root in our lives. Because of the great diversity and character of religious movements today, we may be prone to dismiss them as temporary expressions of the imbalance of the age.

However, it is possible that things of great importance may come from unexpected places. In this connection, I think of the thunder-egg rocks of Oregon in which the central core is the most beautiful agate, though from the exterior one might think to cast it away. It is a viable possibility that even the most bizarre religious group may possess a hint of deeper meaning. However, the fact that there may be positive meaning in any such religious perspectives should not make us uncritical in assessing their overall importance as true alternatives for dealing with the wide range of contemporary problems, for seeing our mappo condition with clear eyes.

The great upsurge of religious involvement today is clearly a protest against the dehumanization of life which we all experience, and a search for the deeper meaning in life which is our common hunger. Religious truth, and how it is to be determined among the multiplicity of visions, claims and experiences, remains the primary problem. If one listens carefully to many discussions of religion among thoughtful people, one may observe that the selection of a religion is frequently a matter of taste rather than truth. Individuals seek groups that already suit their preformed religious sensibilities.

There is also the question as to whether the significance of a religion is fulfilled solely through one's feeling of satisfaction and happiness, or when the life of the persons around him are concretely enhanced through a deeper concern and struggle for justice in human relations. In other words, is religion a purely individual matter, seeking one's own good or is its primary focus the attainment of good for all, even perhaps at one's own sacrifice? Mahayana Buddhism placed the emphasis on the latter, though not ignoring the former entirely. Relating to the issue of the good of others, which is the dominant spiritual principle in Mahayana Buddhism, we may ask whether it is a direct or indirect benefit to mankind.

Is the good of others believed to come about purely through a religious practice which is not involved with the lives of those who are needy, or is it brought about through identity with the sufferings of humanity in relation to its immediate needs? Is religion fulfilled within society or beyond it? For a great many people today, the ultimate goal of religion in some form or other is to bring happiness to the individual themselves. However, when we define the goal of religion as happiness, success, peace of mind or contentment, individuals are tempted to trade their true selves and freedom for a spurious freedom which relieves them of the need to make decisions or to involve themselves in human affairs. It is a subtle problem, but the old saying, "Ye shall know the truth and the truth shall make you free," remains a basic issue in religion today.

The problem of existence is always that of freedom versus security. Many modern groups offer a freedom by way of submission to a master who assures one of the rightness of his choice and assumes all the ambiguities of existence for the devotee. There is relief, but not true freedom, as witness the way in which persons become closed in, split between their minds and their feelings, accepting dogmatism and uncritical in reflecting on their experience. The diversity of religious expression makes the problem of truth very difficult. Most would give it up. However, it is an essential consideration which must be explored if there is to be firm and real commitment.

Commitment implies the truthfulness of that to which we yield ourselves, and we must reflect on that truthfulness. Since plurality can blunt the quest for truth, usually as a defensive measure, there is a tendency to discount and put aside other truth claims as merely interesting. Our age is much like the period at the end of the Hellenistic Age. Cults of all types then flooded the Roman Empire, so much so that when the Apostle Paul in the early Christian church preached at Mars Hill in Athens, where many itinerant religionists discussed their particular cults, he met people who brushed things off because they were dulled by repetitious novelty.

By contrast, search rather than religious novelty or cultism has characterized the history of religion in India. From its beginnings there, more than 2,500 years ago, Buddhism has been a search for truth. It was Gautama's goal to break through the veil of delusion that blinded humanity to things as they really are. Buddhism is a religion of enlightenment. It is not capitulation to taste or conformity to mere custom. In its more than two millennia of tradition, its basic search for truth has provided for a constant renewal and refreshment of that tradition. Shinran's departure from the tradition of his day was such a force of renewal and refreshment. Moreover, his contribution to religious insight as he carried out his own search for truth 800 years ago in Japan is still fresh and clear in its illumination of existential meaning and spiritual reality in this mappo world of our twentieth century.

Religion today has become completely voluntary, losing the many social sanctions of society and family that enforced adherence. There is no reason to belong to, or support, a movement where one does not see the essential truth which that faith offers to humanity. To grasp the depth and relevance of Shinshu today, the place of Shinran's teachings in Buddhism, and the religious roots of Buddhism itself, must be clearly understood, in the perspective of history and the development of Mahayana.

"All human beings have an innate need to tell and hear stories and to have a story to live by. Religion, whatever else it has done, has provided one of the main ways of meeting this abiding need. Most religions begin as clusters of stories, embedded in song and saga, rite and rehearsal ... The Hebrew scriptures are largely stories; so is the New Testament. Rabbis, saints, Zen masters and gurus of every persuasion convey their holy teachings by jokes, koans, parables, allegories, anecdotes and fables . . ."

The story of *Bodhisattva Dharmakara* (Hozo) who finally became Amitabha (Amida Buddha) is the central story of the Pure Land tradition, which establishes its authorization of practice and guarantees its hope. It was, indeed, through the Dharmakara's efforts the Pure Land was said to be created. Another story, that of the White path, was told by Zendo (Shan-tao) to illustrate the character of Pure Land faith and its understanding of life and religion. Throughout Buddhism, parables and stories constituted an essential and fundamental way of transmitting the teaching. The Lotus Sutra is perhaps the most outstanding for this aspect.

It contains numerous famous parables which have been universally employed in Mahayana Buddhism. It describes the *Bodhisattva* who proclaims Buddhism to the people as one whom:

"... preaches the mystic principle to them with a gentle countenance. If there be any difficult question, He answers according to its meaning. By reasonings and parables He expounds and discriminates it."

The major founded religions have developed biographies of their founders as the primary illustrations of the truth of their teachings. From varied traditions in Buddhism, eventually a life of Buddha was formulated and the essential features of his teaching and experience have been included. Teachings and religious experience can never exist disembodied. Religion can only take shape in living persons. Therefore, biography and story have always been essential to religion. In the case of biographies of founders, study will show that they vary from age to age and place to place. There is a correlation between the needs of an age and the way it views the founder of the teaching.

To some extent, we can observe this in the interpretation of Buddha's teaching career in the Tendai system, which had to account for the wide diversity in Buddhist teachings in China. The Mahayanists viewed the Buddha's life as an illustration of compassion, stressing that he desired to remain and teach rather than go directly into Nirvana as a result of his enlightenment. This understanding provided the basis for the *Bodhisattva* discipline, and the ideal of saving all beings. In general, every generation of a religious tradition has to rewrite the biography of its founder to highlight those aspects of his life which are important issues for their own day.

This does not mean to make up a new life and create legend, nor does it mean merely to twist and distort the biography for narrow purposes or deception. In effect, the biography of the founder must become a mirror for our own lives. We must see ourselves in it. It must answer our questions about life and spiritual reality. We cannot simply live with the stories of the past as they were given in the past. We must reinterpret them in terms of fresh meaning and renewed inspiration, for a perspective on our own lives.

Shinran's life is entangled in centuries of tradition. From such a confused historical basis, we must attempt today to discover the character of his experience in a way which we may assess and understand. Initially, Shinran's great-grandson Kakunyo composed the first biography, which he used as the basis for his own authority, and for gaining adherence of the believers to the mausoleum and its caretakers, the descendants of Shinran. Kakunyo clearly presents Shinran as a saint. Other schools of Shinshu composed biographies such as the Shotoden of the Takata School, which exalted Shinran even more in depicting his marriage in Yoshimizu to Tamahi, a daughter of Lord Kanezane, and also the high status which he had attained in Mt. Hiei.

In modern times, there have been important novels which took up Shinran's life. In this regard, the story by Yoshikawa Eiji (and its movie adaptation) is well known. Yoshikawa developed his clearly fictionalized theme against the background of Japanese search for identity in the postwar era. There is a reformist note as Shinran tries to change the corrupt ways of Mt. Hiei. Niwa Fumio in his lengthy work "Shinran To Sono Tsuma," focuses on the human Shinran, the man of passion. Kurata Hyakuzo in his famous works "Shinran and The Priest" and "His Disciples" (Shukke To Sono Deshi), written in the 1920s, presented a more compassionate and sentimental Shinran.

More recently there has been the film "Path of Purity" with Mikuni Rentaro. He portrays Shinran as a reformer and attacking the folk religion. He appears a true man of the people. Our problem today is, what kind of image can we discover in Shinran for our time? In effect, what meaning can he have for us? What meaning can he have for the Shin Buddhist, and for those attracted to Shin Buddhism in America? I believe there are three productive angles from which to observe Shinran's experience.

*First,* there is the outer course of his life, which we may determine through historical analysis. *Second,* there is the inner process of that life, as interpreted by Shinran himself, represented in the process called "Turning through the Three Vows." *Third,* there was the style of life which emerged from his experience, the style he designated as "Neither Priest or Layman," a style which symbolized an entirely new approach to religious existence and meaning.

In relation to the first point, we must locate and take seriously the sources of Shinran's disillusionment with the traditional religious institutions of his time and the direction this disillusionment set for his spiritual development. We must then consider the personal meaning and religio-philosophical importance of the spiritual process through which he passed as the basis for his re-interpretation of Buddhist faith. We must then observe the life principle which emerged from this experience, and which establishes the link between his life and our own.

Shinran can only be relevant to us if we can discover in his experience that which relates to our own. The most significant of the three points, and the one most immediately pertinent to the potential for Shinshu in the modern world, is Shinran's use of religion as self discovery. Historical analysis yields four periods in Shinran's life. From 1181 to 1201, during the period of his entry as a child into the Order and life on Mount Hiei, 20 years of traditionalism and ardent practice culminated in a religious dissatisfaction which led him down from Mount Hiei to seek a new path.

From 1201 until 1207, the second period was his life as a student of Honen, and residence at Honen's hermitage in Yoshimizu where he nurtured a strong commitment to Nembutsu teaching. The third period comprises his life in exile from Kyoto from 1207 to 1211, and the period from 1213 until 1235 he was in the distant provinces, moving from Echigo to Mito-Kanto, teaching the Nembutsu in what might well be termed an evangelistic period. Fourth, after 1235, he returned to Kyoto where until the end of his long life in 1263, he devoted himself to writing.

For him, and for us, the key turning point was at the end of the first period, when with rising spiritual dissatisfaction within himself, and dissatisfaction in relation to the religious institutions of his time, he left Mount Hiei at age 29. This chapter on Shinran's Life, and its potential for impact on our own lives, might well be retitled "Religion as Self Discovery," for such is the potential of his impact on twentieth century men and women. It is my conviction that religion should act to remove our masks and expose our excuses. Religion should penetrate our facades of goodness, our self-esteem, and reveal to us our true natures.

Frequently, religion provides a field for the ego to exalt itself in its piety, by measuring its goodness against those who seem not so good. Not so in the case of Shinran. Perhaps more than any other Buddhist figure in history, Shinran's thought is an outgrowth of his experience of grappling with Buddhist discipline and of plumbing the meaning of that discipline to its deepest level. The singularity of the religious philosophy which he formulated requires that we take seriously the development of his life as the inspiration of that philosophy. That development, that life process was for Shinran a process of self discovery.

When we place Shinran within this framework of self discovery, against the background of Heian Buddhism which had been his environment since age nine, we should be able to perceive how penetrating was his experience, and how unique the understanding which enabled him to shift the basis of religious life not only in face of the traditional Japanese Buddhism of Mount Hiei, but in face of the entire Buddhist tradition.

It is the importance of this religious dissatisfaction, experienced in his 29th year that makes it difficult to take seriously those of Shinran's biographies that are presented in traditional terms and contexts. Generally, ancient biographies were written not to present the reality of the individual but to exalt him and to glorify the group of his followers. Because it is an early biography, and was written by his great grandson, the biography of Shinran by Kakunyo does lay claim to considerable reliability and has been greatly respected in Shin history. Nevertheless, there is reason to believe that Kakunyo's work presents a highly idealized version of Shinran and has given rise to considerable sentimentality in the treatment of his career.

Kakunyo's text begins by congratulating Shinran's aristocratic background, his inclination toward religion and the great advances he made in Buddhist learning. The second chapter briefly states that Shinran visited Honen Shonin in the course of his spiritual search, and that through Honen's explanations, Shinran turned to Honen's teaching. Kakunyo relates that Shinran had a vision of Kannon who took the form of a beautiful woman, presaging Shinran's marriage. Shinran is pictured by Kakunyo as assuming the mission of Honen and Shotoku Taishi in promoting Buddhism among the masses. The exaltation of these personages is observed in the identification of Honen with Seishi, Shotoku with Kannon, and Shinran with Amida.

Undoubtedly, in competition with other schools of Jodo, Kakunyo is attempting to gain the mantle of Honen for Shinran. From that time on, in Shinshu, Shinran was looked upon as a faithful disciple of Honen. There follows in chapter 6 the exaltation of Honen and the influence he gained among the nobility. Two stories are included in which it is shown how Shinran's understanding was closely identified with Honen. Kakunyo details incidents relating to the banishment of Honen, Shinran, and other disciples from Kyoto and of Shinran's mission in the Kanto area as the fulfillment of his earlier vision.

In trying to establish the lineage of Jodo Buddhism through Honen to Shinran and then himself, Kakunyo blurs the whole point and basis for the significant impact which Shinran made in Buddhist history. There is not one word by Kakunyo concerning the inner struggle and momentous decisions which Shinran must have made, and thus it seems likely that the significance of Kakunyo's biography of Shinran was its perspective of authority for Kakunyo himself.

In modern times, a popular treatment by the famous Hyakuzo Kurata in his novel "Shinran" portrays Shinran as a very sensitive and sentimental youth, responding to the sadness of transiency which he experienced in the passing of his father and his mother. He depicts the gradual disillusionment of Shinran in religious practice against the background of the corruption and disruption of Mount Hiei. While Kurata does give insight into Shinran's experience of frustration and failure on Mount Hiei, he too easily parallels it to the experience of Honen and thus subordinates Shinran's experience to that great saint. The story of Shinran's marriage to Tamahi, the daughter of Kujo Kanezane is entirely wrapped by Kurata in romantic and sentimental legend.

These are two examples of the treatment of Shinran's life, one ancient, one modern, which - for purpose of their own - do not come to grips with the historical reality of Shinran as the basis for the unique thought he established. When we explore Shinran's life according to the existing original materials, we discover that when he was a youth he found himself in the monastery. The motives and conditions are quite unknown, but it cannot be because of the early death of his father, since his father also was retired to the monastery as were Shinran's brothers.

The turmoil of the Gempei wars, which marked the collapse of the political power and prestige of the Fujiwara, no doubt affected the fortunes of Shinran's family. Theirs was the Hino clan, a part of the Fujiwara. As fortunes shifted, the monasteries on Hiei, perhaps, became the family's only refuge. On Mount Hiei, rather than achieving high ecclesiastical status as depicted in tradition, Shinran is revealed in his wife Eshin-ni's letters (discovered only as recently as the 1920's) to be a Doso, a priestly functionary in the Hall of Continuous Nembutsu in the monastery. Eshin-ni wrote to her daughter:

"This letter is to certify that your father was a doso at Mt.

Hiei, that he left the mountain . . ."

The Hall of Continuous Nembutsu was concerned with providing ceremonies for nobility through recitation of the Nembutsu, the name of the Buddha, on behalf of the departed, a practice which had been introduced to Tendai through Jikaku Daishi on his return from study in China many years before. The significance of this activity for Shinran was his intensive exposure to Pure Land teaching in the many services. As he reflected on the teaching involved, on his own condition and that of the world about him, he may have become deeply aware of the unavoidable and ineradicable imperfection and weakness of human beings.

After 20 years of such practice and inner reflection upon its meaning, and upon his own human nature, his sense of evil and sin became so intense that it drove him to seek a solution through seclusion in the Rokkakudo, a chapel dedicated to Prince Shotoku in Kyoto. According to Eshin-ni, when he came down from Mount Hiei, convinced he was a failure, and filled with deep religious dissatisfaction and despair, he confined himself in Rokkakudo for 100 days. On the 95th day, he had a vision or dream of the Prince, and as a result, went to visit Honen. Eshinni reports on these events:

"He left Mt. Hiei, remained in retreat for a hundred days at Rokkakudo and prayed for salvation. Then on the dawn of the ninety-fifth day, Prince Shotoku appeared in a dream, indicating the path to enlightenment by revealing a verse. He immediately left Rokkakudo in the morning and he called on Master Honen to be shown the way of salvation. And just as he confined himself for a hundred days at Rokkakudo, he visited Honen daily for a hundred days, rain or shine, regardless of the obstacles.

He heard the Master teach that in order to be saved in the afterlife; regardless of whether one were good or evil, only the recitation of the Nembutsu was necessary. Since he carefully kept this teaching in his heart, he would say the following when people talked about the Nembutsu: 'Wherever

Honen goes, I shall follow him, no matter what others may say - even if they say I would go to hell, because I have wandered since the beginningless beginning and I have nothing to lose.'"

After instruction by Honen, Shinran became a member of his community. According to his own testimony, he became a worthy disciple and received a copy of the Senchaku Hongan Nembutsushu, Honen's autograph, a picture, and some statements in Honen's handwriting. Eventually, master and disciple had to part to go into exile because of persecution of the Nembutsu teaching brought on by the authorities of Mount Hiei. Shinran was virtually ecstatic in later life, as he recalled these crucial events of his 29th through 35th years. In that period, he gained faith in the Original Vow and, with that faith (shinjin), came release from the plaguing sense of his imperfection and anxiety about his destiny:

"What a joy it is that I place my mind in the soil of the Buddha's Universal Vow and I let my thoughts flow into the sea of the Inconceivable Dharma. I deeply acknowledge the Tathagatha's Compassion and sincerely appreciate the master's benevolence in instructing me."

At the heart of Shinran's experience in these times was a deep sense of sin which is reflected in Eshin-ni's brief account and which reached its zenith of expression in Shinran's paradoxical principle that it is easier for an evil person to be saved than a good person. Although we have no writings of Shinran directly from that period when he underwent the most important transition in his life, there are numerous confessions from his later life which represent those feelings and the awarenesses which motivated his search and decisions.

"Even though I take refuge in the Jodo Shinshu It is difficult to have a mind of truth. I am false and untrue and without the least purity of mind. We men in our outward forms display wisdom, goodness and purity. Since greed, anger, evil and deceit are frequent; we are filled with naught but flattery. With our evil natures hard to subdue, our minds are like asps and scorpions as the practice of virtue is mixed poison, we call it false, vain practice."

In the volume of Faith of the "Kyogyoshinsho," Shinran eloquently depicts the condition of beings as he must have realized it in the course of his own arduous endeavors:

"All the ocean-like multitudinous beings, since the beginningless past, have been transmigrating in the sea of ignorance, drowning in the cycle of existences, bound to the cycle of sufferings, and having no pure, serene faith. They have, as a natural consequence, no true serene faith. Therefore, it is difficult to meet the highest virtue and difficult to receive the supreme pure Faith. All the common and petty persons at all times constantly defile their good minds with greed and lust, and their anger and hatred constantly burn the treasure of the Dharma. Even though they work and practice as busily as though they were sweeping fire off their heads, their practices are called poisoned and mixed good deeds and also called deluded and deceitful practices; hence, they are not called true acts. If one desires to be born in the Land of Infinite Light with these deluded and poisoned good deeds, he cannot possibly attain it."

Later, in the same text, Shinran exclaims:

"Truly I know. Sad is it that I, Gutoku Ran, sunk in the vast sea of lust and lost in the great mountain of desire for fame and profit, do not rejoice in joining the group of the Rightly Established State, nor do I enjoy coming near to the True Enlightenment. What a shame! What a sorrow."

How shall we assess these expressions and the sequence of events that surround Shinran's departure from Mount Hiei? The starting point of that assessment must be that of our first chapters; religion today must be existential. By this, we mean that religion must be grounded in the concrete individual consciousness which confronts the multiplicity of problems and challenges of one's own time. The assessment of Shinran's spiritual crises from age 29 to age 35 ought to be so grounded, to be fully meaningful to modern men and women. Shinran, among all the Kamakura Buddhists, was uniquely existentialist, in that his life and his doctrine mirror each other. There is no explanation of his doctrine apart from seeing the inner struggle in his life, while his life inspired an understanding of religion never attained in Buddhist tradition. He was intensely personal and individual. Yuiembo recalled his words:

"The Blessed Sage would say in his confession: 'When looking deeply into Amida's Vow which was meditated upon during five kalpas, I found it was for me, Shinran alone. Hearty thanks to the Original Vow which is intended to save me, burdened with an enormous Karma.'"

The various personal confessions which Shinran made in his writings concerning his own attachments and passions drive home ever more deeply the personal and existential feature of his thought. However, it is a problem for many people that this expression of existential awareness is manifested in a negative way through a consciousness of sin or defilement and imperfection. Buddhism and modern people have a deep confidence in their ability to perfect themselves and to overcome whatever obstacles there may be in one's inner nature to reach the goal of enlightenment.

Human nature is considered as essentially good and concepts of original sin or the burden of Karma which Shinran proclaims are objectionable and inconvenient for most people. As an experience of self-discovery, however, Shinran realized through his practice how deeply rooted in our being are the lusts for power and ego-benefit. The abstract theory of egoism in traditional Buddhism became very real to him. He was undoubtedly unusual since thousands of monks over the centuries had practiced the discipline, experienced their imperfection and went on to do what they could - but, unlike Shinran, they did not leave the monastery nor develop a new philosophy.

In the case of Shinran, it must be recognized that the depth of his feeling went beyond that of the ordinary monk who may have undertaken the various rites of repentance provided by Buddhism, and who then in some confidence went about his duties without being greatly disturbed in his conscience. There is a strong emphasis on purification in Japanese Buddhism. Penitential rites and practices of purification flourished throughout the Heian period, but neither of these traditional avenues of escape or solace were enough for Shinran. Instead, Shinran realized the contradictions of our being and took them seriously. These became the starting point for him, and for him religion was reflection.

Some of Shinran's fellow monks may never have felt serious imperfection or inability. Their eyes were focused outward upon the world and its sins, rather than inward and upon themselves and their own reality. Dogen, for example, never speaks of his own deficiencies, though he was much concerned about the deficiencies of Buddhism in his day. Nichiren excoriates the sins of Buddhism in that same period but he does not show awareness of the potential sin of pride in his own being. Honen generally saw others as more in need of the Nembutsu than himself. He kept the Tendai precepts, which Shinran did not.

Although all these individuals, like their contemporary Shinran, rejected Hiei, they did not do it because they were moved by the deep sense of their own inability to fulfill its ideals. Rather, for them, Hiei was not fulfilling its own ideals, and their departure from tradition was more theoretical and abstract. In contrast, Shinran's was an existential departure; in that he saw he could not fulfill the Tendai ideal himself. With Shinran, there came a total redirection of religious existence, and of an understanding of the nature and basis of religious life.

With others, there was a modification either by intensification as in the case of Dogen - or of narrowing - as in the case of Honen and Nichiren - of principles which were already inherent in the earlier tradition. Shinran, leaving the older institutions totally behind, appears as a truly new departure in the understanding of Buddhism which we will take up in consideration of his thought.

# 2

# Methods of Processing Emotions in the Hinayana

## THE AIM

Buddhism has been described in many ways. It has been called a religion, a philosophy, a way of life and a psychology. Each of these descriptions is correct and emphasizes different aspects. Buddhism is a religion as it deals with questions of life and death and the meaning of life. It is a philosophy as it does not need the hypothesis of a god or of life after death. Buddhism is called a way of life as it teaches the way of non-violence and compassion. Finally, it is called a psychology as it investigates the working of our mind and distinguishes different types of consciousness.

There is yet another way to describe Buddhism, namely as a course. The aim of this course is first the lessening and in the end the elimination of human suffering. This goal is to be reached by using experimental phenomenology: investigation of our consciousness as it is presented to us by means of self-observation. The method, both in theory and in practice, and some methodological considerations will be treated in this chapter.

If we find ourselves in a situation that is not agreeable to us, there are essentially two different ways to attempt to overcome the resulting suffering. On the one hand we can try to change the situation itself. On the other hand we can try to change our consciousness of the situation in such a way that it is no longer experienced as unpleasant. Depending on the circumstances and our possibilities, these attempts will be more or less successful.

It is clear that on the one hand science, technology and democracy have contributed considerably to the way our world can be controlled. On the other hand, we have Buddhism, in particular the 'theravada' school (literary the 'teachings of the elder') that is focussed on the second possibility: eliminating suffering by changing our consciousness. Having completed successfully the course described above implies that one is accomplished in being able to change freely one's consciousness. It may take many years, but the aim is worthwhile.

## THE SMALL AND LARGE VEHICLE

At one time in history the Theravada Buddhists found themselves in a world having poor social-economic conditions. They were then criticized as "thinking only about their own enlightenment, while the world is burning". This criticism was taken seriously. As a result so called `Mahayana' (`large vehicle') Buddhism developed. The followers of this branch of Buddhism worked on improving both their consciousness and the world. To them it did not matter that the goal of overcoming suffering was going to be reached more slowly in this way: "we should reach nirvana as the last ones" became the *bodhisattva* vow of Mahayana Buddhism.

The Mahayana Buddhists used the pejorative term 'Hinayana' ('small vehicle') for the traditional Theravada Buddhism. The difference is, however, a matter of emphasis. A follower of Theravada, too, will find it important to care for our environment. But during the Theravada Buddhist course the attention is focussed on changing consciousness. The sooner one has reached the goal the better, because with an improved state of mind, it is so much easier to create order around ourselves.

Mahayana Buddhism became successful in China, Tibet, Korea and Japan, whereas the Theravada school throve in Thailand, Birma and Sri Lanka. It is tempting to explain this phenomenon by the difference in climate in the countries involved. In the north living conditions are more difficult, therefore controlling the environment is more important and Mahayana developed. As modern society is quite proficient in manipulating the environment, whereas the method of dealing with consciousness is little known, I expect in the future more influence of Theravada Buddhism. This chapter is about theory and practice as taught in this lineage.

**DETACHMENT**

One may wonder whether it is possible at all to overcome suffering by changing consciousness and if it is possible, whether it is desirable to do so. We shall only discuss the first question. The second one is left to the reader. Suppose we are in a restaurant and the waiter does not come. Even if we have plenty of time, we usually get somewhat irritated, often without noticing it. It may happen that we suddenly realize: "O, there is irritation in me", and at once that irritation becomes much weaker or even disappears completely.

This phenomenon is called 'néantiser' by Sartre. It feels like 'melting away' the emotion. It should not be confused with suppressing the emotion. This is the key to the end of suffering: we do not view ourselves as somebody that is irritated, but as somebody that sees irritation. We do no longer identify with the emotion. For a relatively light emotion as described, it is reasonably easy to apply the required detachment. This kind of phenomenon, of melting a light emotion, is relatively well-known.

For stronger forms of irritation or of suffering in general, this method of objectification is more difficult to use. A strong form of concentration is needed in order to do this. Otherwise the irritation, for example, may immediately return after we have objectified it and consequently it keeps control of our consciousness. However, concentration, albeit very essential, will not be the most important tool in reaching complete detachment.

## INSIGHT

In order to follow the Buddhist course one has to develop insight in the way our mind works. One of the fundamental statements of Buddhism is that our consciousness is selfless. Our feeling of 'self' is seen to be a form of attachment that has to be overcome in order to eliminate suffering. It is remarkable that in order to obtain this insight one has to overcome a strong emotional resistance, the so called attachment to self. For example that we are manipulated by our emotions because these consist of several components that diligently reinforce each other.

## THE FRUITS

Having completed the Buddhist path, or part of it, provides us with several sorts of profit. We have already mentioned insight in the functioning of our mind. Another effect is a considerable sharpening of our senses (something that can be obtained also through other kinds of training). Also we acquire the capacity to concentrate quickly. However, the most important result, apart from the elimination of suffering, is freedom. Buddha said,

- As the sea is pervaded by one taste, namely that of salt,
- In the same way my teaching is pervaded by one idea, that of freedom.

Some explanation is due here. Both Spinoza and Freud have remarked that our behavior is determined only partially by our conscious will but much more by something else. For Spinoza this something is our feeling, for Freud it is our unconscious. Often these distinct forces (conscious will versus feeling/unconscious) cause conflicts. Buddhism holds that if we are no longer attached to our feeling, then we are free.

Phenomenology investigates consciousness as it is presented to us, we may say internally. As was mentioned above, progress in the Buddhist course is correlated to gaining insight in the functioning of our mind. In fact it is necessary to have this phenomenological information in order to proceed on 'the path'.

One may question the value of information obtained by self observation: "Is it possible to be objective and precise?" The answer is affirmative. The reason is that Buddhist phenomenology derives its force from the systematic development of an essential discipline, namely meditation. During meditation mental tools are being built that are used for experiments. Experimental phenomenology is the principal method of meditation.

Nevertheless everything is internal, personal: with one's own means one studies the working of one's own consciousness. Therefore the objectivity of Buddhist phenomenology may be questioned. The only thing that really convinces is taking part in the meditation experience. But perhaps the following comparison is reassuring. Mathematics is commonly recognized as a discipline of great precision and objectivity. Yet that subject depends essentially on a notion of truth that is internal ('intuition').

Although in mathematics one uses calculations and formal proofs, there is always a need to have an intuitive judgment that verifies the correctness of the computation or the proof. Thus Husserl and Gödel rightly see mathematics as a part of phenomenology. Even if mathematics is about structures are beyond us and for example about the set of natural numbers 0, 1, 2... it is nevertheless the case that our contact with these structures runs via internal processes. Because of this phenomenological contact we are able to develop an objective mathematics concerning these natural numbers.

It is useful to compare Buddhist phenomenology not only with mathematics, but also with a science, say physics. In physics the theory is built on experimental data. It is not true, however, that in order to study physics; one first learns all the possible experiments and then the development of the theory. On the contrary, experiments and theory are essentially intertwined. At first some simple theory is based on some empirical data. Using these theory new questions may be asked and new and more refined or totally different experiments may be performed. Then the theory is extended.

The situation is analogous with Buddhist phenomenology. To the beginning student it is advised to have some confidence in the theory, but not to have blind faith. When experience is obtained, more and more of the theory can be verified. In this respect the theory is often compared to a map of an unknown country. When during a trip in that country the data on the map turn out to be true, only then we start to have real confidence in it.

## EXPLAINING APPARENT CONTRADICTIONS

Now we will explain how contradictions, which happen to occur in some Buddhist texts, are possible. Suppose some part of reality U is described using some language L. Some of the regularities observed in L are in fact physical laws, but may be confused with logical laws. If we extend the reality U to U+, but keep as the describing language L, then statements may result that contradict statements made about U. Although the contradictions are only apparent, because the statements are about different 'worlds', it may seem that logical laws are violated.

An example will be helpful. Consider a tribe living on an isolated island. Vision of the tribesman is such that they can only see the colors black and white. In their description of the world they say: "Something is either black or white." Although we know that this is for them in fact an empirical law, the people of the island are tempted to consider this as a logical law. Sometimes they use the words `white' and `non-black' interchangeably.

On some day someone has a mystical experience. In our language we can say that person has seen the color green. In the language of the tribe she says: "I have seen something very impressive. It was neither black nor white." For most of the people of her tribe she was saying: "It was neither black, nor non-black." Therefore on the island one may think she is speaking nonsense. However, we know that she is not.

There are, however, stronger contradictions. In his book Exploring Mysticism already mentioned, F. Stal discusses the following so called 'tetra lemma' occurring in Buddhist texts.

Even this contradiction may be explained. Simply consider again the tribe seeing only black and white. But now our mystic sees the color gray. Indeed gray is not white, not black. And it can be said that gray is both white and black. But also that it is neither white nor black and the examples show that contradictions occurring in texts of mystics are not a sign that something essential is wrong. Nevertheless it is preferable that descriptions of altered states of consciousness are free from contradictions in the sense of logic.

## THE PATH

We have already indicated briefly what the key to the elimination of suffering is. For example, by seeing in the right way that we are irritated, this irritation diminishes. This mental act of seeing what happens to us is called mindfulness. The path, as the Buddhist course is often called, consists of learning to become proficient in applying mindfulness. Once one has successfully completed the course, mindfulness is total and without effort. Then the mental formation of suffering can be fully seen and one is not touched by it anymore. This does not imply that one becomes cold or indifferent.

In order to get a better understanding on the nature of the path, it should be compared to a course to learn to swim. One can hear, read and speak about swimming, but progress can be made only by going into the water and doing one's exercises. Something similar holds for the Buddhist path.

## THE LABORATORY

The beginning student of the Buddhist course is advised to practice meditation daily, for example for a period of one hour. However, essential progress is usually only made possible by so called intensive meditation. 'Intensive' means more than eight hours a day; it means engaging oneself every moment of the day with the act of mindfulness. By meditating intensively for a period of ten days, one may make definite progress.

It is clear that for complete devotion to mindfulness one has to live for some time under special conditions that are suitable for 'the work'. Traditionally this happens in the monastery, the 'laboratory' for the mind. The word 'laboratory' may sound peculiar to some readers. Others may object to 'monastery'. What is important are the following conditions.

- Right living. A private room in which one is not disturbed.
- Right temperature. Not too cold, not too hot.
- Right food. Not too much, not too little; sufficiently nutritious.
- Right friends. Persons that take care of preparing food for the students should respect the meditation work that is being done. Moreover an experienced teacher is essential.

During the intensive meditation period (retreat) one does not speak, except with the teacher in a daily interview in which he follows the progress of the student and gives hints. The remainder of the chapter is a description of the exercises and the resulting experience as obtained during some meditation retreats. Although these experiences are my personal ones, the general tendency can be expected by anyone who follows the method.

## THE BASIC EXERCISES

There are three basic exercises: walking, sitting and prostrating (bowing) all with the aim of increasing mindfulness. These exercises have to be performed with the utmost care. To outsiders (and many students of Buddhism as well) they will seem absurd.

### Walking

One starts by standing with the feet next to each other. One says slowly in oneself: "standing, standing, standing". Then very slowly the right foot is lifted and put forward one step. Simultaneously one thinks: "Right goes thus", the thought exactly following the movement. After this step there is a little pause. Then one makes a step with the left foot and the thought follows: "left goes thus". One continues like this for one hour. The next time one walks, the mindfulness may be increased by naming more carefully the movements of the feet.

First "lifting, treading"; "lifting" exactly when the foot leaves the floor and "treading" exactly when the foot touches the floor again. Then one uses consecutively (each phrase for naming the movements is used for at least one hour): "lifting, going, treading"; "heel up, lifting, going, treading"; "heel up, lifting, going, dropping, treading"; and finally "heel up (extremely), lifting, going, dropping, treading, pressing front (foot), pressing back (foot)".

**Sitting**

One sits on the floor on a cushion with one's back straight and cross-legged and for example in full or half lotus position. The eyes are usually closed. One does not move, even if there is pain in the legs, one has an itch or something the like. One pays attention to one's breathing by following the movements of the abdomen: "raising, falling" or "raising, rest, falling". Again the naming follows the body. Sitting is done also for the period of an hour.

**Prostrating**

One starts by kneeling. One put one's hands together with the fingers stretched upwardly. In this position the hands are put before the breast and one thinks 'purity'. Then the hands, still in the same position are put before the forehead and one thinks 'compassion'. Finally one bows deeply, the elbows touching the knees and the lower arms and hands on the floor while keeping one's legs in a straight line. One puts the forehead in front of the hands on the floor, in this way raising one's behind. One thinks 'wisdom'. This prostration exercise is done each time for twenty minutes.

It is important to consider the basic exercises not as a walking, sitting or bowing exercise, but as training in mindfulness. During the retreat only these three exercises are done, one after the other non-stop. The only interruptions consist of the meals, contact with the teacher, practical actions (like washing oneself and dressing) and sleeping. It is important to keep the meditation in the form of mindfulness also during the meals and the practical actions. One continuously pays attention to everything that is there, to the input of our senses.

**The hindrances**

At this moment things are becoming interesting. It turns out to be impossible to perform the basic exercises correctly. In ordinary life we are used to avoid discomfort as much as possible. If our position is uncomfortable, then we move. During meditation this is not done. Therefore all kinds of problems arise as disturbances. These prevent the student from paying attention to the meditation object (like our footsteps). There are five groups of 'hindrances': lust, hatred, drowsiness, doubt and restlessness..

***Lust***

By this we mean feelings (or thoughts) that we like and cause desire. For example, the student may be thinking about the coming meal instead of paying attention to his footsteps or breathing. Lust may arise in many different ways. A characteristic attribute is that one is manipulated by it and cannot escape its grasp.

***Hatred***

This refers to all unpleasant feelings that cause aversion. This emotion manipulates us too. During sitting the student may be in pain, often extremely so. Some part of the body may itch. Or the student may be irritated. Because it is a rule not to move, the student is forced to confront suffering.

***Drowsiness [***

This is a well-known phenomenon. After a period of being bored, the student may rather fall asleep, than pay attention. Sometimes, during sitting, this actually happens. The attentive student will notice that he gets drowsy not because he is tired, but because he has to do something that he does not like and that causes mental and physical resistance.

### *Doubt*

The continuous alternation of pain, boredom and desire for something else makes the student wonder what he is doing. He doubts whether he should not have spent his ten days on a nice holiday. The reasons for coming to the monastery are questioned.

### *Restlessness*

Also this word is self-explanatory. Although it is often a negative experience, it is not classified as hatred. The reason is that restlessness may also be accompanied by lust. As an example in daily life we know the awaiting a meeting with a new love. In meditation restlessness is considered as a hindrance, because it prevents mindfulness.

## USING THE HINDRANCES

At first the student will try to fight the hindrances. Discipline and concentration are said to be important. But even when trying very hard, it turns out impossible to overcome the disturbances. Disappointed and perhaps desperate the student consults the teacher. An important method to continue practice, in spite of the disturbances, consists of so called 'switching'. This will turn the hindrances into something positive. The method is as follows.

As soon as a hindrance arises in the consciousness of the student, he tries to push it away in a gentle but firm fashion. If this succeeds, he then returns immediately to the original object of meditation, like the breathing. In case it is not possible to avoid the influence of the disturbance, the student changes his object of meditation. He switches to the hindrance itself and names it as 'irritation', 'lust' or the name of one of the other hindrances. As soon as the hindrance stops being disturbing, the student switches back immediately to the original object of meditation.

In this way it is almost always possible to exercise in mindfulness. An exception is the hindrance of drowsiness. If this occurs, the student may start the walking or even better the prostration exercise. In this way he does not fall asleep and moreover, obtains new energy. Using the method of switching the student will understand better what genuine mindfulness is. This is not always obvious. It may happen that the student thinks he is mindful, but in fact is not fully so: there is one thing in which the student is more involved, namely concentration. By switching diligently between concentration and the object of meditation, the student will notice the difference between mindfulness and concentration.

## CONFRONTING SUFFERING

Even if the method of switching helps the student with his meditation, it will not always be pleasant. On the contrary, it is almost certain that after skillful switching the hindrances will grow stronger and start alternating rapidly. The resulting hardship will be extreme strong pain or anxiety; restlessness. At this point the student starts complaining to the teacher. He wants to discontinue the retreat. For him meditation has become like dying. However, the teacher advises the student to continue. "In this life we often `die'. Each time when a new desire starts we are `born'. If the desire is strong, then we `burn'.

Finally if it turns out to be impossible to obtain what we want, then we 'die'. It is not that terrible. In our meditation we are working towards cutting through this circle of birth and death, this so called '*samsara*'. Finally we will not be born anymore and then we are free." The student who has managed to endure the retreat so far will usually have enough discipline to continue. He names his suffering: "This is suffering; this is suffering." But as the feeling is very strong, it does not melt away. The student is hoping that this will happen soon.

## SUPER CONSCIOUSNESS

Exactly this hope, this desire causes the discomfort to be even stronger. The situation is constantly deteriorating. Finally the student gives up all hope for improvement. Even then there is extreme suffering. At that point something unexpected happens. Suffering remains, but suddenly it is not bothersome anymore. The student clearly sees the following. "This is my body, this is my mind; both are burning, but it does not matter."

From that point on the method of mindfulness also works for strong forms of suffering. This probably has been made possible as the student has developed a strong form of concentration. This all may sound unbelievable. Perhaps the following may relieve some doubts. Suppose one pronounces repeatedly a particular word, for example the word 'rubber', then it may seem that the word looses its meaning. Or rather the sound 'rubber' and the concept 'rubber' are being separated. Usually these two components are melded together in our consciousness.

This phenomenon is well-known and is called a 'jamais vu' or a 'semantic fatigue'. Something similar may also happen with our suffering. Pain is being decomposed into two components: 'pain as pure feeling' and 'pain as something to run away from'. After this decomposition, using mindfulness, it is relatively easy to melt away the second part. This method of splitting consciousness into various parts is characteristic for meditation as taught in Theravada Buddhism, the so called vipassana meditation. As a result one is able to understand better the functioning of consciousness. The word 'vipassana' means 'insight'.

The consciousness of the student is now getting more and more 'pure'. The hindrances are less and less frequent. And if they do happen to come, it is easy to use mindfulness in order to melt them away. The student is able to see the growing of every hindrance; and then he uses mindfulness "as a gun to shoot it away". This is how it feels at least. If the student is a 'good boy' and applies mindfulness also to feelings of lust, then a strong and stable consciousness will result. All phenomena are the same as before and all mental faculties are the same. But there are almost no disturbances anymore. Pain is strong, but far away.

The hindrance of doubt seems to be conquered completely. "It is true indeed that it is possible to improve one's consciousness by means of meditation" the student is thinking. [As the student would find out later, a remarkable aspect of the new consciousness is that some of one's ordinary skills are impaired. Writing is rather difficult, as if one is doing it with the wrong hand. Reading is extremely tiresome. Estimating distances does not work well either. Objects seem nearer than they really are. Sometimes one is not well-balanced while walking. After some trial and error one quickly is able to re- establish correct estimation of distances. The left-right aspects of the walking exercises play an important role in repairing the disturbances in one's equilibrium.]

The altered state of consciousness satisfies descriptions occurring in mysticism. The student is taken by rapture and feels omnipotent. By melting away these kinds of narcissistic feelings the consciousness of the student is getting to be even more stable. It satisfies the statement of the Hindi "Atman is Brahman" (the self is god). The student thinks he is enlightened. However, as will turn out soon, there is still a long way to go.

## DISGUST

The student is now continuing to meditate having a consciousness that is neither pleasant nor unpleasant, but is nevertheless very exalted. There is almost nothing to do. The hindrances are gone and being mindful on for example breathing is effortless. At one moment the student notices that it becomes difficult to keep his super consciousness. More and more pressure is growing on his mind (or is it the head?). Even if it does not bother him, it is a threatening omen.

At any price the student wants to keep his exalted consciousness. But most unfortunately he cannot keep his strong concentration any longer and he falls back on what used to be his old consciousness. It turns out that this consciousness is totally neglected. It looks like a giant abyss. Desperately the student tries to regain his exalted consciousness. It does not work. Then suddenly the student looses all grip and falls in the abyss. The experience is indescribable. The following symptoms are some indications of what happens.

- Chaos: perception is completely confused; everything is turning.
- Anxiety: there is an 'infinitely' strong anxiety; all other anxieties seem to be derived from this basic one.
- Disgust: one is extremely sick; the stomach turns and one has to vomit.
- Craziness: it feels as if one is crazy; the mind and the body are present, but there is no ego anymore that controls everything.

The experience is more terrible than death at least that is how it feels like. Nevertheless thinking operates as usual. Panic stricken the student goes to the teacher, who is available 24 hours a day during the intensive meditation retreat, precisely for these cases of depersonalization. The student hopes that the teacher can perform some miracle. But that is not what happens.

The teacher reacts in an unexpected way. He says the following. "Remember the theory. Our existence has three characteristics: changeability, suffering and selflessness. Changeability means that no phenomenon is permanent. Even the visual image that we have of a solid object is not constant. If we look well, we will see many small fluctuations in the image as perceived. In this changing world we look for some hold, something that is constant. In our ignorance we consider our ego, our self, as a fixed remaining entity. But that is an illusion.

Why would our ego feel the need to be consolidated, if it were really permanent? Well, the changeability causes the circumstances in which we live to be often in conflict with the ideas of the ego and friction results. That is suffering. Finally, selflessness means that the phenomena, out of which our consciousness is built up, are essentially beyond our control. These three attributes of our existence, changeability, suffering and selflessness are in fact three aspects of one single truth. Now you have experienced yourself these three characteristics. This is important. Just continue your practice."

But the student is not at all interested in meditation anymore. He just wants to stop his depersonalization. The teacher notices this and gives specific instructions. "Instead of prostrating for twenty minutes, you should do it from now on each time twenty minutes longer. That is, first twenty minutes, then forty, then sixty and so on. Work well on your mindfulness. Then the nausea will disappear by itself. However, if it comes back, do not name it as `nausea' but as `knowing'. Do not feed it it."

## EMERGENCY

Back in his room the student has lost all motivation and does not want to continue the practice. However, stopping for a rest deteriorates the situation: the abyss becomes more threatening and nauseating. In utter despair he follows the instructions of the teacher. After a couple of hours it turns out that the exercises have a calming effect. Especially the prostrations function well against the sickness. Then the student wants to relax. But each time he slackens his mindfulness, he is pushed back into the abyss. It is like having a knife on one's throat forcing one to meditate fully. It is a matter of life or death. Being tired, the prostration exercises give new energy.

After having worked for many hours like this, being exhausted, the student is not sure whether he can go to bed. It may induce the nausea again. The student goes to the teacher and asks whether it is possible to go to sleep. "All right, sleep with mindfulness", is the answer. The student sleeps remarkably well. However, the next morning the emergency is still there. Only after some days of extremely hard work, the student re-establishes a stable consciousness without nausea. His ego feeling returns, albeit in another more light form. The student keeps some suspicion towards the method.

## BACK IN THE WORLD

Returning from the laboratory the student enters 'the world'. It turns out that he can function normally. Eventually this brings back some confidence to the student. However, sometimes there is nostalgia for the feeling of ego that he has left behind. But the new form of ego also has its advantages. An irritating situation can be relativized more easily. And indeed it turns out that all anxieties are corollaries to the fundamental one. By knowing this one, all other anxieties have become less serious.

## AGAIN

It may take a while before the student is motivated again to join an intensive meditation retreat. One of the possible motives is the memory of the super consciousness. Another reason may be, that on the one hand the student has gained confidence in the theory as parts of it turned out to be true, and on the other hand the theory promises much more. A description will be given now of the work done after one has chosen to continue the practice.

## REPEATING

The student notices that he has to start from scratch. The technique learned at the previous retreat has been lost. Fortunately progress is much faster now. Again there are hindrances. Again they can be used to increase mindfulness. Again there is strong pain or strong suffering. Again there arises strong concentration, making the extreme pain easy to take- again a stable consciousness results.

However, the teacher is not satisfied. "If there is strong pain, but you do not mind, then you first form the pain, while you throw it out later. That is a waste of the energy that it all takes. You should prevent the formation of the pain and in general of your feelings. Then you do not need to throw away anything. Cut through the addiction to your feeling. Stay with the input, with the contact of your senses."

The student is not able to do that. He again develops a super consciousness. Again he notices that he cannot keep it up. When he falls this time, the nausea is less strong, as it is a known phenomenon by now. After only an hour the consciousness of the student is stable again.

## THE FIVE GROUPS

In order to proceed from here, the following facts from the theory should be known.

Our phenomenological awareness (as always both physical and mental) can be divided into five groups ('*skandha*' in Pali; usually translated with 'aggregate'):

1. Input (of our senses) - Everything that we are aware of enters through one of the six senses. These are characterized by the following verbs: to see, to hear, to taste, to smell, to feel (to perceive by touch) and to think. The first four senses, namely the eyes, the ear, the tongue and the nose do not need further description. The fifth sense, bodily feeling, has many manifestations for example itch, pain and cold.

   There is no special location for this sense. The sixth sense is the mind. This is usually not considered as a separate sense, but rather as the place where all senses come together and are being processed. There are, however, some good arguments for classifying the mind as a sense. If we look up something in our memory, we obtain information that was not there before. If we have some thoughts after seeing some object, then, although that thinking is a consequence of the seeing, it is a separate input for our awareness. In the Buddhist theory there is also processing of the input, but this is placed in the groups (2) - (5).
2. Perception- This group will be discussed first, because group (2) is somewhat more complicated. After the senses have delivered the input to us, perception makes recognizable units from the data. It makes a classification; as they say "it distinguishes this from that".
3. Feeling- This group should not be confused with sense number five, the feeling of touch, itch, cold, etc. In group two we give a value judgment to our sense input. We say "This is pleasant, this is unpleasant and this is neutral." Our feeling indicates whether we like to have a phenomenon in our consciousness or whether we don't;

or that we are indifferent to it. Indeed, according to the theory feeling comes in three forms: positive, negative and neutral. Because Buddhism sees feeling as the direct cause of our behavior, group (2) is considered as very important. Positive feeling is equated with lust; negative feeling with hatred; and finally neutral feeling with ignorance. Lust, hatred and ignorance are seen as the three fundamental sins. Of these three ignorance is the most persistent one, since it is hidden and can change suddenly into lust or hatred. The reader may wonder why positive and negative feeling ('desire and sadness') are repudiated. One may reason as follows: "All right, one is better off not having negative feelings, but don't the positive ones form the meaning of life?" To this one may reply that it is certainly the case that for example sex and good food are pleasant. But the desire for it has a hold on us, it manipulates us.

The goal of Buddhism is to be free from this desire. The mentioned delights will remain pleasant, even after one is enlightened. But then they are pleasant on the level of group (1), the sensory data. Although the following simile is not perfect, one may compare the enlightened enjoying-without-desire to listening to beautiful music. We enjoy the music of Mozart, but we do not cry when the symphony is over. Having 'positive feeling', in the technical sense of Buddhism, means desire that is constantly directed to the object of desire, even if it is absent. A comparison with Calvinism is appropriate here. In this persuasion just as in Buddhism lust is considered a sin. However, in Calvinism it is something that is given a negative value: it is something that is not allowed and one should be ashamed of it. In Buddhism lust is considered as something that is present in us. It is considered a sin because it is the cause of suffering and bondage. But that is all.

4. Output (conditioning, volition) - According to Buddhism our behavior is conditioned. This applies to everything we do, both with our body and with our mind.

Cybernetically this conditioning can be viewed as the output of our body-mind complex: our nerves are firing to control our movements and our thoughts. Phenomenologically conditioning is correlated to volition: we usually have the impression that we want to do whatever we are doing. However, this volition can be seen as a side effect. Therefore it is adequate to describe group (4) simply as output.

5. Consciousness (state of consciousness) - In the first place consciousness is the integrating factor that unifies our input and its processing. So there is a difference between input, perception and consciousness. Input as such is still disconnected. (Sometimes when it is dark we may see that our visual input consists of small fluctuating parts.) Then, perception classifies the input, but only locally so. Finally consciousness gives a global image.

In the second place group (5) refers to our mood, to our mental state. It will turn out that the way our consciousness unifies our awareness is strongly dependent on our feeling. There is a strong interaction between the five groups. Feeling results from input, but in a manner that depends on perception and consciousness. If someone says something rude to us, then the resulting feeling depends on who has spoken to us, that is, depends on perception. Moreover the result of the unfriendly words depends on our mood of the moment. That is, our state of consciousness (group (5)) also influences our feeling.

Conversely, feeling plays a central role in perception, conditioning and consciousness. In the next sections we will give evidence for this. Because of its central role, feeling is therefore placed as second group, directly after input. The views of Spinoza and Freud concerning the bondage of our behavior are related to this theory. According to Spinoza our feeling determines our actions. According to Freud the determining factor is our unconscious. Buddhism reconciles these two views. Also according to this theory feeling determines our actions; however, large parts of that feeling are unknown. That is another reason why our ignorance is considered to be a sin: it determines our actions without our realizing it. And in addition we usually make rationalizations about our motives for those actions.

## SUBLIME CONSCIOUSNESS

The student analyses his experiences in the light of the theory of the five groups. Using strong concentration, he is able to endure strong pain, without being bothered by it. Probably that is because the connection between feeling and conditioning is interrupted. A drawback is that it takes a considerable amount of energy. If one could disconnect the link between input and feeling, then perhaps suffering could be overcome much more easily. For this it is necessary to know exactly how feeling is formed.

Work is resumed. As usual the pain slowly develops during sitting. As soon as the pain becomes unbearable the student automatically switches to super consciousness: "Ouch, now I can take it." But the teacher is dissatisfied: "You should not hide your pain, but stop forming it!" The student is increasing his mindfulness. As soon as a little pain arises, he sees it. But he also notices, that directly after the pain is melted away using mindfulness, a whiff of pleasure arises because the pain is gone. Previously he had failed to notice this.

It now becomes an exercise in swiftness of the factor mindfulness. It runs as follows. Pain; melting; pleasure; melting; pain; melting; pleasure; melting; etcetera. At first the student is not well synchronized with this flux of phenomena. Then it goes better. Suddenly the student gains momentum. Part of consciousness is disappearing. Almost the student becomes nauseated again. But using mindfulness the formation of the sickness is prevented. And then, quite unexpectedly, he can do it: siting quietly for a long period without having pain. It simply is not being formed.

Now things are going quite well and effortless. Consciousness is becoming calm and stable because little effort is required much more calm as before. As compared to the present consciousness that previous super consciousness is thick and treacly, due to the presence of neutral feeling. At the time it seemed to be the utmost experience. The student enjoys his present sublime consciousness. It is stable. Having had previous experience with an altered state of consciousness the student wonders whether he can loose it again. At first sight there seems nothing to loose.

## BROKEN CONSCIOUSNESS

Suddenly something happens. There is new pain. The student is unable to prevent its formation. How come? The pain-pleasure method does not work. Moreover it is not clear whether or not the student is bothered by the pain. But it is quite strong. The teacher is consulted. He says: "The pain (and more generally the feeling) is supported by your perception and consciousness." The student does not understand this remark. The teacher continues: "While working with the pain, you may try to notice small fluxes in your consciousness."

The student asks: "Should I name this and make it melt away using mindfulness?" The teacher: "Yes, but only do this when you have confidence in your practice. You will interrupt the continuity of your consciousness, of your existence. Everything will start turning like being in a roller coaster. Then continue your practice, even if you feel sick. After a while-no one can say how long it will take-the turning will stop. Do not try to step out of the roller coaster, otherwise you will fall down."

The student, who by now has got used to strange phenomena, is quite intrigued by these words. He continues the practice walking, sitting, etc. Pain is not being formed and after long sitting pain is being formed. At one moment it becomes almost impossible to melt away the pain then comes a strong outburst of pain. An even stronger blast of mindfulness is able to melt away the pain. By properly paying attention the student notices that his perception-right after the melting away of the pain-disappears locally for a short moment. The vision of an object lying in front of the student melts away for less than a second. It leaves a hole in his perception.

The student tries again. Pain; melting; and hole in perception. Pain, hole, pain, hole... faster and faster. Then suddenly pain is not formed anymore. But consciousness collapses also. There is only awareness, with every now and then a puff of perception or consciousness. Intellect appears to be functioning normally. The holes in consciousness are turning around quickly.

During the nausea this must have happened also. But then the student did not see any details because of lack of mindfulness. Also perception of the body is disturbed. During walking the room seems to be a jolting carriage. The student does not become sick, because mindfulness watches his stomach well. The experience is not pleasant, but not terrible either. However, when after two hours everything still keeps turning, the student starts to worry. Then he develops restlessness and wants to have a stable consciousness. There is nevertheless no nausea nor anxiety.

## GLUING CONSCIOUSNESS

The student decides to consult the teacher. His room is at a different wing of the monastery. Walking there, while developing strong mindfulness, the consciousness of the student suddenly is glued together. It just happened, without doing anything special. It is a new consciousness; yet everything in it is the same as before. The student changes his mind and starts walking back to his room. Then his mindfulness weakens and he falls back to his broken consciousness. This makes him decide to go to the teacher after all.

After the student has told what had happened, the teacher says: "Your practice is going well. Especially the way your consciousness has been glued together. Feeling will be substituted by mindfulness. In case your consciousness breaks again, name it as `knowing'. Do not identify with either the new consciousness, or the broken old consciousness." After the return to his room, it takes a couple of hours for the student's consciousness to stabilize.

Then he starts analyzing what has happened. The functioning of consciousness is apparently analogous to that of a television screen, consisting of rapidly fluctuating images. Normally we have the impression of continuity. Probably the reason is that feeling works as a kind of glue for these separate fluctuating images. By the meditation technique feeling is (temporarily) switched off. Therefore there is no more glue and consciousness will show itself in its broken form. The student does not understand well how everything works, but the phenomena are interesting.

## TYPES OF CONSCIOUSNESS

Back to work. The exercises are going well. There are few disturbances and sublime consciousness results. Pain is not being formed. However, later pain arises again. When this pain is being melted away, consciousness starts breaking again. The student thinks "O, that is all right; I know how to depersonalize!" But he is wrong; it is going to be tough. The depersonalization is different this time and as this was unexpected, the student is getting restless again. Working hard makes consciousness stable. It becomes sublime again, even more so than before.

After continuing the work, the student falls again in a depersonalization. He becomes angry: "There is no end to this!" This emotion of angriness has an unexpected effect. The broken consciousness is glued together instantaneously. But how ugly it is. Everything exhales malignity: the walls are angry, each footstep is angry, everything is angry. Work is continued. Consciousness breaks and the angriness in the walls suddenly disappear. The student tries whether consciousness can be glued together also with other feelings.

First he tries lust. It works; when consciousness is glued together with lust everything becomes luscious. The student has no objection and keeps this type of consciousness. In the dining room he notices, however, that he is taking too much food. A habit he had overcome already at the beginning of the retreat. When the desert comes he promises to himself not to take too much. Nevertheless, he is taking more than he can eat comfortably. Apparently his hands took more than his mind wanted.

Back in his room the student decides that a consciousness glued together with lust is undesirable and he gives it up. During the resulting depersonalization the student happens to feel insecure. This time, by accident, the broken consciousness is glued together with anxiety. Everything exhales this emotion. The student is walking around in the surrealistic world of a phobic. After having made a more quiet consciousness, the student goes to the teacher for his daily interview.

The teacher is dissatisfied about these experiments. "You have to continue the basic exercises. Feeling has to be substituted by mindfulness. Do not glue with feeling, but with mindfulness. The difference is that you are dependent on your feeling. Mindfulness on the other hand sets you free. Be not attached to particular forms of consciousness. Let them come and go by themselves. The final goal is freedom. When you will have it, sublime consciousness may arise as often as you want. However, if you make some type of consciousness now, then you want to do that. As a result there is hidden feeling in it and you will not be free. This means that for example your sublime consciousness will depend on something. Therefore it will be impossible to keep it. When finally you will be free, then you do not depend on anything, you have become `unconditioned'."

The period of intensive training is over, however. With good feeling the student returns home. So the work is not finished yet.

## POSTSCRIPT

The way to the elimination of suffering is the way to eliminate attachment to self. This means the elimination of our addiction to feeling. Personal experience of a small part of the way is described here. Striking occurrences were the following.

- Strong pain, without minding it;
- Super concentration and super consciousness;

- Depersonalization (very strong withdrawal symptoms);
- Sublime consciousness;
- Stabilization either by means of feeling or by means of mindfulness.

The possibility of using mindfulness to relativize problems is commonly known, albeit that usually no terminology for this act is given. The most striking aspect of the method of vipassana meditation is that this mindfulness, if combined with effort and concentration, can be used in a very powerful way. The path is not always pleasant, but it is quite varied and remarkable.

In the Mahayana tradition we experience a sense of gentleness toward ourselves, and a sense of friendliness to others begins to arise. That friendliness or compassion is known in Tibetan as nyingje, which literally means "noble heart." We are willing to commit ourselves to working with all sentient beings. But before we actually launch into that project, we first need a lot of training. The obstacle to becoming a Mahayanist is not having enough sympathy for others and for oneself-that is the basic point. And that problem can be dealt with by practical training, which is known as lojong practice, "training the mind."

That training gives us a path, a way to work with our crude and literal and raw and rugged styles, a way to become good Mahayanists. Ignorant or stupid students of the Mahayana sometimes think that they have to glorify themselves; they want to become leaders or guides. We have a technique or practice for overcoming that problem. That practice is the development of humility, which is connected with training the mind. The basic Mahayana vision is to work for the benefit of others and create a situation that will benefit others. Therefore, you take the attitude that you are willing to dedicate yourself to others. When you take that attitude, you begin to realize that others are more important than yourself.

Because of that vision of Mahayana, because you adopt that attitude, and because you actually find that others are more important - with all three of those together, you develop the Mahayana practice of training the mind. Hinayana discipline is fundamentally one of taming the mind. By working with the various forms of unmindfulness, we begin to become thorough and precise, and our discpline becomes good. When we are thoroughly tamed by the practice of samatha discipline, or mindfulness practice, as well as trained by vipasayana, or awareness, in how to hear the teachings, we begin to develop a complete understanding of the dharma.

After that, we also begin to develop a complete understanding of how, in our particular state of being tamed, we can relate with others. In the Mahayana we talk more in terms of training the mind. That is the next step. The mind is already tamed, therefore it can be trained. In other words, we have been able to domesticate our mind by practicing Hinayana discipline according to the principles of the Buddhadharma. Having domesticated our mind, then we can use it further. It's like the story of capturing a wild cow in the old days. Having captured the cow, having domesticated it, you find that the cow becomes completely willing to relate with its tamers. In fact, the cow likes being domesticated. So at this point the cow is part of our household. Once upon a time it wasn't that way-I'm sure cows were wild and ferocious before we domesticated them.

Training the mind is known as lojong in Tibetan: lo means "intelligence," "mind," "that which can perceive things"; jong means "training" or "processing." The teachings of lojong consist of several steps or points of Mahayana discipline. The basic discipline of mind training or lojong is a sevenfold cleaning or processing of one's mind. In Tibetan the commentary is called Changchup Shunglam. Shung is the word used for "government" and also for "main body." So shung means "main governing body." For instance, we could call the Tibetan government po shung-po meaning "Tibet," shung meaning "government."

The government that is supposed to run a country is a wide administration rather than a narrow administration: it takes care of the country, the economics, politics, and domestic situations. Shung is actually the working basis, the main working stream. Lam means "path." So shunglam is a general highway, so to speak, a basic process of working toward enlightenment. In other words, it is the Mahayana approach. It is the highway that everybody goes on, a wide way, extraordinarily wide and extraordinarily open. Chanchup means "enlightenment," shung means "wide" or "basic," and lam means "path." So the title of the commentary is *The Basic Path Toward Enlightenment.*

The main text is based on Atisha's teachings on lojong and comes from the Kadam school of Tibetan Buddhism, which developed around the time of Marpa and Milarepa, when Tibetan monasticism had begun to take place and become deep-rooted. The Kagyupas received these instructions on the proper practice of Mahayana Buddhism through Gampopa, who studied with Milarepa as well as with Kadam teachers. There is what is known as the contemplative Kadam School and the intellectual Kadam School. What we are doing here is related to the Kadam School's contemplative tradition. The Gelukpas specialized in dialectics and took a more philosophical approach to understanding the Kadam tradition.

The word kadam has an interesting meaning for us. Ka means "command," as when a general gives a pep talk to his or her troops or a king gives a command to his ministers. Or we could say "Logos," or "word," as in the Christian tradition: "In the beginning was the Word." That kind of Word is a fundamental sacred command, the first that was uttered at all! In this case, ka refers to a sense of absolute truth and a sense of practicality or workability from the individual's point of view. Dam is "oral teaching," "personal teaching," that is, a manual on how to handle our life properly.

So ka and dam mixed together means that all the ka, all the commands or messages, are regarded as practical and workable oral teachings. They are regarded as a practical working basis for students who are involved with contemplative disciplines. That is the basic meaning of kadam. The few lists presented here are very simple ones, nothing particularly philosophical. It is purely what one of the great Kagyu teachers regarded as a "grandmother's fingerpoint."

When a grandmother says, "This is the place where I used to go and pick corn, collect wild vegetables," she usually uses her finger rather than writing on paper or using a map. So it is a grandmother's approach at this point. You can just follow the book and do as it says which is extraordinarily powerful and such a relief. And that sense of simplicity still continues. It is so precious and so direct. I do not know what kind of words to use to describe it. It is somewhat rugged, but at the same time it is so soothing to read such writing. That is one of the characteristics of Jamgon Kongtrul-he can change his tone completely, as if he were a different author altogether.

Whenever he writes on a particular subject, he changes his approach accordingly, and his basic awareness to relate with the audience becomes entirely different. Jamgon Kongtrul's commentary on the Kadampa slogans is one of the best books I studied in the early stages of my monastic kick. I was going to become a simple little monk. I was going to study these things and become a good little Buddhist and a contemplative-type person. Such a thread still holds throughout my life.

In spite of complications in my life and organizational problems, I still feel that I am basically a simple, romantic Buddhist who has immense feeling toward the teachers and the teaching. What has been said is a drop of golden liquid. Each time you read such a book it confirms again and again that there is something about it which makes everythin very simple and direct. That makes me immensely happy. I sleep well, too.

There is a hard-edged quality of cutting down preconceptions and other ego battles that might be involved in presenting the teaching. But at the same time there is always a soft spot of devotion and simplicity in Mahayana Buddhism which you can never forget. That is very important. I am not particularly trying to be dramatic. If it comes through that way, it's too bad. But I really do feel extraordinarily positive about Jamgon Kongtrul and his approach to this teaching.

## THE PRELIMINARIES OR BASIS FOR DHARMA PRACTICE

In practicing the slogans and in your daily life, you should maintain an awareness of the preciousness of human life and the particular good fortune of life in an environment in which you can hear the teachings of Buddhadharma; the reality of death, that it comes suddenly and without warning; the entrapment of karma-that whatever you do, whether virtuous or not, only further entraps you in the chain of cause and effect; and the intensity and inevitability of suffering for yourself and for all sentient beings. This is called "taking an attitude of the four reminders."

With that attitude as a base, you should call upon your guru with devotion, inviting into yourself the atmosphere of sanity inspired by his or her example, and vowing to cut the roots of further ignorance and suffering. This ties in very closely with the notion of maitri, or loving-kindness. In the traditional analogy of one's spiritual path, the only pure loving object seems to be somebody who can show you the path. You could have a loving relationship with your parents, relatives, and so forth, but there are still problems with that: your neurosis goes along with it. A pure love affair can only take place with one's teacher. So that ideal sympathetic object is used as a starting point, a way of developing a relationship beyond your own neurosis.

Particularly in the Mahayana, you relate to the teacher as someone who cheers you up from depression and brings you down from excitement, a kind of moderator principle. The teacher is regarded as important from that point of view. This slogan establishes the contrast between *samsara*-the epitome of pain, imprisonment, and insanity-and the root guru-the embodiment of openness, freedom, and sanity-as the fundamental basis for all practice. As such, it is heavily influenced by the vajrayana tradition.

## ULTIMATE AND RELATIVE BODHICHITTA

The ultimate or absolute *bodhichitta* principle is based on developing the paramita of generosity, which is symbolized by a wish-fulfilling jewel. The Tibetan word for generosity, jinpa, means "giving," "opening," or "parting." So the notion of generosity means not holding back but giving constantly. Generosity is self-existing openness, complete openness. You are no longer subject to cultivating your own scheme or project. And the best way to open yourself up is to make friends with yourself and with others. Traditionally, there are three types of generosity. The first one is ordinary generosity, giving material goods or providing comfortable situations for others. The second one is the gift of fearlessness.

You reassure others and teach them that they don't have to feel completely tormented and freaked out about their existence. You help them to see that there is basic goodness and spiritual practice, that there is a way for them to sustain their lives. That is the gift of fearlessness. The third type of generosity is the gift of dharma. You show others that there is a path that consists of discipline, meditation, and intellect or knowledge. Through all three types of generosity, you can open up other people's minds. In that way their closedness, wretchedness, and small thinking can be turned into a larger vision. That is the basic vision of Mahayana altogether: to let people think bigger, think greater.

We can afford to open ourselves and join the rest of the world with a sense of tremendous generosity, tremendous goodness, and tremendous richness. The more we give, the more we gain-although what we might gain should not be our reason for giving. Rather, the more we give, the more we are inspired to give constantly. And the gaining process happens naturally, automatically, always. The opposite of generosity is stinginess, holding back-having a poverty mentality, basically speaking. The basic principle of the ultimate *bodhichitta* slogans is to rest in the eighth consciousness, or alaya, and not follow our discursive thoughts.

Alaya is a Sanskrit word meaning "basis," or sometimes "abode" or "home," as in Himalaya, "abode of snow." So it has that idea of a vast range. It is the fundamental state of consciousness, before it is divided into "I" and "other," or into the various emotions. It is the basic ground where things are processed, where things exist. In order to rest in the nature of alaya, you need to go beyond your poverty attitude and realize that your alaya is as good as anyone else's alaya. You have a sense of richness and self-sufficiency. You can do it, and you can afford to give out as well. And the ultimate *bodhichitta* slogans are the basic points of reference through which we are going to familiarize ourselves with ultimate *bodhichitta*.

Ultimate *bodhichitta* is similar to the absolute *Sunyata* principle. And whenever there is the absolute *Sunyata* principle, we have to have a basic understanding of absolute compassion at the same time. *Sunyata* literally means "openness" or "emptiness." *Sunyata* basically understands nonexistence. When you begin realizing nonexistence, then you can afford to be more compassionate, more giving. A problem is that usually we would like to hold on to our territory and fixate on that particular ground. Once we begin to fixate on that ground, we have no way to give. Understanding *Sunyata* means that we begin to realize that there is no ground to get, that we are ultimately free, nonaggressive, and open. We realize that we are actually nonexistent ourselves. We are not-no, rather.

Then we can give. We have lots to gain and nothing to lose at that point. It is very basic. Compassion is based on some sense of "soft spot" in us. It is as if we had a pimple on our body that was very sore-so sore that we do not want to rub it or scratch it. During our shower we do not want to rub too much soap over it because it hurts. There is a sore point or soft spot which happens to be painful to rub, painful to put hot or cold water over. That sore spot on our body is an analogy for compassion. Why? Because even in the midst of immense aggression, insensitivity in our life, or laziness, we always have a soft spot, some point we can cultivate-or at least not bruise. Every human being has that kind of basic sore spot, including animals.

Whether we are crazy, dull, aggressive, ego-tripping, whatever we might be, there is still that sore spot taking place in us. An open wound, which might be a more vivid analogy, is always there. That open wound is usually very inconvenient and problematic. We don't like it. We would like to be tough. We would like to fight, to come out strong, so we do not have to defend any aspect of ourselves. We would like to attack our enemy on the spot, single-handedly. We would like to lay our trips on everybody completely and properly, so that we have nothing to hide. That way, if somebody decides to hit us back, we are not wounded. And hopefully, nobody will hit us on that sore spot that wound that exists in us.

Our basic makeup, the basic constituents of our mind, is based on passion and compassion at the same time. But however confused we might be, however much of a cosmic monster we might be, still there is an open wound or sore spot in us always. There always will be a sore spot. Sometimes people translate that sore spot or open wound as "religious conviction" or "mystical experience." But let us give that up. It has nothing to do with Buddhism, nothing to do with Christianity, and moreover, nothing to do with anything else at all. It is just an open wound, a very simple open wound. That is very nice-at least we are accessible somewhere. We are not completely covered with a suit of armor all the time. We have a sore spot somewhere. Such a relief! Thank earth!

Because of that particular sore spot, even if we are a cosmic monster-Mussolini, Mao Tse-tung, or Hitler-we can still fall in love. We can still appreciate beauty, art, poetry, or music. The rest of us could be covered with iron cast shields, but some sore spot always exists in us, which is fantastic. That sore spot is known as embryonic compassion, potential compassion. At least we have some kind of gap, some discrepancy in our state of being which allows basic sanity to shine through. Our level of sanity could be very primitive. Our sore spot could be just purely the love of tortillas or the love of curries. But that's good enough. We have some kind of opening.

It doesn't matter what it love is of as long as there is a sore spot, an open wound. That's good. That is where all the germs could get in and begin to impregnate and take possession of us and influence our system. And that is precisely how the compassionate attitude supposedly takes place. Not only that, but there is also an inner wound, which is called tathagatagarbha, or Buddha nature. Tathagatagarbha is like a heart that is sliced and bruised by wisdom and compassion. When the external wound and the internal wound begin to meet and communicate, then we begin to realize that our whole being is made out of one complete sore spot altogether, which is called "*bodhisattva* fever."

That vulnerability is compassion. We really have no way to defend ourselves anymore at all. A gigantic cosmic wound is all over the place-an inward wound and an external wound at the same time. Both are sensitive to cold air, hot air, and little disturbances of atmosphere which begin to affect us both inwardly and outwardly. It is the living flame of love, if you would like to call it that. But we should be very careful what we say about love. What is love? Do we know love? It is a vague word. In this case we are not even calling it love. Nobody before puberty would have any sense of sexuality or of love affairs. Likewise, since we haven't broken through to understand what our soft spot is all about, we cannot talk about love; we can only talk about passion.

It sounds fantastic, but it actually doesn't say as much as love, which is very heavy. Compassion is a kind of passion, compassion, which is easy to work with. There is a slit in our skin, a wound. It's very harsh treatment, in some sense; but on the other hand, it's very gentle. The intention is gentle, but the practice is very harsh. By combining the intention and the practice, you ae being "harshed," and also you are being "gentled," so to speak-both together. That makes you into a *bodhisattva*. You have to go through that kind of process. You have to jump into the blender. It is necessary for you to do that. Just jump into the blender and work with it. Then you will begin to feel that you are swimming in the blender.

You might even enjoy it a little bit, after you have been processed. So an actual understanding of ultimate *bodhichitta* only comes from compassion. In other words, a purely logical, professional, or scientific conclusion doesn't bring you to that. The five ultimate *bodhichitta* slogans are steps toward a compassionate approach. A lot of you seemingly, very shockingly, are not particularly compassionate. You are not saving your grandma from drowning and you are not saving your pet dog from getting killed. Therefore, we have to go through this subject of compassion. Compassion is a very, very large subject, an extraordinarily large subject, which includes how to be compassionate.

And actually, ultimate *bodhichitta* is preparation for relative *bodhichitta*. Before we cultivate compassion, we first need to understand how to be properly. How to love your grandma or how to love your flea or your mosquito-that comes later. The relative aspect of compassion comes much later. If we do not have an understanding of ultimate *bodhichitta*, then we do not have any understanding of the actual working basis of being compassionate and kind to somebody. We might just join the Red Cross and make nuisances of ourselves and create further garbage. According to the Mahayana tradition, we are told that we can actually arouse twofold *bodhichitta*: relative *bodhichitta* and ultimate *bodhichitta*.

We could arouse both of them. Then, having aroused *bodhichitta*, we can continue further and practice according to the *bodhisattva*'s example. We can be active *bodhisattvas*. In order to arouse absolute or ultimate *bodhichitta*, we have to join samatha and vipasayana together. Having developed the basic precision of samatha and the total awareness of vipasayana, we put them together so that they cover the whole of our existence-our behavior patterns and our daily life-everything. In that way, in both meditation and postmeditation practice, mindfulness and awareness are happening simultaneously, all the time. Whether we are sleeping or awake, eating or wandering, precision and awareness are taking place all the time. That is quite a delightful experience.

Beyond that delight, we also tend to develop a sense of friendliness to everything. The early level of irritation and aggression has been processed through, so to speak, by mindfulness and awareness. There is instead a notion of basic goodness, which is described in the Kadam texts as the natural virtue of alaya. This is an important point for us to understand.

Alaya is the fundamental state of existence, or consciousness, before it is divided into "I" and "other," or into the various emotions. It is the basic ground where things are processed, where things exist. And its basic state, or natural style, is goodness. It is very benevolent. There is a basic state of existence that is fundamentally good and that we can rely on.

There is room to relax, room to open ourselves up. We can make friends with ourselves and with others. That is fundamental virtue or basic goodness, and it is the basis of the possibility of absolute *bodhichitta*. Once we have been inspired by the precision of samatha and the wakefulness of vipasayana, we find that there is room, which gives us the possibility of total naivete, in the positive sense.

The Tibetan for naivete is pak-yang, which means "carefree" or "let loose." We can be carefree with our basic goodness. We do not have to scrutinize or investigate wholeheartedly to make sure that there are no mosquitoes or eggs inside our alaya. The basic goodness of alaya can be cultivated and connected with quite naturally, in a pak-yang way. We can develop a sense of relaxation and release from torment-from this-and-that altogether.

## RELATIVE BODHICHITTA AND THE PARAMITA OF DISCIPLINE

That brings us to the next stage. Again, instead of remaining at a theoretical, conceptual level alone, we return to the most practical level. In the Mahayana our main concern is how to awaken ourselves. We begin to realize that we are not as dangerous as we had thought. We develop some notion of kindness, or maitri, and having developed maitri we begin to switch into karuna, or compassion. The development of relative *bodhichitta* is connected with the paramita of discipline. It has been said that if you don't have discipline, it is like trying to walk without any legs. You cannot attain liberation without discipline. Discipline in Tibetan is tsultrim: tsul means "proper," and trim means "discipline" or "obeying the rules," literally speaking. So trim could be translated as "rule" or "justice."

The basic notion of tsultrim goes beyond giving alone; it means having good conduct. It also means having some sense of passionlessness and nonterritoriality. All of that is very much connected with relative *bodhichitta*. Relative *bodhichitta* comes from the simple and basic experience of realizing that you could have a tender heart in any situation. Even the most vicious animals have a tender heart in taking care of their young, or for that matter, in taking care of themselves. From our basic training in samatha- vipasayana, we begin to realize our basic goodness and to let go with that. We begin to rest in the nature of *alaya*-not caring and being very naive and ordinary, casual, in some sense. When we let ourselves go, we begin to have a feeling of good existence in ourselves.

That could be regarded as the very ordinary and trivial concept of having a good time. Nonetheless, when we have good intentions toward ourselves, it is not because we are trying to achieve anything-we are just trying to be ourselves. As they say, we could come as we are. At that point we have a natural sense that we can afford to give ourselves freedom. We can afford to relax. We can afford to treat ourselves better, trust ourselves more, and let ourselves feel good. The basic goodness of alaya is always there. It is that sense of healthiness and cheerfulness and naivete that brings us to the realization of relative *bodhichitta*.

Relative *bodhichitta* is related with how we start to learn to love each other and ourselves. That seems to be the basic point. It's very difficult for us to learn to love. It would be possible for us to love if an object of fascination were presented to us or if there were some kind of dream or promise presented. Maybe then we could learn to love. But it is very hard for us to learn to love if it means purely giving love without expecting anything in return. It is very difficult to do that. When we decide to love somebody, we usually expect that person to fulfill our desires and conform to our hero worship. If our expectations can be fulfilled, we can fall in love, ideally.

So in most of our love affairs, what usually happens is that our love is absolutely conditional. It is more of a business deal than actual love. We have no idea how to communicate a sense of warmth. When we do begin to communicate a sense of warmth to somebody, it makes us very uptight. And when the object of our love tries to cheer us up, it becomes an insult. This is a very aggression-oriented approach. In the Mahayana, particularly in the contemplative tradition, love and affection are largely based on free love, open love which does not ask anything in return.

It is a mutual dance. Even if during the dance you step on each other's toes, it is not regarded as problematic or an insult. We do not have to get on our high horse or be touchy about that. To learn to love, to learn to open, is one of the hardest things for all of us. Yet we are conditioned by passion all the time. Since we are in the human realm, our main focus or characteristic is passion and lust, all the time. So what the Mahayana teachings are based on is the idea of communication, openness, and being without expectations. When we begin to realize that the nature of phenomena is free from concept, empty by itself, that the chairs and tables and rugs and curtains are no longer in the way, then we can expand our notion of love infinitely.

There is nothing in the way. The very purpose of discussing the nature of *Sunyata* is to provide us that emptiness, so that we could fill the whole of space with a sense of affection-love without expectation, without demand, without possession. That is one of the most powerful things that the Mahayana has to contribute. In contrast, Hinayana practitioners are very keen on the path of individual salvation, not causing harm to others. They are reasonable and good-thinking and very polite people. But how can you be really polite and keep smiling twenty-four hours a day on the basis of individual salvation alone, without doing anything for others? You are doing everything for yourself all the time, even if you are being kind and nice and polite. That's very hard to do.

At the Mahayana level, the sense of affection and love has a lot of room-immense room, openness, and daring. There is no time to come out clean, particularly, as long as you generate affection. The relationship between a mother and child is the foremost analogy used in developing relative *bodhichitta* practice. According to the medieval Indian and Tibetan traditions, the traditional way of cultivating relative *bodhichitta* is to choose your mother as the first example of someone you feel soft toward. Traditionally, you feel warm and kind toward your mother. In modern society, there might be a problem with that. However, you could go back to the medieval idea of the mother principle.

You could appreciate her way of sacrificing her own comfort for you. You could remember how she used to wake up in the middle of the night if you cried how she used to feed you and change your diapers, and all the rest of it. You could remember how you acted as the ruler of your little household, how your mother became your slave. Whenever you cried, she would jump up whether she liked it or not in order to see what was going on with you. Your mother actually did that. And when you were older, she was very concerned about your security and your education and so forth. So in order to welcome relative *bodhichitta*, relative wakeful gentleness, we use our mother as an example, as our pilot light, so to speak.

We think about her and how much she sacrificed for us. Her kindness is the perfect example of making others more important than you. Reflecting on your own mother is the preliminary to relative *bodhichitta* practice. You should regard that as your starting point. You might be a completely angry person and have a grudge against the entire universe. You might be a completely frustrated person. But you could still reflect back on your childhood and think of how nice your mother was to you. You could think of that, in spite of your aggression and your resentment. You could remember that there was a time when somebody sacrificed her life for your life, and brought you up to be the person you are now.

The idea of relative *bodhichitta* in this case is very primitive, in some sense. On the other hand, it is also very enlightening, as *bodhichitta* should be. Although you might be a completely angry person, you cannot say that in your entire life nobody helped you. Somebody has been kind to you and sacrificed him or herself for you. Otherwise, if somebody hadn't brought you up, you wouldn't be here as an adult. You could realize that it wasn't just out of obligation but out of her genuineness that your mother brought you up and took care of you when you were helpless. And because of that you are here. That kind of compassion is very literal and very straightforward. With that understanding, we can begin to extend our sense of nonaggression and nonfrustration and nonanger and nonresentment beyond simply appreciating our mother.

This is connected with the paramita of discipline, which is free from passion and has to do with giving in. Traditionally, we use our mother as an example, and then we extend beyond that to our friends and to other people generally. Finally, we even try to feel better toward our enemies, toward people we don't like. So we try to extend that sense of gentleness, softness, and gratitude. We are not particularly talking about the Christian concept of charity; we are talking about how to make ourselves soft and reasonable. We are talking about how we can experience a sense of gratitude toward anybody at all, starting with our mother and going beyond that to include our father as well-and so forth until we include the rest of the world.

So in the end we can begin to feel sympathy even toward our bedbugs and mosquitoes. The starting point of relative *bodhichitta* practice is realizing that others could actually be more important than us. Other people might provide us with constant problems, but we could still be kind to them. According to the logic of relative *bodhichitta,* we should feel that we are less important and others are more important-any others are more important! Doing so, we begin to feel as though a tremendous burden has been taken off our shoulders.

Finally, we realize that there is room to give love and affection elsewhere, to more than just this thing called "me" all the time. "I am this, I am that, I am hungry, I am tired, I am blah-blah-blah." We could consider others. From that point of view, the relative *bodhichitta* principle is quite simple and ordinary. We could take care of others. We could actually be patient enough to develop selfless service to others. And the relative *bodhichitta* slogans [slogans 7-10] are directions as to how to develop relative *bodhichitta* in a very simple manner, a grandmother's approach to reality, so to speak.

## ULTIMATE BODHICHITTA SLOGANS

This slogan is an expression of compassion and openness. It means that whatever you experience in your life-pain, pleasure, happiness, sadness, grossness, refinement, sophistication, crudeness, heat, cold, or whatever-is purely memory. The actual discipline or practice of the *bodhisattva* tradition is to regard whatever occurs as a phantom. Nothing ever happens. But because nothing happens, everything happens. But in this case, although everything is just a thought in your mind, a lot of underlying percolation takes place. That "nothing happening" is the experience of openness, and that percolation is the experience of compassion.

You can experience that dreamlike quality by relating with sitting meditation practice. When you are reflecting on your breath, suddenly discursive thoughts begin to arise: you begin to see things, to hear things, and to feel things. But all those perceptions are none other than your own mental creation. In the same way, you can see that your hate for your enemy, your love for your friends, and your attitudes toward money, food, and wealth are all a part of discursive thought.

Regarding things as dreams does not mean that you become fuzzy and woolly, that everything has an edge of sleepiness about it. You might actually have a good dream, vivid and graphic. Regarding dharmas as dreams means that although you might think that things are very solid, the way you perceive them is soft and dreamlike. For instance, if you have participated in group meditation practice, your memory of your meditation cushion and the person who sat in front of you is very vivid, as is your memory of your food and the sound of the gong and the bed that you sleep in. But none of those situations is regarded as completely invincible and solid and tough.

Everything is shifty. Things have a dreamlike quality. But at the same time the production of your mind is quite vivid. If you didn't have a mind, you wouldn't be able to perceive anything at all. Because you have a mind, you perceive things. Therefore, what you perceive is a product of your mind, using your sense organs as channels for the sense perceptions.

## EXAMINE THE NATURE OF UNBORN AWARENESS

Look at your basic mind, just simple awareness which is not divided into sections, the thinking process that exists within you. Just look at that, see that. Examining does not mean analyzing. It is just viewing things as they are, in the ordinary sense. The reason our mind is known as unborn awareness is that we have no idea of its history. We have no idea where this mind, our crazy mind, began in the beginning. It has no shape, no color, no particular portrait or characteristics. It usually flickers on and off, off and on, all the time. Sometimes it is hibernating; sometimes it is all over the place.

Look at your mind. That is a part of ultimate *bodhichitta* training or discipline. Our mind fluctuates constantly, back and forth, forth and back. Look at that, just look at that! You could get caught up in the fascination of regarding all dharmas as dreams and perpetuate unnecessary visions and fantasies of all kinds. Therefore it is very important to get to this next slogan, "Examine the nature of unborn awareness." When you look beyond the perceptual level alone, when you look at your own mind (which you cannot actually do, but you pretend to do), you find that there is nothing there. You begin to realize that there is nothing to hold on to.

Mind is unborn. But at the same time, it is awareness, because you still perceive things. Therefore, you should contemplate that by seeing who actually perceives dharmas as dreams. If you look further and further, at your mind's root, its base, you will find that it has no color and no shape. Your mind is, basically speaking, somewhat blank. There is nothing to it. We are beginning to cultivate a kind of *Sunyata* possibility; although in this case that possibility is quite primitive, in the sense of simplicity and workability. When we look at the root, when we try to find out why we see things, why we hear sounds, why we feel, and why we smell-if we look beyond that and beyond that-we find a kind of blankness.

That blankness is connected with mindfulness. To begin with, you are mindful of some thing: you are mindful of yourself, you are mindful of your atmosphere, and you are mindful of your breath. But if you look at why you are mindful, beyond what you are mindful of, you begin to find that there is no root. Everything begins to dissolve. That is the idea of examining the nature of unborn awareness.

## SELF-LIBERATE EVEN THE ANTIDOTE

Looking at our basic mind, we begin to develop a twist of logic. We say, "Well, if nothing has any root, why bother? What's the point of doing this at all? Why don't we just believe that there's no root behind the whole thing?" At that point the next slogan, "Self-liberate even the antidote," is very helpful. The antidote is the realization that our discursive thoughts have no origin. That realization helps a lot; it becomes an antidote or a helpful suggestion. But we need to go beyond that antidote. We should not hang on to the so-whatness of it, the naivete of it.

The idea of [that] antidote is that everything is empty, so that you have nothing to care about. You have an occasional glimpse in your mind that nothing is existent. And because of the nature of that *Sunyata* experience, whether anything great or small comes up, nothing really matters very much. It is like a backslapping joke in which everything is going to be hoo-ha, yuk-yuk-yuk. Nothing is going to matter very much, so let it go. All is *Sunyata*, so who cares? You can murder, you can meditate, you can perform art, you can do all kinds of things-everything is meditation, whatever you do. But there is something very tricky about the whole approach. That dwelling on emptiness is a misinterpretation, called the "poison of *Sunyata*."

Some people say that they do not have to sit and meditate, because they have always "understood." But that is very tricky and very hard to fight such people and never trust them at all-unless they actually sit and practice. You cannot split hairs by saying that you might be fishing in a Rocky Mountain spring and still meditating away; you might be driving your Porsche and meditating away; you might be washing dishes (which is more legitimate in some sense) and meditating away. That may be a genuine way of doing things, but it still feels very suspicious.

Antidotes are any notion that we can do what we want and that as long as we are meditative, everything is going to be fine. The text says to self-liberate even the antidote, the seeming antidote. We may regard going to the movies every minute, every day, every evening as our meditation, or watching television, or grooming our horse, feeding our dog, taking a long walk in the woods. There are endless possibilities like that in the Occidental tradition or for that matter in the theistic tradition.

The theistic tradition talks about meditation and contemplation as a fantastic thing to do. The popular notion of God is that he created the world: the woods were made by God, the castle ruins were created by God, and the ocean was made by God. So we could swim and meditate or we could lie on the beach made by God and have a fantastic time. Such theistic nature worship has become a problem. We have so many holiday makers, nature worshipers, so many hunters. In Scotland, at the Samye Ling meditation center, there was a very friendly neighbor from Birmingham, an industrial town, who always came up there on weekends to have a nice time.

# 3

# Hinayana and the West

Buddhism can be split into two main schools, Hinayana and Mahayana. The Lesser Vehicle, Hinayana, focuses on the teachings of the Gautama Buddha as recorded in the lessons known as sutra that he gave whilst in the flesh on the physical plane. With these teachings the intent is to rid one's mind of mental afflictions in order to free oneself from suffering. The Greater Vehicle, Mahayana, as followed by His Holiness (H.H.) Dalai Lama and the Tibetan people, adhere to sutra as well. Yet they take it one step further. The purpose for attaining an enlightened mind is so that you can then be in a position to assist all sentient beings. If carried out sincerely this pledge generates great compassion and a feeling of interconnectedness -the oneness of all.

It is called *Bodhisattva*, and can act as the fuel to propel one toward the ultimate goal. Once there you realise the true interdependence of everything. The Mahayana teachings can be further divided, as there is a set of "secret" teachings. The fact that they exist is no secret and you aren't required to roll your trousers up and do a funny handshake to receive them. They are secret because the masters only revealed them to the students of the highest intent and greatest mental capacity. Often to receive the teachings it requires taking the *Bodhisattva* Vow, in which the student vows to remain in the cycle of existence until all sentient beings are saved (enlightened).

Quite a big thing, a little bit more than giving up your

seat on a packed bus for someone else and waiting in the rain for the next one -it could mean several hundred more incarnations of suffering, losses and frustrations whilst the murderer down the street gets his act together and probably even means you helping him. It both comes from and generates the knowledge and feeling of the interconnectedness of life -a big part of the goal. These secret teachings are called Tantra or Tantric Teachings. Don't get too excited, there is no actual cavorting -not on the physical plane at least.

And most of the highest Tantric Masters are virgins! It is more to do with channelling and transmuting energy, sometimes sexual, for higher spiritual attainment. The Hinayana path just follows the teachings orated by Sakayamuni Buddha (the historical Buddha also known as Gautama Buddha) to his disciples whilst in his home of flesh. It is believed by the Mahayanists that Buddha was simultaneously teaching his more advanced students the secret Tantric teachings on other planes of existence. Some Hinayanists dispute this. The Tantric teachings are then split into a hierarchy of four; with Kalachakra being in the elite bracket known as Anuttara Tantra (Supreme Tantra).

This does not necessarily make it the automatic first choice for one's spiritual practice, as there are many factors to take into account when making a selection of this manner -a Porsche doesn't suit everybody's needs. Before I get on to the juicy stuff, just let me share with you a little of how a Tantric practice works. The aim, as in all Buddhism, is to achieve an omniscient mind and Tantra is the superhighway to achieving this goal. It works by meditating on the effect -basically you pretend that you already have a perfectly enlightened body.

More than that, through the empowerment conferred by the Tantric Master, you actually merge various aspects of your bodies both physical and subtle, with the Tantric Master and/ or the deity in question. Modern day personal development practices employ similar strategies to this; from axioms like "be the change you want to see in the world" and "fake it till you make it" to advanced NLP (Neuro Linguistic Psychology) processes where you merge yourself with and become your future selves. With Tantric Guru Yoga and Deity Yoga practices you mix your energy bodies with those of enlightened beings.

You can see why it's the superhighway. But before you can gain access to this wonderful freeway to *Nibbana* and beyond you require to be initiated. That's were the Kalachakra Empowerment comes in. A lot of us have received Reiki empowerments. When done properly this too is a Tantric Empowerment. Well, the Kalachakra empowerment is not dissimilar in principle, the difference is it will often take four or five full days, and you may be taking it simultaneously with as many as 250,000 people if you attend a ceremony on the Indian Subcontinent or a mere 10,000 if the ceremony is in the West.

To receive the empowerment you require to take certain vows of general behaviour and respect for the teachings and to receive the full empowerment you must take the *Bodhisattva* Vow. It is only for the open-hearted and those intending to be this way. Kalachakra attendees choose which vow they wish to take and the tantric teacher imparting the Kalachakra gives different practices for people taking the different vows.

People attend a Kalachakra Empowerment for different reasons. A few because it is their chosen spiritual practice for this lifetime; some desire the imprint on their mind-stream to assist with their practices in future lifetimes and other people because of the blessing it bestows upon them in a more mundane sense. The amount of people of differing spiritual backgrounds who attend for the latter reason or out of curiosity is growing, particularly in the West. For this reason and because of the significance of the times in which we are living H.H.

The 14$^{th}$ Dalai Lama (he is the same being that has reincarnated 14 times in a row to be a Tantric Master and leader of a Mahayana lineage) has greatly increased the bestowal of the Kalachakra in recent times. In long distant incarnations it may have been granted only once or twice in a lifetime with people flocking from far corners of the Tibetan plateau and beyond to attend, just to get the imprint to be able to practice in future lifetimes. Now H.H. Dalai Lama gives it twice a year, once somewhere in India and once in the West.

In fact he will give it for the $30^{th}$ time, in his current incarnation, next January in Amaravati, India. This will be a very auspicious ceremony, as it is in the place where Sakyamuni Buddha first brought this powerful teaching into the physical plane. It is said that whilst the Lord Buddha gave a discourse at Vultures Peak in Bihar, North India, twelve lunar months after having achieved full enlightenment under the bodhi tree he simultaneously propounded.

The Kalachakra to a host of Buddhas, gods and goddesses near Amaravati in South India is an old practice. King Suchandra of Shambhala (the Buddhist realm of spiritual warriors -a higher dimensional reality of peace and spiritual prosperity) miraculously descended to Earth to attend the teachings, record and take them back to Shambhala where Kalachakra became the spiritual practice of choice. And as legend would have, it is being held until such time as the world and human beings are ripe for it to be revealed en masse to assist in bringing about the fabled reign of Shambhala on Earth; an unparalleled time of peace and opportunity to practice spiritual advancement.

It is no mistake that in this time of planetary change from the Piscean to the Aquarian age, the age many people believe to be the time as prophesied in the Book. of Revelation and referred to by the Mayan elders many, many moons ago, that H.H. Dalai Lama has greatly stepped up the dissemination of Shambhala's prized teaching. Could the 1,000 years of peace spoken of in the bible be equated with the reign of Shambhala on Earth? Buddhists realise that for this to come about it requires a critical mass of people in society to take responsibility for their own mind and what it contributes to the collective interdependent whole.

Hence the fields are ploughed and fertile now the seeds are being sown. It is said that if you have received the seeds of a Kalachakra Empowerment in a previous lifetime you will be drawn to it again. The imprint will be on your mind stream and you will be strangely and irresistibly drawn to Kalachakra again. Perhaps the name will ring in your mind once you have heard it or you will have a strange fascination with the symbol or *mandala*. They may even cause noticeable activations in your body.

You may, even feel the urge to fly half way round the world to sit on a mat on a dusty floor amongst 250,000 people in the baking heat, spending your nights huddled up in a mud hut just to attend it. Many thousand Tibetans travel by foot for weeks over high mountain passes, using up their life savings, to attend and get a glimpse of H.H. Dalai Lama.

Chakra as most of us know is Sanskrit for "wheel", and Kala translates as "Time". So Kalachakra is the "Wheel of Time". The teaching tells us that there are three wheels of time. The outer, which concerns the machinations of interactions between bodies in the world; from who we bump into on the way to the shops, to the moon dragging currents of water across the globe, to Jupiter's trajectory around the Sun and beyond. Then there is the inner, which is the internal processes within our bodies, physical and subtle; the things that you may say are you and of your sense.

And then there is the Wheel of Time that is Kalachakra it is neither of the former and provides us with a gateway to enlightenment and out of sense phenomena. The whole body of teaching that forms Kalachakra is huge with its own astrology, psychology and much much more, a parallel universe, if you will. For the lovers of pomp and ceremony and beautiful intricacies the Kalachakra has it all, especially on the Indian Subcontinent. It takes about a fortnight for the whole event to take place. It's a cross between a University Conference and a Buddhist Jamboree, with monks by the thousands trotting around town.

Makeshift food and accommodation tents are put up and there are market stalls with Tibetan goods and souvenirs. Even ferris wheels and dodgems, there certainly is a carnival atmosphere in the lead up, as everyone waits and anticipates Santa Lama and the spiritual gifts he will bestow. I think of it as Buddstock! It all starts with a few days of preparatory rituals to gain permission from the local earth spirits to perform the ceremony, they generally require appeasing. Then the meticulous construction of the sand *mandala* commences. The *mandala* is the palace and abode of the deity Guru Kalachakra and exists in the higher realms. Fantastically talented and dedicated monks construct a 2-D version of it out of coloured grains of sand.

No glue and definitely no mistakes -probably the hardest jigsaw you are ever likely to find and several monks working round the clock for 5 days on hands on knees. Whilst the *mandala* is under construction the Tantric Master gives several days of preparatory teachings. Some directly relevant to Kalachakra but mainly vital Buddhist foundation teachings, with the message firmly drummed home that it is practicing the basic virtues day in and day out that is the basis of achieving Buddhahood, the higher teachings being the bauble or icing on the cake.

After four or five days of preliminary teachings the excitement really starts to grow, more and more people arrive from out of town to receive just the empowerment, either because of time commitments or most likely using the same principle as licking off the chocolate and throwing the biscuit away. The excitement peaks as proceedings stop for a day, it's almost like the last day of term at school when you can come in mufty (casual dress). Everyone relaxes and there are ritual offering dances and other goodies. Then to exams, or rather the initiation begins.

There is one day of preliminary empowerments and then 7 empowerments spread over 3 further days. It is on the day of the preliminary empowerment that you can choose to take the *Bodhisattva* vows in order to be conferred the full empowerment or to simply receive the ceremony as a blessing. You are also given 2 blades of kusha grass, the short one for under your pillow and the big one under your mattress.

Especially those attending for the first time -or simply have greater obscuration to clear? The camaraderie between Vajra brothers and sisters (those who have shared the same tantric empowerment) is truly beautiful to be a part of, an understated unspoken yet very deep love (compassion and interconnectedness) seems to float through the next three days, gliding in and out of the hall and spending a lot of time sleeping, resting and contemplating- contemplating nothing, just a stillness of mind and very warm temples, my neurology being reconfigured no doubt.

For two and a half thousand years, people have followed a Buddhism religion based on the teachings of a man they called the Buddha, meaning the Enlightened One. The starting pint in Buddism is mankind and the way in which they suffer not just physical pain but the general feelings of dissatification with life, the craving to achieve or have something more, the fear of change and death. It seeks to give a person peace of mind and to encourage and develop loving compassion towards all living beings.

To many, Buddhism goes beyond religion and is more of a philosophy or 'way of life'. It is a philosophy because philosophy 'means love of wisdom' and the Buddhist path can be summed up as:

1. To lead a moral life,
2. To be mindful and aware of thoughts and actions, and
3. To develop wisdom and understanding.

Buddhism is not a dogmatic religion in the sense that it does not required a person to accept fixed beliefs and ideas. It does not concern itself by debationg whether or not there is a God. It regards all such beliefs as secondary importance. The main thing is to help people overcome suffering and to achieve a full life. The goal of Buddism religion is enlightenment which means to be fully awake to the reality of life, to have an understanding of why there is suffering in the world and how it man be overcome. Buddhists claim that in the teaching of the Buddha they find a path which will eventually lead them to achieve this enlightement for themselves.

There is great variety within Buddhism. Ther are two main Branches of the religion - Theravada or Hinayana Buddhism in the North. Nevertheless there is a common basis to all Buddhism expressed in what is called the Triple Jewel (*Tri Ratna*) - the Buddha (the enlightened one), the Dharma (teaching) and the *Sangha* (community of monks.)

Difference of opinons and arguments arising from time to time caused the formation of new sects. Finally there arose two sects of thought which are known as Hinayana and Mahyana. The Hinayana adhered more to the concept of four noble truths and eightfold paths which were primarly a philoshophy with rules of conducts and ethics. For them the worship of deities was secondary. The conception of Nirvana was the freedom from the cycle of rebirth. Hinayana got its name because this doctrine is meant for the individual salvation where each person has to work out his own destiny comparatively few are able by their own efforts to obtain emancipation and chieve Nirvana. Hinayan Buddhism is alos called Theravada Buddhism.

Early Buddhism stressed that the goal of each individuals was to seek freedom from the chain of rebirth and thus from all sufferings and death. The word used to describe this goal was Nirvana. Although there were many different philosophical schools, the religion centered on the instituiton of the monastery with its ordained monks and a lay congregation that supported the monastery. The ritual was simple and minimum. Mediation and introspection were encouraged. Each individual sought his own Nirvana where as in Mahayana Buddhism the concept of *Boddhisattva,* the being who desired highest enlightnment for the welfare of other and his practice of six *Parmita* (*Dana, Sila, Kshanti, Birya, Bhyana,* and *Prajna*) is emphaised.

The function of the *Boddhisattva* was to postpone his own final leap into Nirvana and to remain in the round as long as a single sentient beings remained undelivered form suffering. This form of Buddhism came to be known as Mahayana (the great way) or the *Boddhisattvayana.* The goal of Mahayana is attain Buddhahood. The method of attaining was modified. Buddhism changed through Mahayana into an altruistic faith oriented system in wihch in addition to meditative practices, devotion to a *Boddhisattva* was as an equally valid way to reach Buddhahood. The goal was now characterised as the state of Tatatha, emptiness and nonduality.

Mahayana which is dominated by Mantras is known as mantryana. Tantrayana or Vajrayana is characterised as the path which leads to perfect enlightenment. Vajrayana literally means the adamantine path or vehicle, but its technical meaning is the 'Sunya Vahicle' where *Sunya* is used to special sense to represent *vajra* means "Thunderbolt" or 'diamond' and *Yana* means 'Path, Way or Vehicle'. *Vajra,* connoting diamond, was chosen as the name of the tantric Buddhist tradition because of the diamond's industructability as well as of its physical ability to cut through all substances. Vajrayana constitutes the last major stage in the development of Buddhism.

Vajrayana Buddhism accepts all assumptions of Mahayana, but expands and elaborates them futher adding a few of its own. The goal is now characterised as Boddhi Nature (the matrix of Enlightment). Every sentient being is a potential Buddha, but he or she is unware of it beacuse of the dense fog of ignorance that clouds the mind.

The fog is said to be discursive thought, which discriminates and polarises all concepts. Once it is moved Boddhi nature will emerge like a clear ligh. This state of reality it achieved by combining "Prajna" (Knowledge, wisdom or insight) with "Upaya" (means of fitness of action which is the same as karuna or compassion). Thus, both literally and figuratively, Vajrayana is the belief in the twin principles of insight and compassion and in their "Sahaja" (co-emergence) which leads one to the state of *Mahasukha* (great bliss).

## MAJOR COMPONENT OF BUDDHISM

Every religion has a set of ideas that serve as the basis for the teachings that it offers. These are called presuppositions. These are concepts about the nature of existence that are the basis for the teachings of the religion. For example, the major Judeo-Christian-Islamic presupposition is that there is a universal creator God who can affect our day to day existence. The Buddhist presuppositions originated in early philosophical and religious speculation that took place in India between 4500 and 2500 years ago. They are as follows:

## THE BUDDHIST THEORY OF EXISTENCE (ONTOLOGY)

All physical existence is in a cycle much like the "big Bang" theory of modern astro-physics where all matter come together in a big ball and then explodes. It expands for billions of years and then collapses back into a ball for billions of years until it and explodes again. This Buddhist system this cycle is called a kalpa and these cycles will repeat infinitely. The physical form of the world is a Vast mountain in the center of the universe, with all of the continents around it: At the top are 28 heaven worlds, next, below them there are the five realms of Mount Meru itself, after that there are alternating rings of mountains and seas and after that there is a great sea with the continents in it.

Various heavenly beings live in the heaven worlds, human's animals and ghosts live on the continents, and beings who have been reborn in the hells live in six realms that are under the continents. They are not shown in this drawing. All life emerges from disturbances in the dharma. Life is also eternal and any individual may be reborn an infinite number of times. He or she can be reborn as anything from bacteria to a heavenly being in the highest heaven. The cycle of lives of an individual continues so often and in so many ways that some Buddhists have developed a saying.

"Every being now alive has been your mother at some time in the past," and they really do mean to count all of the insects, and even earthworms. The Buddhist theory of the end of the being/world/universe (eschatology) states that the universe will go on for all infinite time. World cycles, or kalpas, will repeat over and over and the life cycle of individual beings will repeat over and over- infinitely!

The Buddhist view of personal salvation (soteriology) is that the individual may escape the endless cycle of rebirths by attaining enlightenment. Enlightenment is essentially knowledge of how the system works and how the individual is literally identical with the totality of the universe. This knowledge is called enlightenment. It may be attained through:

1. Faith
2. Practice
3. Ethical/moral behaviuor/well being

All of these beliefs were in existence before the lifetime of the person we call the Buddha. Its founder was Gotama Siddhartha who became known as the Buddha or "Enlightened One." He lived about 2500 years ago in a small kingdom in the Indian-Nepalese border region. There are four main events in his life.

The first was his birth which was accompanied by many good omens and events. After his birth, he grew up as a well educated prince of his kingdom and married a young woman who gave birth to their son. However, he tired of the princely life and, feeling dissatisfied, soon left home to become a wandering ascetic, a beggar. He joined a band of such beggars and wandered about from place to place seeking teaching from great masters. What he sought from these teachers was a special kind of knowledge that would allow him to understand the nature of the universe. For six years the young prince lived a beggar's life. During this time he nearly starved to death through deliberately depriving himself of food.

The second great event is his enlightenment in which he attained that special knowledge. There is a very long story of this event. Essentially it is as follows. Prince Gotama, having nearly starved to death from his ascetic practices, resolved to eat again and to then meditate (essentially sitting quietly and thinking about it) until he attained the knowledge that he was seeking. To gain this knowledge, he sat down under a big tree and begins to meditate.

At one point in his meditations, an evil being, named Mara attacked the prince with an army of evil warriors representing hate, lust and greed. A great battle followed in which the weapons of the evil army turned into flowers and Mara, the evil being, was defeated. At the defeat of Mara, Prince Gotama had won the right to the knowledge he sought. That knowledge is called enlightenment or bodhi. Once he attained that knowledge, Gotama became known as the Buddha which means the "enlightened one." The name is actually the word bodhi combined with the verb ta, "to be," combined into one word, i.e. bodhi+ta = Buddha. So when we say Gotama the Buddha we are actually saying "Gotama the Enlightened One."

The third great event is the first sermon. After he had attained his special knowledge, Gotama the Buddha decided to teach his special way of attaining this knowledge to others. He went to a place known as the deer park where the ascetics who had been his former companions were living. They quickly realized that Gotama the Buddha had attained the special knowledge and asked him to teach them how to attain it. What he taught them will be talked about later. The act of teaching it to his former fellow ascetics is called the first sermon.

From this first teaching arose all future teachings by Gotama the Buddha and his followers. He would teach for over forty years. The fourth event is his last death, which is called the parinirvana. The word parinirvana means something quite different than just death. The Buddhists believe that an individual life force would live forever. It does this by being born and dying over and over again. If one has been good, he or she will be reborn in the higher levels of birth such as in the human realms or in the worlds of the heavenly beings.

However, if one has been bad, he or she will be reborn in the lower levels of birth, as an animal, a ghost or even in one of many hells. To die to be reborn is ordinary death to the Buddhists. However the Buddha was not to be reborn again. Thus his death was like the flame of a candle going out. It was the cessation of all rebirths. Gotama the Buddha had attained his final release. What would happen to his individual being? He would reunite with the totality of the universe- like a drop of water falling into the ocean.

## FOUNDERS OF TEACHINGS IN BUDDHISM

Based on the presuppositions we have just learned about Buddhism, Gotama Buddha taught that others could also attain the special knowledge and thereby attain release from the cycle of rebirth by fully realizing the following.

The teachings of the Buddha as explained by the teachers who followed him is a truly vast subject. This covers thousands of volumes of literature and more than a hundred different approaches or sects of Buddhism. There are three divisions of major approaches and each of those major sub-schools is divided into many sub-schools. One can spend lifetime learning about them.

Some believe that there will be very few Buddhas while others believe that there can be many Buddhas; others believe that to attain Buddhahood takes many thousands of lifetimes while others believe that one can attain Buddhahood in this lifetime; some believe in detailed and secret rituals while others believe in totally unstructured individual approaches. Yet others believe in rebirth in a kind of Buddhist paradise while some believe that the final attainment is to be made right here and now in this very life time. By Buddhist definition all these approaches are valid and each is free to follow the teachings of his or her own choosing.

In addition, as Buddhism was spread into countries near India and throughout the rest of Asia, adaptations to local concerns were made in the teachings. Thus a Thai Buddhist may believe one thing, a Tibetan Buddhist another and a Chinese yet another. All of this adaptation was done by the teachers who followed the original teachings of Gotama Buddha.

The community of followers is divided into four categories:

1. The male beggars or, as they are usually called, "monks."
2. The female beggars, or nuns
3. The male lay followers
4. The female lay followers

Each order has its own rules, essentially defining right, views, intentions, speech, conduct and livelihood. The lay community is, as with all lay populations, deeply concerned with the problems of daily life and they have many rituals and ceremonies concerned with:

1. Good health
2. Prosperity
3. Well being
4. Death

## BUDDHISM IN ASIA

From the outset Buddhism was a missionary religion. The Buddha travelled over a large area spreading his teachings, and explicitly charged his disciples to do likewise with the words: 'Go, monks, and wander for the good and welfare of the multitudes.' The spread of Buddhism was given a considerable boost in the third century BC when one of the greatest figures in Indian history - Ashoka Maurya - became emperor of India around 268 BC. Through conquest Ashoka extended the Mauryan Empire, making it the largest Indian empire to be seen until the British Raj.

After a bloody campaign on the east coast, in the region of present-day Orissa, he experienced remorse and turned to Buddhism. For the remainder of his long reign he ruled according to Buddhist principles, and under his patronage Buddhism flourished. As well as helping to establish Buddhism within India, Ashoka also dispatched ambassadors to the courts of rulers in the Near East and Macedonia, and, according to the Sinhalese chronicles, to South-East Asia. The record of these early missions is found in the stone inscriptions Ashoka left throughout his realm, which provide some of the most reliable data on early Indian history.

It is not known with any certainty what became of the missions, but the ones to the West seem to have had little impact, as the earliest surviving mention of Buddhism in Western documents is found in the writings of Clement of Alexandria in the second century AD (earlier classical references to the Indian sarmanes and samanaioi may also refer to Buddhism). There is a wide-spread belief, particularly in the West, that the ideal of the Theravada, which they conveniently identify with Hinayana, is to become an Arahant while that of the Mahayana is to become a *Bodhisattva* and finally to attain the state of a Buddha.

It must be categorically stated that this is incorrect. This idea was spread by some early Orientalists at a time when Buddhist studies were beginning in the West, and the others who followed them accepted it without taking the trouble to go into the problem by examining the texts and living traditions in Buddhist countries. But the fact is that both the Theravada and the Mahayana unanimously accept the *Bodhisattva* ideal as the highest. The terms Hinayana (Small Vehicle) and Mahayana (Great Vehicle) are not known to the Theravada Pali literature. They are not found in the Pali Canon (Tripitaka) or in the Commentaries on the Tripitaka.

Not even in the Pali Chronicles of Ceylon, the Dipavamsa and the Mahavamsa. The Dipavamsa (about the 4th Century A.D.) and Pali Commentaries mention Vitandavadins, evidently a sect of dissenting Buddhists holding some unorthodox views regarding some points in the teaching of the Buddha. The Vitandavadin and the Theravadin both quote the same authorities and name the sutras of the Tripitaka in order to support their positions, the difference being only in the mode of their interpretations.

The *Mahavamsa* (5th Century A.D.) and a Commentary on the Abhidhamma refer to Vetulla - or Vetulyavadins (Sanskrit: Vaitulyavadin) instead of Vitandavadin. From the evidence of the texts, it may not be wrong to consider that these two terms - Vitanda and Vetulya - represented the same school or sect. We learn from the *Abhidhamma-Samuccaya,* an authoritative Mahayana philosophical text (4th Century A.D.) that the terms Vaitulya and Vaipulya are synonymous, and that Vaipulya is the *Bodhisattva-Pitaka*. Now, the *Bodhisattva-Pitaka* is definitely Mahayana. Hence Vaitulya undoubtedly denotes Mahayana.

So we can be certain that the terms Vitanda, and Vetulya used in the Pali Chronicles and Commentaries refer to Mahayana. But the terms Hinayana and Mahayana were not known to them, or ignored or unrecognised by them. It is universally accepted by scholars that the terms Hinayana and Mahayana are later inventions. Historically speaking, the Theravada already existed long before these terms came into being. That Theravada, considered to be the original teaching of the Buddha, was introduced to Ceylon and established there in the 3rd Century B.C., during the time of Emperor Asoka of India.

At that time there was nothing called Mahayana. Mahayana as such appeared much later, about the beginning of the Christian Era. Without Mahayana there could not be Hinayana. Buddhism that went to Sri Lanka, with its Tripitaka and Commentaries, in the 3rd Century B.C., remained there intact as Theravada, and did not come into the scene of the Hinayana-Mahayana dispute that developed later in India. It seems therefore not legitimate to include Theravada in either of these two categories. The Mahayana mainly deals with the *Bodhisattva*-yana or the Vehicle of the *Bodhisattva*. But it does not ignore the other two: *Sravaka*-yana and *Pratyeka-Buddha*-yana.

For example, Asanga, the founder of the Yogacara system, in his *Magnum Opus*, the *Yogacara Bhumisastra,* devotes two sections to *Sravaka*-bhumi and *Pratyeka-Buddha*-bhumi to *Bodhisattva*-bhumi, which shows that all three yanas are given due consideration in the Mahayana. But the state of a *Sravaka* or a *Pratyeka-Buddha* is inferior to that of a *Bodhisattva*.

This is quite in keeping with the Theravada tradition which, too, holds that one may become a *Bodhisattva* and attain the state of a fully Enlightened Buddha; but if one cannot, one may attain the state of a *Pratyeka-Buddha* or of a *Sravaka* according to one's capacity. These three states may be considered as three attainments on the same Path. In fact, the *Sandhinirmocana Sutra* (a Mahayana Sutra) clearly says that the

*Sravakayana* and the Mahayana constitute one *Yana* (*ekayana*) and that they are not two different and distinct 'vehicles'.

## THE THREE INDIVIDUALS

Now, who are these three individuals: *Sravaka, Pratyeka-Buddha* and *Bodhisattva*? Very briefly:

- A *Sravaka* is a disciple of a Buddha. A disciple may be a monk or a nun, a layman or a laywoman. Bent on his or her liberation, a *Sravaka* follows and practises the reaching of the Buddha and finally attains Nirvana. He also serves others, but his capacity to do so is limited.
- A *Pratyeka-Buddha* (Individual Buddha) is a person who realizes Nirvana alone by himself at a time when there is no *Samyaksambuddha* in the world. He also renders service to others, but in a limited way. He is not capable of revealing the Truth to others as a *Samyaksambuddha*, a fully Enlightened Buddha does.
- A *Bodhisattva* is a person (monk or layman) who is in a position to attain Nirvana as a *Sravaka* or as a *Pratyeka-Buddha*, but out of great compassion *(maha karuna)* for the world, he renounces it and goes on suffering in *samsara* for the sake of others, perfects himself during an incalculable period of time and finally realizes Nirvana and becomes a *Samyaksambuddha*, a fully Enlightened Buddha. He discovers The Truth and declares it to the world. His capacity for service to others is unlimited.

The definition of the three *Yanikas* (followers of the three yanas) given by Asanga is very instructive and clarifies some points. According to him, a *Sravaka*yanika (one who takes the vehicle of disciples) is a person who, living according to the law of the disciples. By nature having feeble faculties (qualities), bent on his own liberation through the cultivation of detachment, depending on the Canon of the Disciples *(Sravaka-pitaka)*, practising major and minor qualities, gradually puts an end to suffering.

A *Pratyeka-Buddha-Yanika* (one who takes the Vehicle of the Individual Buddha) is a person who, lives according to the law of the Individual Buddha, By nature having medium faculties, bent on his liberation through the cultivation of detachment, he has the intention of attaining Enlightenment exclusively through his own mental development, depending on the *Sravaka*-pitaka, practising major and minor qualities, born at a time when there is no Buddha in the world and gradually puts an end to suffering.

A *Mahayanika (one* who takes the Great Vehicle) is a person who, living according to the law of the *Bodhisattvas*, by nature having sharp faculties, bent on the liberation of all beings, depending on the Canon of the *Bodhisattvas*, matures other beings, cultivates the pure Buddha-domain, receives predictions or declarations *(Vya-Karana)* from Buddhas and finally realizes the perfect and complete Enlighten*ment (Samyaksambodhi)*.

From this we can see that anyone who aspires to become a Buddha is a *Bodhisattva*, a Mahayanist, though he may live in a country or in a community popularly and traditionally regarded as Theravada or Hinayana. Similarly, a person who aspires to attain Nirvana as a disciple is a *Sravakayanika* or Hinayanist though he may belong to a country or a community considered as Mahayana. Thus it is wrong to believe that there are no *Bodhisattvas* in Theravada countries or that all are *Bodhisattvas* in Mahayana countries. It is not conceivable that *Sravakas* and *Bodhisattvas* are concentrated in separate geographical areas.

Further, Asanga says that when a *Bodhisattva* finally attains Enlightenment *(Bodhi)* he becomes an Arahant, a Tathagata (i.e. Buddha). Here it must be clearly understood that not only a *Sravaka* (disciple) but also a *Bodhisattva* becomes an Arahant when finally he attains Buddhahood. The Theravada position is exactly the same: the Buddha is an Arahant -*Araham Samma-SamBuddha* - "Arahant, Fully and Perfectly Enlightened Buddha." The Mahayana unequivocally says that a Buddha, a

*Pratyeka-Buddha* and a *Sravaka* (disciple), all three are equal and alike with regard to their purification or liberation from defilements or impurities *(Klesavaranavisuddhi).*

This is also called *Vimukti-Kaya* (Liberation-body), and in it there is no difference between the three. That means that there are no three different Nirvanas or Vimuktis for three persons. Nirvana or Vimukti is the same for all. But only a Buddha achieves the complete liberation from all the obstructions to the knowable, i.e., obstructions to knowledge *(Jneyyavaranavisuddhi),* not the *Sravaka*s and *Pratyeka-Buddha*s. This also is called *Dharma-Kaya* (Dharma-body), and it is in this and many other innumerable qualities, capacities and abilities that the Buddha becomes incomparable and superior to *Sravaka*s and *Pratyeka-Buddha*s.

This Mahayana view is quite in keeping with the Theravada Pali Tripitaka. In the *Samyutta-Nikaya* the Buddha says that the Tathagata (i.e. Buddha) and a bhikkhu (i.e. *sravaka,* disciple) liberated through wisdom are equal with regard to their *Vimutta* (liberation), but the Tathagatha is different and distinguished from the liberated bhikkhus in that he (Tathagata) discovers and shows the Path (Magga) that was not known before.

These three states of the *Sravaka,* the *Pratyeka-Buddha* and the Buddha are mentioned in the *Nidhikanda Sutta* of the *Khuddakapatha,* the first book of the Khuddaka-nikaya, one of the five Collections of the Theravada Tripitaka. It says that by practising virtues such as charity, morality, self-restraint, etc., one may attain, among other things, "the Perfection of the Disciple" *(Savaka-Parami),* "Enlightenment of the *Pratyeka-Buddha*" *(Paccekabodhi)* and "the Buddha-domain" *(Buddhabhumi).* They are not called *Yanas* (vehicles). In the Theravada tradition these are known as *Bodhis,* but not *Yanas.*

The *Upasaka-janalankara,* a Pali treatise dealing with the ethics for the lay Buddhist written in the 12th century by a Thera called Ananda in the Theravada tradition of the Mahavihara at Anuradhpura, Sri Lanka, says that there are three Bodhis: *Savakabodhi (*Skt: *Sravakabodhi), Paccekabodhi (*Skt: *Fratyekabodhi)* and *Sammasambodhi (*Skt: *Samyaksambodhi).*

## THE BODHISATTVAS

Just like the Mahayana, the Theravada holds the *Bodhisattva* in the highest position. The Commentary on the *Jataka,* in the tradition of the Mahavihara at Anuradhapura, provides a precise example: In the dim past, many incalculable aeons ago, Gotama the Buddha, during his career as *Bodhisattva,* was an ascetic named Sumedha. At that time there was a Buddha called Dipankara whom he met and at whose feet he had the capacity to realise Nirvana as a disciple *(Sravaka).* But Sumedha renounced it and resolved, out of great compassion for the world, to become a Buddha like Dipankara to save others.

Then Dipankara Buddha declared and predicted that this great ascetic would one day become a Buddha and offered eight handfuls of flowers to Sumedha. Likewise, Dipankara Buddha's disciples who were with him and who were themselves Arahants offered flowers to the *Bodhisattva.* This story of Sumedha distinctly shows the position a *Bodhisattva* occupies in the Theravada. Although the Theravada holds that anybody can be a *Bodhisattva,* it does not stipulate or insist that all must be *Bodhisattva* which is considered not practical. The decision is left to the individual whether to take the Path of the *Sravaka* or of the *Pratyeka-Buddha* or of the *Samyaksambuddha.* But it is always clearly explained that the state of a *Samyaksambuddha* is superior and that the other two are inferior. Yet they are not disregarded.

In the 12th Century AD., in Myanmar (a strictly Theravada country), King Alaungsithu of Pagan, after building Shwegugyi Temple, set up an inscription in Pali verse to record this act of piety in which he publicly declared his resolution to become a Buddha and not a *Sravaka.* In Sri Lanka, in the 10th Century, King Mahinda IV (956-972 AD.) in an inscription proclaimed that "none but the *Bodhisattvas* would become kings of Sri Lanka (Ceylon)". Thus it was believed that kings of Sri Lanka were

*Bodhisattvas*. A Thera named Maha-Tipitaka Culabhaya, who wrote the *Milinda-Tika* (about the 12th Century AD.) in the Theravada tradition of the Mahavihara at Anuradhapura, says at the end of the book in the colophon that he aspires to become a Buddha: *Buddho Bhaveyyam* "May I become a Buddha," which means that this author is a *Bodhisattva.*

We come across at the end of some palm leaf manuscripts of Buddhist texts in Sri Lanka the names of even a few copyists who have recorded their wish to become Buddhas, and they too are to be considered as *Bodhisattvas*. At the end of a religious ceremony or an act of piety, the bhikkhu who gives benedictions, usually admonishes the congregation to make a resolution to attain Nirvana by realising one of the three *Bodhis* - *Sravaka*bodhi, *Pratyekabodhi* or *Samyaksambodhi* - as they wish according to their capacity. There are many Buddhists, both bhikkhus and laymen, in Sri Lanka, Myanmar, Thailand and Cambodia which are regarded as Theravada countries, who take the vow or resolution to become Buddhas to save others.

They are indeed *Bodhisattvas* at different levels of development. Thus one may see that in Theravada countries all are not *Sravakas*. There are *Bodhisattvas* as well. There is a significant difference between the Theravada and the Mahayana with regard to the *Bodhisattva* ideal. The Theravada, although it holds the *Bodhisattva* ideal as the highest and the noblest, does not provide a separate literature devoted to the subject. The teachings about the *Bodhisattva* ideal and the *Bodhisattva* career are to be found scattered in their due places in Pali literature.

The Mahayana by definition is dedicated to the *Bodhisattva* ideal, and they have not only produced a remarkable literature on the subject but also created a fascinating class of mythical *Bodhisattvas*. It took Buddha a whole lifetime to discover and refine the secrets to enlightenment, but a meager forty-nine days after reaching enlightenment he was asked to teach all he had learned. Buddha rose without question from his deep meditation to help the monks in there quest for knowledge. The lesson Buddha taught when he rose from meditation was first the wheel of Dharma.

Among these teachings of the first wheel of Dharma is the sutra of the four noble truths... 1. This is suffering, 2. The causes of suffering, 3. Suffering can end, nirvana is peace, 4. The true path or eight-fold noble path. These truths must be realized and accepted in order to move on to the next stage. This is also the source of the Hinayana known as the lesser vehicle of Buddhism.

The second wheel of Dharma teaches us the perfection of wisdom sutra, which is a profound saying paying homage to the holy Perfection of Wisdom! The third sutra or wheel of Dharma is about discriminating the intention, it is a long conversation about abandoning our self-cherishing personalities and cherishing only others we can begin to experience true peace and happiness. These two wheels of Dharma make up the Mahayana, or the great vehicle of Buddhism. The Hinayana teaches us how we can attain liberation from suffering for ourselves, no one can do it for you and it is not for you to force anyone else to follow Buddha's teachings. Wisdom is the end to suffering.

In Buddhism wisdom can refer to conventional and ultimate wisdom, these cannot be forced on anyone who does not accept it into their hearts. The Mahayana teaching explains the way to reach full enlightenment or Buddhahood as it is sometimes called for the sake of others. In Asia, where the Buddha grew and learned both the Hinayana and Mahayana traditions flourished. It started in India and then over time spread in to other surrounding countries like Tibet. Gradually these teachings are spreading in to the west.

## ORIGIN OF BUDDHISM IN AMERICA

In America, followers of Buddhism are found primarily in the states of Utah, Arizona, Washington, Oregon, California, and Hawaii. American Buddhists are predominately Americans of Japanese ancestry and Southeast Asians who have immigrated to the United States. The first Buddhist church or temple in the United States was consecrated in San Francisco in 1905. The Buddhist Mission of North America was started in San Francisco in 1898 and incorporated in 1942 as the Buddhist Church of America.

## BRANCHES OF BUDDHISM

After the death of Gautama, his followers divided into two groups, the Hinayana (small vehicle) and the Mahayana (great or larger vehicle). Hinayana Buddhism has maintained the original simple and austere rules of discipline left by Gautama. This form of Buddhism is the religion of most of the people of Burma, Cambodia, Sri Lanka, Laos, Thailand, and Vietnam. Mahayana Buddhism expanded the original teachings of Gautama.

This group believes that there are many Buddhas and saints. Mahayana also includes a doctrine of heaven and hell, and salvation by faith and grace. This form of Buddhism has been a major faith in China, Japan, Korea, and Mongolia for hundreds of years. Tibetan Buddhism, a form of Mahayana, is called Lamais and is com- prised of a number of different sects. They range from the Shin sect (notable for its love of pageantry) to the austere Zen. Zen's emphasis on meditation gives it much in common with Hinayana Buddhism.

## ORGANIZATIONAL STRUCTURE

The organizational structure of Buddhism varies with the branches. There is usually a national headquarters, which is the Office of the Bishop. Buddhist churches are divided geographically into districts. Organizations are maintained by each congregation to meet the spiritual, social, and educational needs of the members.

Any qualified member of the congregation may conduct worship services. Weddings, funerals, and other religious functions are conducted by senior members of the congregation.

## BUDDHIST LEADERSHIP

The titular head of the American Buddhist Church bears the title of Bishop. In parts of Asia, Buddhist clergymen are addressed as "Bhikku" and belong to the Buddhist monastic order called the *Sangha*.

## WORSHIP REQUIREMENTS

The place of worship is the Temple, *Pagoda,* or *Dagobas*. The statue of Buddha is the key symbol of Buddhism and is the central figure in most temples and pagodas. Reverence should be shown in and around this area as a sign of respect for the Buddhists and their religious beliefs.

# 4

# Discipline and Austerity

Buddhist tradition has it that shortly after the passing away of the Lord Buddha five hundred of his Arhats and disciples, led by Kasyapa, met in council at Rajagaha for the purpose of recalling to mind the truths they had received from their beloved Teacher during the forty-five years of his ministry. Their hope was to implant the salient principles of his message so firmly in memory that they would become a lasting impetus to moral and spiritual conduct, not alone for themselves and the brethren in distant parts of the land, but likewise for all future disciples who would seek to follow in the footsteps of the Awakened One.

With the Teacher no longer among them, the monks found themselves with the responsibility of handing on the teaching and discipline of the Order as faithfully as possible. Having no written texts to rely on, they did as their forebears had before them and prepared their discourses "for recitation," that is, basic themes were repeated with variations in order to impress the ideas on their hearers. At that time, according to the Sinhalese, the *Dhammapada* was orally assembled from the sayings of Gautama given on some three hundred different occasions.

Put in verse form the couplets contrast the vanity of hypocrisy, false pride, heedlessness, and selfish desire with the virtues of truthfulness, modesty, vigilance, and self-abnegation. The admonitions are age-old, yet they strike home today, their austerity of purpose fittingly relieved by gentle humor and earthy simile. Subsequently, several renditions of the *Dhammapada* in the Sanskrit and Chinese languages came into circulation; likewise, a number of stanzas are to be found almost verbatim in other texts of the canonical literature, testifying to the esteem in which its content was anciently held.

Since first collated, the *Dhammapada* has become one of the best loved of Buddhist scriptures, recited daily by millions of devotees who chant its verses in Pali or in their native dialect. It was inevitable that differences in interpretation of teaching as well as of disciplinary practices would arise, with the result that about a century after the First Council was held a second gathering was called to affirm the purity of the doctrine. It was at this Second Council that the Arhats divided into two main streams, namely, the *Mahasanghika* or "Great Assembly" and the *Theravada* or "Doctrine of Elders."

These gradually developed into the Mahayana or Northern School of Buddhism espoused chiefly in India, Tibet, China, and later Japan, and the Hinayana or Southern School whose stronghold is Sri Lanka, Burma, and the countries of Southeast Asia. The range of Buddhist literature is vast, and much is made of the difference in emphasis between the Mahayana and the Hinayana: *Mahayana* or the "great way or vehicle" is the large "ferryboat" or fuller doctrine of the Lord Buddha that will ferry all beings across the ocean of births and deaths to the "other shore"; *Hinayana* or "incomplete or deficient way or vehicle" is, the Mahayanists say in contempt, the "ferryboat" of inferior quality because it contains less of the vital essence of the Master's wisdom.

The Theravadins, the largest branch of Southern Buddhism, repudiate the title, and never refer to themselves as Hinayanists; because they hold that as the Pali Canon represents the oldest records of Buddha's life and message they are closer to the source than are the later and more elaborate doctrines of the Mahayanists. In fact, the Theravadins reverently state that the *Dhammapada* preserves the *Buddhavacana* or "word of Buddha." Without doubt it carries the spirit of the Master's teaching, but there is no firm assurance that the Pali texts represent the most primitive Canon, for there appears to have been more than one collection of scriptures at a very early stage, from which both Pali and Sanskrit Canons may have developed.

With the passage of years, although both derive inspiration from the same source, the two Schools diverged rather widely. To put it almost too simply, the basic difference lies in this: the goal of the Theravadin is to transmit in utter fidelity the teaching and example of Buddha-Gautama and by the steadfast practice of the virtues to become, in the course of time, an Arhat, one "worthy" of attaining the supreme nirvana or bliss of omniscience; the goal of the Mahayanist is to become a *Bodhisattva*, one whose "essence is bodhi or wisdom," and when nirvana is reached to renounce it for the sake of the world and the "weal of gods and men." In this sublime act of compassion is the promise that all beings are potential Buddhas, having the same intrinsic capacity for enlightenment.

Significantly, the same character training and purification process must be undergone by all devotees, by those who would become Buddha and enter nirvana, and by those who would refuse nirvana, as did Gautama Sakyamuni in the manner of his predecessor Buddhas. But let it not be thought that because the Theravadins do not explicitly delineate the *Bodhisattva* ideal they lack compassion. In actuality, the power of the Compassionate One is implicit in every word and incident recorded in the Pali Canon, the *Tripitaka* or "Three Baskets," the second of which, namely *Sutta-Pitaka,* includes the *Dhammapada* and the famed *Jatakamala* or "stories" that relate the previous "births" of Buddha.

One has only to read a little in this extensive literature to feel the depth of love that filled the Tathagata. He comes through not as a god or far-off divinity, but as a wonderfully wise and compassionate friend who understands human weakness yet has the gift of inciting the least of us to noble endeavor. His very presence on earth was witness of the "earnest resolve" he had made "a hundred thousand cycles vast and four immensities ago" to join the line of *Bodhisattva*s who periodically fulfill their dhamma of bringing light and hope to a troubled humanity.

Were this still not a potent influence in every Buddhist land today the populace would not gather in villages and groves, as they do in Sri Lanka, on full moon nights of their holy days, particularly in the month of Vesak (April/May), to hear once again the monks chanting the sacred verses of how Prince Siddhartha became Gautama-*Bodhisattva* out of love for all beings everywhere. The present translation of the *Dhammapada* by Dr. Harischandra Kaviratna originally appeared as a serial in Sunrise magazine from August 1970 through September 1971. It has been revised by the translator where needed, and a Glossary of Pali philosophical terms with Sanskrit equivalents added.

Dr. Kaviratna, a native of Sri Lanka, is equally versed in Sinhalese, Pali, and Sanskrit, and since youth has been a dedicated researcher into the esoteric implications behind the Vedas, Vedanta, and Buddhist canonical and noncanonical literatures of both Northern and Southern Schools. It is our sincere hope that readers will find food for contemplation in this ancient devotional scripture which for more than twenty centuries has inspired in its hearers a genuine conversion, a "turning about" of the soul from the limitations of the personal toward the light within, the light that is our Self, our refuge, and our strength.

Ballads and folklore are the most precious remnants of a glorious and prolific culture that disappeared from the surface of our globe many centuries prior to the dawn of our present civilization. Embedded in age-old legendary poems are the loftiest speculations of our most ancient forebears and, although their culture vanished in the prehistoric past, we may discern its indelible impress upon the extant literature that is the universal heritage of mankind.

The *Dhammapada, the Bhagavad-Gita,* and the ascetic poems of the Jains, for instance, perpetuate ethics and norms that were promulgated by the sages of an age that is still shrouded in mystery. Valmiki and Vyasa of Aryavarta, Homer and Pindar of Greece, Druid bard and Mayan priest, Chinese lawgiver and Egyptian hierophant - all echoed these moral values in their epics and systems of thought. It is evident that even in the earliest dawn of prehistory men used a universal system of signs and symbols to transmit ideas and impressions - without doubt a symbol can more adequately represent a philosophical conception than the written word.

Among ancient peoples, such as the Indo-Aryans, literacy and education were not considered of primary importance but merely as aids to interior illumination and religious insight. And indeed, throughout the centuries, mystics of both East and West have attained enlightenment and union with supreme Reality not through scholastic study, not through dialectic discourses, but through self-abnegation and intuitive direct comprehension. Rarely do those of great intellectual stature alone penetrate to the deepest esoteric truths embodied in the symbology of scriptural texts. With this in mind, we can better understand the conviction of the Brahmans that the sacred knowledge would be perverted when put into writing: the Vedas had to be *heard*.

The art of writing, therefore, did not become popular, as the emphasis of education was on the development of memory and its retentive power. If the expounder of a special branch of knowledge wished to protect his system from falling into oblivion, he rendered it into verse, to be sung or chanted; only on rare occasions did he commit it to writing. Paleographic evidence indicates also that writing, in its earliest stages, was used mostly to chronicle historic events; it was not used to impart instruction in mysticism and philosophy, exorcism and religion, for Druid bard and Brahman sage alike considered this a profanation of the esoteric wisdom. In that golden epoch of intuition and memory culture no teacher ever attempted to hand down the sacred knowledge through the medium of script.

The immortal epics of poet-philosophers, such as the *Iliad* of Homer and the *Ramayana* of Valmiki, were learned by professional bards and minstrels who recited them in the courts of kings and in the pleasure gardens of the great cities where they drew large cosmopolitan gatherings. They wandered from land to land reciting the traditional ballads in order to entice a zealous following from among the curious. In those days erudition was judged not by a scholar's literary achievements, but by his ability to inspire his bearers to seek wisdom. It was customary also in every court throughout the world for a professional royal minstrel to chant the dynastic history from its beginning up to the time of the living king.

For example, in pre-Columbian America, in the palaces of the Incas and Aztecs, reciters were employed who had memorized the genealogy of the solar rulers from the most remote eras. In this way the hoary wisdom of the Vedas as well as of the non-Vedic literature of India was safely passed from generation to generation by word of mouth for many thousands of years with the utmost preservation of their purity, until in later times they were recorded and printed in book form. Even today in traveling through India, Sri Lanka, or Burma, one may come across numerous individuals who can dictate for days the great works of scripture, grammar, astrology, medicine, and those of other branches of ancient knowledge.

Some of this ancient lore is still being orally transmitted, having never been recorded. In Sri Lanka and Burma it is customary for every Buddhist novice to learn the Pali grammar, lexicons, and the *Dhammapada* by heart. Of course, most of these works are metrical compositions which make the memorizing of them quite easy. It is rare to find a Buddhist monk in those countries who cannot recite the *Dhammapada* verbatim. It is well known that even the physical philosophers of Miletus and Athens presented their speculations in poetic form.

The versification of the *Dhammapada* was done in the Audience Hall of Jeta's Grove at Sravasti to enable the followers of Buddha to learn them by rote. Most people think that the versification of these discourses was done after the demise of the Great Master, but my own research leads me to question this. Although at a certain phase of human culture, learning by rote and oral transmission as a mode of preserving knowledge were admired by the philosophers both in East and West, we cannot underestimate the magnitude of the disadvantages involved.

Natural catastrophe, pestilence, war, or other large-scale disasters could destroy the line of priests, bringing to an abrupt end the collective wisdom of untold centuries. This is the exact cause of the disappearance of most of the spoken languages of the archaic past, before the emergence of Sanskrit, Sumerian, Hamitic, and Semitic which, according to our modern philologists, can rightfully claim to be of very early antiquity. How many languages with their literary treasures have vanished from the surface of our planet is still an unsolved question. Dialects which we now know only by name have left us no more than their imprint on the grammatical structures and vocabularies of our modern tongues.

While the age-old method of oral instruction had intrinsic esoteric merit, the ancient philosophers caused neglect of the written word, which did not reemerge before the sixth century B.C. at the dawn of the new intellectual epoch in India. Throughout the Buddhist canon are passages which presuppose the existence of that very ancient religious tradition known as the Vedas, of which the Great Mendicant, Buddha, had acquired mastery under the renowned sage Visvamitra, "the universal friend." Yet the source of this literature is lost in the mists of time.

Although its system of philosophy differs vastly in some of its cardinal tenets from Brahmanism, any critical student is aware that Buddhism contains many of the teachings of the earliest Upanishads. For a fuller understanding of Buddha's spiritual teachings, a regard for the atmosphere in which they developed at the convergence of Vedic and non-Vedic streams is indispensable. The sacred tradition of the Vedas was already in the possession of the Aryans many millennia ago. Its mystic religio-philosophy was not only closely related to that of their relatives in Iran (where it took the form of the Avesta), but is also similar to the Eleusinian and Orphic traditions of the Western Aryans who migrated to and established their cultural empires in Greece, Central and Northern Europe, and the Emerald Isle.

It should be noted, however, that the seeds of desuetude had been germinating in the Aryan religion before that great family divided. Orthodox Hindus hold that the Vedas existed even before the creation of the world, coeternal with Brahman. Consequently, most of the hymns of the *Rig-Veda* are not just odes to the beauty of nature, but are musings about a transcendental reality *beyond* visible natural phenomena. It is said that the rishis, while in spiritual trance, came in direct contact with celestial beings of whom they sang, and whom they considered as expressions of the cosmic intelligence, manifestations of the immanent divine principle. Thus they conceived of nature as a living organism controlled by conscious, intelligent entities.

To denote these deities, the poets coined a special appellative term, *deva,* for which there is no adequate equivalent in modern European languages. It literally means the "shining one" or the "donor." The rain, therefore, is a deva, because it gives nourishment to all life on earth. Sun, moon, and stars are devas, because they shed light throughout the solar system and universe. The Ganges, Indus, and Sarasvati are deified rivers, because they irrigate the arable lands of Aryavarta. In addition, many gods of the pluralistic pantheon once were great heroes, warriors, or philanthropists, who later were venerated as devas for their valor or benevolence.

The religion of the Vedas is neither naturalism nor anthropomorphism, polytheism or monotheism, but a unique mysticism, a synthesis of religious streams known to the ancient Aryans. But when esotericism was ousted by exotericism, symbolism by ritualism, idealism by sacerdotalism, this early spiritual vision dwindled into a polytheistic sacrificial creed, and the cultural life of the Aryans became completely dominated by priesthood.

The Brahman priests made every effort to monopolize for themselves the religious hymns of the Vedas and the ballads which the Aryans sang in praise of the deified natural forces, thus arrogating to themselves as much power as possible. Dr. T. W. Rhys Davids writes in *Buddhist India:*

> We cannot, therefore, be far wrong if we suppose they [the Brahmans] were not merely indifferent to the use of writing as a means of handing on the books so lucrative to themselves, but were even strongly opposed to a method so dangerous to their exclusive privileges. And we ought not to be surprised to find that the oldest manuscripts on bark or palm leaf known in India are Buddhist; that the earliest written records on stone and metal are Buddhist; that it is the Buddhists who first made use of writing to record their canonical books; . . .

And so it was that with the advent of the Buddha the art of writing was given renewed impetus, and began to rise again from the gloomy limbo where it had been concealed for so long by the Brahman priesthood. For a genealogy of Prince Siddhartha Gautama Sakya Muni, full-blown lotus of the solar dynasty, Lion of the Sakya clan, prince and heir-apparent of the city state of Kapilavastu, we have to rely mostly on the literary material embedded in the immortal Sanskrit poetical works of Avaghosha and Kshemendra. Asvaghosha flourished in the second century A.D. at the court of the Kushan King Kanishka in Northern India and recorded the Buddhist chronicles which had been handed down through oral tradition.

Kshemendra, a great Buddhist poet of Kashmir in the eleventh century, wrote a poetical chronology of the dynastic history of the Sakya clan in his *Avadana Kalpalata,* an epic work which was translated into Tibetan in 1272 A.D. by Sovi-rton Lochava under the supervision of Phags-pa, spiritual instructor of Kublai Khan. The original Sanskrit text was lost for many centuries but recovered in 1882 by the Buddhist scholar Sri S. C. Das in the Tibetan printing establishment at Potala. The Sakya-utpatti ("Birth of the Sakya clan") of Kshemendra, as well as Pali commentaries and Tibetan legends, together give a comprehensive account of the origin of the Sakya clan.

Almost thirty miles to the south of the foothills of the Himalayas, a rolling plain extends for hundreds of miles along the Nepalese frontier, verdant and picturesque, rich in scenic delights and silent forest glades through which flow sparkling streams. In this ideal retreat Buddhist tradition has it that a *bodhisattva*, Kapila Gautama Muni, lived about three centuries before the advent of Gautama Buddha. Sometime between 950 and 900 B.C. there reigned a mighty king named Virudhaka, lord of a vast confederation of vassal states, and descendant of the Ikshvaku dynasty.

On a pleasure trip he beheld a most charming young princess and felt himself compelled to make her a matrimonial proposal, which the princess accepted only on condition that the king appoint her youngest son, instead of her eldest, to be his heir to the throne of Kosala. In due time the queen reminded her lord of the promise he had made; the king was distressed by the demand that he break the Vedic convention, but the four older sons volunteered to accept banishment. They loaded their chariots and rode towards the Himalayas whose snow-covered peaks glittered on the far horizon. After some days they reached the monastery of the celebrated sage Kapila Gautama.

The princes were well received and, instructed by the sage; they founded a flourishing metropolis which became known as Kapilavastu. After many centuries of benign rule, the sovereignty of the Sakya kingdom fell to King Sinhaharm. During his reign Kapilavastu became a center of international trade, learning, and spiritual culture. King Sinhahanu had four sons and four daughters. The oldest son was Prince Suddhodana. He became known as King of Law, for he governed in accordance with the rules prescribed by Manu for righteous kings, and was loved by all his subjects.

King Suddhodana married his cousin Maya and, after her death, another cousin, Maha-Prajapati. Queen Maya was the personification of beauty and purity, compassion, cosmic love, and intelligence. In esoteric schools she was considered the materialization of a divine vision: Queen Maya had all the virtues to become the mother of the universal Lord of

Compassion, and yet after several years of married life the royal couple had not been blessed with a child.

The account of the annunciation of the Sakya prince who was to become Buddha, known to every Buddhist in Sanskrit, Pali, or his native vernacular, is charmingly rendered into English by Sir Edwin Arnold, one of the great poets of the nineteenth century who spent a large part of his life in India. His classic, *The Light of Asia,* relates:

That night the wife of King Suddhodana,

Maya the Queen, asleep beside her Lord,

Dreamed a strange dream; dreamed that a star from heaven –

Splendid, six-rayed, in color rosy-pearl,
Whereof the token was an Elephant
Six-tusked, and white as milk of Kamadhuk –
Shot through the void; and, shining into her,
Entered her womb upon the right. Awaked,
Bliss beyond mortal mother's filled her breast,
And over half the earth a lovely light
Forewent the morn. The strong hills shook; the waves
Sank lulled; all flowers that blow by day came forth
As 'twere high noon; down to the farthest hells
Passed the Queen's joy, as when warm sunshine thrills
Wood-glooms to gold, and into all the deeps
A tender whisper pierced. "Oh ye," it said,
"The dead that are to live, the live who die,
Uprise, and hear, and hope! Buddha is come!"
Whereat in Limbos numberless much peace
Spread, and the world's heart throbbed, and a wind blew
With unknown freshness over lands and seas.
And when the morning dawned, and this was told,
The grey dream-readers said "The dream is good!

The Crab is in conjunction with the Sun;
The Queen shall bear a boy, a holy child
Of wondrous wisdom, profiting all flesh,
Who shall deliver men from ignorance,
Or rule the world, if he will deign to rule."
In this wise was the holy Buddha born.

It was the age-old custom that the first confinement of a young mother should take place in the home of her parents, so, when Queen Maya felt that the blessed day was drawing near, she intimated her desire to go to her childhood home for the great event which the whole world was anticipating. The Lord of Kapilavastu caused the road connecting the two cities of the Sakyas to be swept and decorated, embellished with festoons and garlands. It was the month of flowers; the day was Vaisakha (Vesak) Full Moon Day in the year 623 B.C.

Between the two cities lay the famous pleasure garden Lumbini, and it was here, as the cortege paused on the journey, that the holy child saw the light of day among blossoming trees and warbling birds, while strains of heavenly music filled the air and soft breezes enriched with a celestial aroma blew throughout the Sakya kingdom. Buddhist tradition records that as soon as Prince Siddhartha was born, King Suddhodana summoned the most erudite scholars and astrologers to the palace of Kapilavastu to cast the horoscope of the newborn babe.

After examining the planetary positions, seven of the eight astrologers announced that the prince would become either the universal monarch of the present cycle, or he would retire from the world and become Buddha. Kaundanna alone, youngest member of the Astrological Council, predicted that Siddhartha would indeed abdicate the throne of the Sakyas and become omniscient Buddha to save suffering humanity. Later, when the prince renounced the throne, Kaundanna also gave up the "householder life" and joined a small group of contemplatives in the forest.

It was this community of five ascetics with whom Gautama-Siddhartha spent six years practicing austerities so severe that, when near death, he perceived that enlightenment was not to be attained by this means. It was then he adopted the system of moderation that came to be known as the Middle Way. After Gautama's illumination under the Bodhi tree, these five monks became his earliest disciples. Another who correctly foresaw the infant's destiny was the venerable sage Asita (or Kala Devala), who was spiritual guide and mentor to King Suddhodana and to his father before him.

On learning of the birth of Siddhartha, the sage hastened to the palace and, observing the distinguishing marks on the child, the aged Asita wept - not for the prince, but for himself, as his great age would prevent him from seeing the child grow up to become Buddha. As King Suddhodana strongly believed in the prediction that his son would be a world monarch, he had him instructed by Visvamitra in the extensive curriculum befitting such a prince, including the Vedas and all systems of mysticism then current. It is noteworthy that the young man was taught to decipher pictographs as well as the sign language of cave dwellers and those plying the seas.

In fact, from the vivid descriptions in ancient Sanskrit and Tibetan Buddhist works, and even from those in the rival literatures of the Jains and Vedantins, we may safely deduce that the Buddha had mastered all the sciences, arts, and languages known in India at that time. We have here an interesting parallel between King Suddhodana of Kapilavastu appointing the sage Visvamitra as teacher to Prince Siddhartha and the selection by King Philip of Macedonia of the great philosopher Aristotle to be preceptor to Prince Alexander.

In both Aryan princes the age-old dream of establishing an invincible brotherhood of peoples was ingrained in their racial soul; but while Alexander spent most of his short life in military expeditions in an effort to expand the borders of his empire, Prince Siddhartha bade adieu to a worldly realm in order to establish an imperishable, eternal kingdom of the spirit. The seventh-sixth centuries B.C. marked a new historical epoch in the religious evolution of Northern India. The racial intellect of the time was compelled to face two opposing psychological trends.

The solution lay in the emergence of a magnetic individual who could successfully synthesize the realism of the physical philosophers with the idealism of the ancient Vedas, one who could blend the best of the old with the vigorous and constructive elements of the new. This mighty task, undertaken by Gautama Sakyamuni, was successfully accomplished by setting the "Wheel of the Sacred Law in motion" - that eternal Law which is forever valid, for the past, the present, and for eternities to come.

This Law is preserved for posterity in the *Dhammapada*, a sublime ethical treatise of twenty-six cantos, which is to millions of Buddhists what the *Bhagavad-Gita* is to Hindus. Although it is not known when it was first committed to writing, its content suggests a direct descent from spiritual instruction given by Gautama Buddha. Extensive research confirms that these teachings express a universal wisdom, a rediscovery of the eternal Buddha Dharma which could rightly be termed the Sanatana Dharma or "eternal wisdom."

Dhammapada - the path of *dhamma* (Sanskrit *dharma*, a word comprising the essential ideas contained in the words truth, virtue, and law) - was compiled at the First Council of Buddhist Elders three weeks after the Master's passing. It is therefore the oldest anthology on Buddhism extant. The work consists of a systematic collection of stanzas, terse yet elegant, giving the quintessence of Buddhist wisdom. These stanzas were the distillation of various sermons delivered by Buddha to kings and queens, to ministers and merchants, cowherds and peasants, to grieving mothers, distressed lovers, monks, paupers, saints, and criminals.

The first verse of the *Dhammapada* is a direct attack on the dialectical materialism prevalent at the time of Buddha. Mind is not a by-product of physical elements; according to Buddha, mind precedes everything that exists. Nor is the destruction of the physical body the end of human existence. The external cosmos is a creation of mind integrated into a cosmic order of cause and effect. The Master admonished his leading Arhats not to compel his followers to learn Ardha-Magadhi in order to understand his doctrine.

Therefore, when Buddhism expanded, as it rapidly did, beyond the frontiers of Aryavarta, the missionaries began to translate the Dharma into numerous dialects and vernaculars. We know, for example, that *Dharmapadam,* an early Prakrit treatise, was composed during the fourth century B.C., and that about a century later, the first Buddhist king, Asoka, sent his son, Arhat Mahinda, to Sri Lanka, where he and his disciples made the first Sinhalese version of this ethical manual, titled *Dhampiya.*

Unfortunately, this earliest rendition of *Dhammapada* in Sinhalese-Prakrit fell into oblivion soon after Buddhist prelates retranslated it into Pali along with the other works of the *Tripitaka* in 88-76 B.C. It may be noted that Pali, like most European languages, has no alphabet of its own; in Sri Lanka it was written in Sinhalese script, while Burmese Buddhists used their own characters to write the Pali text. The language used by Buddha, Ardha-Magadhi dialect, is very similar to the literary language of the Jains. Pali has the coloring of this dialect.

Because in a living language terms undergo continual modification as the thought life of the nation changes, the Theravada scholars tried to retranslate the Buddha Dhamma from Sinhalese back into Pali, which has the Sinhalese idiom unaltered with very little Sanskrit influence upon it. Most of the Indian versions are no longer extant, either in printed or manuscript form, in any of the museum libraries of the world. Only a few birchbark manuscripts in Prakrit were discovered in the early part of the nineteenth century in northwestern India.

A Chinese *Dhammapada,* translated from the Sanskrit, was not lost; it was the first book, along with the rest of the *Tripitaka,* ever to be produced in a printing press and was made from wooden blocks in 972 A.D. But not until 1885 was the Pali Dhammapada, which had been lost to India for twenty-two centuries or so, reintroduced into that country in Devanagari transliteration by my paternal uncle, Ven. B. Sri Dharmapala Nayaka Thero of Batapola, under the guidance of Rt. Ven. C. A. Silakkandha Nayaka Thero of Dodanduwa, Sri Lanka.

Thirty years earlier, in 1855, a young Danish scholar, Victor Fausboll, published the first European edition of the *Dhammapada* in a Latin translation, with Pali text, and selections of native commentary. Subsequent renditions in German, English, and French followed, making the scripture more readily available to Western students. Later, Dr. E. W. Burlingame's three-volume translation of the voluminous commentary on the *Dhammapada,* written by the renowned Indian scholar Buddhaghosha in the early part of the fifth century A.D., provided the modern reader with a wealth of legendary and historic details regarding the various episodes and circumstances which led to the utterance of these verses.

Were Buddha to come to the world today, however, he would probably not countenance some of the stories that accompany his ethical teachings. For instance, he did not totally deny the existence of spirit in his and anatman *(Pali anatta*) doctrine, but used negative terms to illustrate and clarify the state of spirit.

In this luminous kalpa one thousand Buddhas will appear. Due to this auspiciousness it is known as a fortunate aeon. The historical Buddha, Sakyamuni, who appeared over 2500 years ago, was the fourth Buddha. Before him were the Buddhas Krakuchchanda, Kanakamuni and Kashyapa. Prior to his life as Prince Siddartha, Buddha Sakyamuni, as a *bodhisattva,* had generated the enlightened aspiration to benefit limitless sentient beings, and consequently accumulated a vast stock of merit and wisdom, during many lives.

Then, while teaching in the Buddha field of Tushita, the Buddhas and *bodhisattvas* of the ten directions requested him to manifest the supreme birth in our world. Thus, proclaiming the *bodhisattva* Maitreya as his regent, he looked carefully, chose the place and conditions of his birth and then entered his mother's womb. He took birth in Lumbini, to Queen Mahamaya and King Sudodhana, of the royal family of the Shakya caste, and displayed great qualities of intelligence and compassion, quickly mastering many subjects without even being taught.

However, Prince Gautama Siddhartha was not destined for a worldly life: seeing impermanence and the inevitability of suffering, old age and death, he stepped out of his sheltered home, abandoning the temporary pleasures of wealth, power and family. He searched for the wisdom to end suffering and endeavoured to understand life. He wandered the countryside as a mendicant, studying under the most renowned yogins and gurus of his time. Being naturally gifted, he quickly mastered the various practices he was taught, but still his goal eluded him.

One day, he realised the path must lie somewhere between the extremes of indulgence in sensuality, and austerity, neither of which, he had found, lead to liberation: indulgence intoxicates the mind, while mortification places undue stress on the mind. Having adopted a more moderate approach, he then, with single-pointed concentration, sat under the shade of a bodhi tree, at present day Bodhgaya in India, and meditated on the nature of reality.

Finally, he achieved his goal: he recognised the fundamental, eternal, unchanging nature of mind, and, in so doing, he became free from all delusion. Transcending dualistic experience, he saw through the conventional notion of a self that conceives of the rest of the world as "other" and thereby experiences pleasure and pain in relation to it. Emerging from this profound realisation, he became "Buddha," which means "Fully Awakened." The truth he realised is expressed in the four seals that characterise all Buddha's teachings:

All compounded phenomena are impermanent;

All defiled phenomena have the nature of suffering;

Whether totally afflicted or completely pure,

All phenomena are empty and without a self;

Nirvana alone is liberation and peace.

Soon after attaining enlightenment, Buddha began teaching and sharing his vast wisdom with those who sought guidance. He first turned the wheel of dharma in Varanasi, and continued to teach extensively throughout India. After showing the path, Buddha said "Although I have shown the means of liberation, you must know that it depends on you alone." This being so, we must validate all teachings through sincere investigation and personal experience. After Buddha's paranirvana in Kushinagar, a council of 500 Arhats assembled and collected all his teachings, so that the lamp of wisdom would abide in the world and dispel the darkness and suffering of all beings.

The three presiding Arhats at the council, Upali, Buddha's oldest disciple, Ananda, the Buddha's cousin and Mahakashyapa, the most learned of Buddha's disciples, each repeated Buddha's teachings and discourses. They were divided into three sections, which became known as the Tripitaka, or three baskets:

1. The Vinaya-pitaka: moral discipline, repeated by Upali.
2. The Sutra-pitaka: the collection of major discourses, repeated by Ananda.
3. The Abhidharma-pitaka: the collection of metaphysical teachings, repeated by Mahakashyapa.

**THE BASICS**

Although we trace our lineage and tradition to Buddha Sakyamuni, the teachings of Buddhism are beginningless, and, as a living truth, they are realised directly. Buddha taught the Middle-way: the most profoundly validated path, which lies between the extremes of asceticism and indulgence, and between the two extreme views of eternalism (taking what is impermanent to be permanent) and nihilism (denying karma and conventional truth).

Buddha taught that we are totally responsible for ourselves, and no one else can save us. He said there is no external creator, just the unfailing principle of Karma or cause and effect. He taught about Buddha nature: our potential for Buddhahood, which is inherent in every being, and, for that reason, our purpose is to realise and manifest this.

The foundation of Buddhism is the Four Noble Truths:

Suffering, Its causes, Cessation of suffering and The Eight-Fold Path leads to its end.

Buddha said that to accomplish liberation, suffering must be comprehended, its cause given up, its cessation mastered and the path developed. The origin of suffering is ignorance, which means "not knowing" the true nature of existence. From this confusion arise all the manifestations of *samsara*. We project things which do not exist: a self and other, and permanence onto what is impermanent. We also believe such things as the notion that lasting happiness can be obtained from material possessions. This all gives rise to the emotions of desire, aggression, jealousy and pride, which can overwhelm our mind and so determine our actions, which then result in karma.

The momentum of this carries the consciousness from one life to the next, to experience the results of our actions. Only liberation can break this cycle. Liberation from suffering is possible by following the Eight-fold Path: Right View, Right Thought, Right Speech, Right Action, Right Livelihood, Right Effort, Right Mindfulness, and Right Concentration.

The ten actions to avoid are Taking life, Taking what is not given, Sexual misconduct, Lying, Sowing Discord, Harsh words, Worthless chatter, Covetousness, Wishing harm to others, Wrong views. The ten virtuous actions consist of giving up the ten negative actions and practicing their positive antidotes: To renounce killing and instead protect the lives of living beings; to renounce taking what is not given, and instead practice generosity; to give up sexual misconduct, and instead to follow the rules of discipline; to renounce lying, and instead tell the truth; to give up sowing discord, and instead to reconcile disputes; to abandon harsh words, and instead speak pleasantly; to put an end to useless chatter, and instead to recite prayers; to renounce covetousness, and instead to learn to be generous; to give up wishing to harm others, and instead to cultivate the desire to help them; to put an end to wrong views, and instead to establish in yourself the true and authentic view. This involves developing the six perfections: Generosity, Discipline, Patience, Diligence, Concentration, Discriminating knowledge.

The fundamental teachings of the Buddha are: to avoid any harmful actions, to cultivate positive actions, and to tame your own mind.

## BUDDHIST PRACTICE

Besides urging us to correct our external behaviour, Buddhism provides meditative practices which help us to correct the mental and emotional causes of our actions and our suffering. Such practices range from those of great simplicity to those of extreme complexity, and may be widely applicable, or suited only to very experienced practitioners.

Good instructions on meditation can be found in books, but, to be safe and most effective, it is best to first make contact with a qualified teacher who is connected to an unbroken lineage from the Buddha. This is because it is through this relationship that we form a personal connection to the enlightened nature, and receive the blessings of the lineage. Having connected with a teacher, we enter the path by Taking refuge (trusting):

In the Buddha - his life shows that enlightenment can be accomplished,

In the Dharma - the teachings that clearly show the profound path to Buddhahood,

In the *Sangha* - the guidance and support of the community of spiritual friends.

The Buddha's teachings are divided into the "Three Turnings of the Wheel of Dharma." The first turning includes his teachings on Vinaya, or moral discipline, and the practice of the four mindfulnesses. The second turning was for the countless *bodhisattvas*, to whom he taught the Perfection of Wisdom: teaching that all phenomena are empty and lack true existence. In the third turning, Buddha explained the clear light nature of mind, which is inseparable from emptiness and has, inherent within it, all the qualities of Buddhahood.

The Buddha was only concerned with the here and now with the present reality of the moment in each of our lives. In the present moment, distinctions between the theoretical concept called Hinayana and the theoretical concept called Mahayana come down to the relationship between what one thinks and says and what one does. Cause and effect is the law of real time. And we each continue to receive the effects of our causes. Everything else is just ideality (fantasy). In the last eight years of his life, Sakyamuni Buddha taught that the law of cause and effect comprises ten suchnesses that are common to all phenomena, even Buddha's.

The ten suchness are the appearance, nature, entity, power, influence, internal cause, relation, latent effect, manifest effect and consistency from beginning to end." These ten factors or suchnesses give rise to the realms of experience that we undergo as human beings. These ten factors give rise to the six lower realms from hell, insatiable desire, animality, hatred, tranquility and to bliss, the three noble paths from arharts, pretyakas, and *bodhisattvas*, as well as Buddhahood itself. This principles establishes that the lower nine worlds of common mortals and the world of Buddhahood are powered by the same Law and are not separate realms of existence.

Each of these ten realms in turn possesses the other nine as latent conditions thereby comprising 100 worlds in total. In turn each of these ten worlds are comprised of the ten factors mentioned above and so they comrpise actually 100 factors. And finally the thoousand factors of reality exist on three realms, the realm of the self, the immediate dependency or group and the larger natural environment or universe. This philosophy is the Tien Tai School known as the three thousand realms in a single life moment. The life moment contains the past, present and future and it permeates all of space of the ten directions in a single instance of thought. Tien Tai developed this philosophy of Life on the basis of the Lotus Sutras teachings.

This constitutes the actual life experience of living beings and is manifested throughout all of eternity throughout time and space. If you dont believe they exist in both time and space, then lets consider the world of hell. We know that at any given moment in time, the various worlds are manifesting themselves across space. Inmates in jail awaiting a death sentence, like say John Gotti, are probably transmigrating through the four lowest worlds of hell, insatiable desire, animality and hatred. Maybe at times, when his daughter pays a visit he enters a momentary state of tranquility and enjoys a fleeting state of humanity.

He just breaks the news about a new grandchild on the way; he may experience a moment of heavenly bliss. This is the transmigration through the lower six paths from moment to moment in our lives. Under such states, it is the outer environment that controls our karmic effects. Maybe once in a blue moon John Gotti thinks about the biblical expression, "what you sow, so shall you reep". This is probably the closest he gets to cause and effect, but nonetheless, since he doesnt know of Buddhism, he prays to God to change his karma for him. Annothe good example is the difference in world view between when we get up to read the paper bout Israel and Palestine in our cozy *pajamas* while the people over there are actually suffering through it.

The *Lotus Sutra* is the only sutra where the Buddha does not speak from the capacity of his listeners, discards expedient means and employs words and phrases to descirbe his actual enlightened state. You guys will continue to remain stuck, speaking only on the basis of abstract concepts as you continue indulging a false understanding of matters concerning the Buddhist philosophy. In the end you'll all be faulted for entertaining erroneous assumptions and you will receive effects accordingly. It's really not about schools, my good friends. Buddhism is a discipline related to actual life outcomes occurring from moment to moment and day to day in the actual world.

It's about the life condition we are able to manifest and the amount of karma we can purify. Look deeply at the unity, work and outcomes of the Soka Gakkai International. It is an organization of people united behind and who take action in perfect accord with the deep wisdom of the Lotus Sutra. Purifying karma (oneness of inner and outer conditions) deepens our own sense of self identity and the quality of our life experience (non duality) in the context of our relationships and associations in this actual world.

The Lotus Blossom of the Fine Dharma sprouts only under certain conditions and only for those of a true seeking mind, and only for those willing to put away their arrogance and attachments and those willing to enter the Buddha's realm based on faith alone. The Buddha wisdom is the oneness of master and disciple in the realm of dependent co-arising. The realm of dependent co-arising is the only actual world of reality. Emptiness and the Middleway is the Buddha's trancendental inner wisdom and eternal inner true identity. We each comprise this same fundamental reality. Severing attachments to desires is only an expedient device and the first step on this path.

The bodhissatva path is a higher path and the path that finds the most effective means and measures of bringing the Dharma wisdom to the greatest number of people in the course of the Buddha's actual life time. This is why when the Buddha was ready to open up his teachings to the greater lot of humanity he introduced the easy doctrines of Amithaba so that the people can begin to learn the true nature and power of the mind. This is called an expedient Mahyana teaching precisely because Amitahba is merely a spiritual quality existing in the mind universe only.

It is the *Sambhogakaya* aspect of the Buddha within us. We can know that this was an expedient device because in the end there was no greater joy for disciples than to be in the company of Sakyamuni the actual person himself. The greatest standard to uphold in Buddhism is the standard that all the Buddha's disciples attained enlightenment before they died by awakening to the Buddhanature within themselves through their association with the Buddha.

No other description of events is more perfect. The Buddha never intended for the earlier teachings (latter to be called Hinayana) or the expedient Mahayana teachings (gradual introduction of three bodies to be the vehicle of their deliverance in and of themselves as separate teachings).

These were merely preparatory teachings. Without revealing the actual true Cause for enlightenment (delivering others along with oneself through the revelation of the eternity of our actual life) Buddhism appears to be nothing but an endless painfull austerity. This is the source of Mike's anxiety. And Bruce has no answers for him.

## TEACHINGS OF THE BUDDHA

Buddhist doctrine can be considered as a marked departure from the Brahmanical tradition. Buddhist philosophy did not focus on abstract thinking nor did it indulge in idle speculations on such questions as the origin and end of the world or on the existence of a god. The Buddha said, 'if by the absolute is meant something out of relation to all known things, its existence cannot be established by any reasoning. The whole universe is a system of relations. We know nothing that is or can be unrelated.

If the absolute is devoid of qualities, the all things arising from him ought likewise to be devoid of qualities. But in reality all things are circumscribed by qualities. Hence the absolute cannot be their cause'. The gospel of the Buddha avoided all hypotheses regarding the unknown and concerned itself only with the present day to day happenings in life. Distancing itself from ritualism, theology and metaphysics Buddhism stressed on the perfection of character and devotion to virtues.

According to Buddhist philosophy the idea of self is an imaginary false belief which produces harmful thoughts of 'me' and 'mine', selfish desire and other problems. This false belief is considered as the root cause of all evils in the world. The basic teachings of the Buddha are centered on the reality of human suffering and the need to find way of lasting relief from all forms of discontent. Buddha's philosophy may be simply explained in three words, *Anatman, Anitya* and *Dukkha*. Except Nirvana, all things are Anitya and so are painful and devoid of any everlasting substance. It is the Four Noble Truths which provide the key to the understanding of the Buddha's teachings.

The Four Noble Truths are as follows:

- That all forms of being, human and otherwise, are afflicted with sufferings,
- That the cause of this suffering is craving, born of the illusion of a soul,
- That this suffering has a lasting end in the Experience of Enlightenment (Nirvana) which is the complete letting go of the illusion of a soul and all consequent desire and aversion,
- That this peaceful and blissful Enlightenment is achieved through a gradual training, a Path which is called the Middle way or the Eightfold Path.'

The Eightfold Path which consists of the diligent cultivation of virtue, meditation and wisdom is as follows:

- Right Understanding
- Right Thought
- Right Speech
- Right Action
- Right Livelihood
- Right Effort
- Right Mindfulness
- Right Concentration

Right understanding means right way of interpreting and viewing the world. It involves the abandonment of all dogmatically held wrong views and understanding the truth that the world is filled with endless sorrow generated by selfishness and non-controlled desire. Right thought is 'free from greed and lust, free from ill-will, free from cruelty'. Right speech includes proper way of communication without hurting others sentiments and abstaining from lies.

Right action refers to unselfish action and involves acts of kindness, compassion, etc. Right livelihood means that one should not make his living by questionable means and follow honest methods. Right effort has been described as the right frame of mind, i.e. controlling passions so as to prevent the rise of bad thoughts. Through right frame of mind one can destroy attachments, anger, jealousy, etc. Right mindfulness is considered as technique of cultivating awareness which is viewed as meditation for the removal of worldly evils.

Right concentration is an effort towards achieving of wholesome consciousness through systematic cultivation of meditation. The Buddhist goal is the achievement of human perfection which is considered as the real purpose of life. It is essential to follow the Buddhist path in order to attain happiness, contentment and freedom from fear.

## THE BENARES SERMON

The Blessed One thus addressed the five Bhikkhus; 'There are two extremes, O Bhikkhus, which he who has given up the world ought to avoid. What are these two extremes? A life given to pleasures, devoted to pleasures and lusts: this is degrading, sensual, vulgar, ignoble, and profitless; and a life given to mortifications: this is painful, ignoble, and profitless.

By avoiding these two extremes, O Bhikkhus, the Tathagata has gained the knowledge of the Middle Path which leads to insight, which leads to wisdom, which conduces to calm, to knowledge, to the Sambodhi, to Nirvana. 'Which, O Bhikkhus, is this Middle Path the knowledge of which the Tathagata has gained, which leads to insight, which leads to wisdom, which conduces to calm, to knowledge, to the Sambodhi, to Nirvana?

It is the Holy Eightfold Path, namely, Right Belief, Right Aspiration, Right Speech, Right Conduct, Right Means of Livelihood, Right Endeavour, Right Memory, Right Meditation. This, O Bhikkhus, is the Middle Path the knowledge of which the Tathagata has gained, which leads to insight, which leads to wisdom, which conduces to calm, to knowledge, to the Sambodhi, to Nirvana. 'This, O Bhikkhus, is the Noble Truth of Suffering: Birth is suffering; decay is suffering; illness is suffering; death is suffering.

Presence of objects we hate, is suffering; separation from objects we love, is suffering; not to obtain what we desire, is suffering. Briefly, the fivefold clinging to existence is suffering. 'This, O Bhikkhus, is the Noble Truth of the Cause of Suffering: Thirst, that leads to re-birth, accompanied by pleasure and lust, finding its delight here and there. [This thirst is threefold] namely, thirst for pleasure, thirst for existence, thirst for prosperity.

'This, O Bhikkhus, is the Noble Truth of Cessation of Suffering. [it ceases with] the complete cessation of this thirst - a cessation which consists in the absence of every passion - with the abandoning of this thirst, with the doing away with it, with the deliverance from it, with the destruction of desire. 'This, O Bhikkhus, is the Noble Truth of the Path which leads to the cessation of suffering; That holy eightfold Path, that is to say: Right Belief, Right Aspiration, Right Speech, Right Conduct, Right Means of Livelihood, Right Endeavour, Right Memory, Right Meditation.

The 'five clingings' are: corporality, feeling, perception, mental formation, consciousness. Buddhism sums up in this way all the elements of our (illusory) bodily and spiritual personality.

## THE WORLD RELIGIONS READER

The philosophy of Buddhism is based on rationalism and the Buddha talked about the law of Karma and rebirth. According to Buddhism every event in individual's life is determined by the Karma of his or her previous life. Life is thought of as an unbroken chain and the present existence of an individual is the consequence of his/her past activities. The Buddhist doctrine of Karma is not fatalism and it is based on morality and the law of causation. The belief in Karma was very much there in the Upanishads but the Buddha explained and formulated this doctrine in a different way.

According to the Buddha, 'All living beings have actions (Karma) as their own, their inheritance, their congenital cause, their kinsman, their refuge. It is Karma that differentiates beings into low and high states'. It is Karma that explains the circumstances that living beings find themselves in. The Buddha did not believe in Atman (soul) but accepted the continuity of individual consciousness even after death. In Buddhism rebirth is not transmigration but continuity in life series in which process Karma serves as a casual connection. Karma becomes the force behind and reason for the practice of morality.

The story of Angulimala illustrates the Buddhist notion of Karma. Angulimala was a robber and later on became a Buddhist monk. Even after becoming Buddhist monk one day he could not escape people's wrath because people could recognize him as an earlier robber. When Angulimala complained to the Buddha about this incident the Buddha said, 'you are suffering in this life itself for the evil deeds you have committed. Endure it, you will be all right. It is not better to suffer small punishment in this life itself than to suffer greater punishment in the life to come'. Next to Karma, come the concepts of rebirth and nirvana.

The Buddha did not belief in the existence of soul but how does then rebirth occur. This has been explained in the following way. 'On a Buddhist shrine one candle, burnt low, is about to expire. A monk takes a new candle lights it from the old. The old candle dies, the new candle burns bright. What went across from the old candle to the new? There was a causal link but nothing went across! In the same way, there was a causal link between your previous life and your present life, but not soul has gone across.'

When a person dies, physical body goes but the dying consciousness in this life migrates to a fresh body as a fresh consciousness. The concept of rebirth has been popularized in Buddhism through the Jataka stories related to the previous births of the Buddha. Attainment of nirvana is the ultimate goal in Buddhism. Nirvana means the annihilation of passion, hatred and delusion. Nirvana is the cessation of all sufferings.

Through self-control and pursuing the eightfold path one can attain nirvana in this life itself. Buddhism is essentially a philosophy of eternal change. The Buddhist teachings emphasize on individual to take responsibility on his/her deeds, no god or priest or anyone else can help you out from your misdeeds. Even the Buddha had no power to save. Shift of emphasis from deities to karma in Buddhism is explained as an attempt to undermine religious differentiations and a move towards the idea of a universal religion.

**THE ROUND OF EXISTENCE**

The king said: 'when you speak of transmigration [rebirth], Nagasena, what does that mean? 'A being born here, O king, dies here. Having died here it springs up elsewhere. Having been born there, there it dies. Having died there, it springs up elsewhere. That is what is meant by transmigration.' 'Give me an illustration.' 'It is like the case of man, who after eating a mango should set the seed in the ground. From that a great tree would be produced and give fruit. And there would be no end to the succession, in that way of mango trees...' Are all subject to rebirth?

The king said: 'Nagasena, is there anyone who, after death, is not reindividualised [reborn]?' 'Some are, some are not,' 'Who are they?' 'A sinful being is reindividualised, a sinless one is not.' 'Will you be reindividualised?' 'If, when I die, I die with craving for existence in my heart, yes; but if not, no....' Is this my last existence? The king said: 'Is a man, Nagasena, who will not be reborn, aware of the fact? 'Yes, O king.' 'And how does he know it?' 'By the cessation of all that is cause, proximate or remote of rebirth.' 'Give me an illustration.' 'Suppose a farmer, a great king, had ploughed and sown and filled his granary; and then, for a period should neither plough nor sow but live on the stored- up grain, or dispose of it in barter, or deal with it as he has need.

Would the farmer be aware, great king, that his granary was not getting filled?' 'Yes, he would know that.' 'But how? 'He would know that the cause, proximate and remote, of the filling of the granary had ceased. Just so, with the man you spoke of. By the cessation of all that leads to rebirth, he would be conscious of having escaped his liability to it.' What follows after him? What thing is (a man's) own? What takes he hence? What dogs his steps, like shadow in pursuit? Man's merits and the sins he here hath wrought. That is the thing he owns, that takes he hence. That dogs his steps, like shadow in pursuit.

Hence let him make good store for life elsewhere. Sure platform in some other future world, rewards of virtue on good being wait. The cause of inequality among living men.

The king said: 'Why is it, Nagasena, that all men are not alike but some are short-lived and some long-lived, some sickly and some healthy, some ugly and some beautiful, some without influence and some of great power, some low-born and some high-born, some stupid and some wise? 'Why is it, O great king, that all vegetables are not alike, but some sour and some salt, and some pungent, and some acid, and some astringent, and some sweet?' 'I fancy, Sir, it is because they come from different kinds of seeds.' 'Just so, O great king, are the differences you have mentioned among men to be explained.

For it has been said by the Blessed One: Beings, O Brahmin, have each their own karma, are inheritors of karma, belong to the tribe of their karma, and are relatives by karma, have each their karma as their protective over lord. It is karma that divides them up into low and high and the like divisions.

## DEVELOPMENT OF BUDDHISM

In the development of Buddhism the *Sangha* or the order of Monks had played a significant role. During the Buddha's life time the *Sangha* came into existence and gradually it developed into a democratic set up by making its doors open to all irrespective of caste or sex. Following the order of Monks the order of Nuns was also set up, although it did not get much prominence. The *Sangha*s were known for austerity, discipline and egalitarian ethos.

However, over a period of time because of various regional traditions from which the monks came and interest in particular branch of study or a teacher different sects emerged within the *Sangha*. We will discuss the emergence of various sects within Buddhism later on. Now let us have some idea on the Buddhist literature. The Buddha's teachings were communicated through oral tradition. The Pali Canon developed in stages by additions and alterations, expositions and deliberations, is respected as the word of the Buddha. The main division of the Pali Canon is threefold, Vinaya Pitaka, Sutta Pitaka and Abhidhamma Pitaka and the Canon itself is called Tripitaka.

Although the Tripitaka is referred as the word of the Buddha, there are texts within the Canon either attributed to specific monks or related to an event postdating the time of the Buddha or that can be shown to have been composed after that time. The Vinaya Pitaka deals with the monastic rules and essentially consists of two parts, the Vinaya-Vibhanga and the Vinaya-Vastu. The Sutta Pitaka is a religious discourse and forms the principle source of our knowledge of the Dhamma. The Sutta Pitaka comprises of five collections or Nikayas: Digha, Majjhima, Samyutta, Anguttara and Khuddaka.

The Abhidhamna Pitaka is a collection of philosophical treatises analysing the texts of the Sutta Pitaka. It consists of seven books of which *Kathavatthu* is the most important. Besides the Pali canonical literature Buddhist literature in Sanskrit was written by the followers of the Mahayana Buddhism. The *Vaipulya Sutras*, written in Sanskrit, form the basic of the Mahayana texts. There are also about 550 Jataka stories and each story is about Buddha's previous birth as a *bodhisattva*. Though this vast Buddhist literature is basically spiritual in nature yet this literature has great historical value because this helps us in understanding the life and customs of ancient society and the changes that came in values over the years.

According to tradition, immediately after the Buddha's death a gathering of the monks took place during which Upali and Ananda, two chief disciples of the Buddha, said to have recited the Vinaya Pitaka and the Sutta Pitaka. About a hundred years after the Buddha's death the second council was held in Vaishali. By this time there were divisions among the Buddhist monks on various issues, especially over the true interpretation of the Buddha's teachings.

The two prominent groups that emerged out of this schism in the Buddhist order were the Sthaviravadins (Theravadins) and the Mahasanghikas. The third Buddhist council was held during the reign of Asoka at Pataliputra. At this council differences of opinions were not confined to the Vinaya, but also concerned the Dhamma. The President of the Council, Moggaliputta Tissa, compiled a book called the Kathavatthu which refuted the heretical, false views and theories held by some sects.

## THE ABHIDHAMMA

Pitaka was included at this council. The fourth council was held in Kashmir under the leadership of Vasumitra and Asvaghosa during the reign of Kanishka. Thus differences among the monks on the interpretation of Buddhism got more crystalized in the successive council meetings and the two major schools of Buddhist philosophy that emerged are known as the Hinayana and the Mahayana. The fact is that both Hinayanism and Mahayanism derived their views from the identical sayings of the Buddha, but they differ in interpreting these sayings.

The Hinayanists also called the Theravadins believe that there is no permanent self or soul and that an individual is the only a combination of what they call the five aggregates - matter, sensation, perception, predisposition and consciousness. It is through eradication of ignorance, lustful cravings and selfish thoughts that one can eliminate Karma and repeated rebirths and achieve nirvana. Hinayana stresses on individual efforts towards gradual enlightenment. This doctrine is meant for the individual salvation where each person has to work out his own destiny. Meditation and introspections are encouraged for attaining enlightenment.

The countries where the Theravda tradition is currently alive are Sri Lanka, Thailand, Burma, Combodia and Laos. The Mahayana tradition appears to have developed between 1st century B.C. and 2nd centuries A.D. The Mahayana philosophy is based on the Buddha's original teachings but it does not belief traditional interpretations. It tried to expand the scope of Buddhism by introducing new theories and practices so as to make it more familiar and meaningful for the lay Buddhists. It also elevated the status of the Buddha to that of God so that all questions and doubts regarding the existence of the Buddha after his nirvana would be cleared.

The Mahayana philosophy teaches that every sentinent being can become a Buddha, the only thing preventing enlightenment is the failure to improve one's own actions and state of mind. It promotes the ideal of the *bodhisattva* who shuns entering nirvana until all sentinent beings can do so as well, willingly remaining in the painful cycle of birth and death to perform works of compassion. Followers of this tradition conceive of the Buddha as an eternal being to whom prayers can be made and add a polytheistic dimension to the religion. It is also known as 'Great Vehicle' because of its all-inclusive approach to liberation as embodied in the *bodhisattva* ideal and the desire to liberate all beings.

Compassion along with wisdom is considered as the path of enlightenment. In addition to meditative practices devotion to a *bodhisattva* is considered important to reach Buddha- hood. Let us have a look at the important points of differences between the Hinayana and the Mahayana traditions. In Hinayana Buddhism the immediate goal is achieving Nirvana, individual salvation, where each person has to work out his/her own destiny whereas for the Mahayana Buddhists immediate goal is achieving *bodhisattva.*

A *bodhisattva* is an individual who has gained spiritual enlightenment but puts off his own final state of Nirvana in order to assist all sentinent beings (human, animals and insects) to attain salvation.

- Hinayana sees suffering as real while Mahayana tradition considers it as an illusion.

- In the Hinayana tradition main thrust is on the Buddha's teachings, where as deification of the Buddha and worship of deities are considered integral part of the Mahayana tradition.
- Although both the schools believe in the basic philosophy of Buddhism but the differences that they have mainly are in terms of interpretation of the Buddhist philosophy and in its practices.
- Hinayana Buddhism became popular in Sri Lanka, Burma and the countries of South-East Asia, where as Mahayana Buddhism became the dominant sect in India, Central Asia, Tibet, China and Japan.

The Vajrayana constitutes the last major stage in the development of Buddhism. The Vajrayana, meaning both thunderbolt and diamond, is predominently yogic and magical in character. It accepts all assumptions of Mahayanism but expands and collaborates them further adding a few of its own. The goal of Vajrayana Buddhism is the realization of *Sunyata,* both mentally and physically. It believes in yogic exercises for spiritual evolution and the concept of an enlightened Guru (teacher) in transmission of spiritual power. Vajrayana developed in parts of northern India and Tibet.

## UPANISHADS AND BUDDHISM

In the Upanishadic thought we find a clear shift from Vedic ritualism and sacrifices. Notion of individual soul (*Atman*) seeking union with the universal soul (Brahman) is considered as the ultimate liberation or Moksha in the Upanishads. It is suggested that relief from rebirth can be achieved better through meditation and yoga than by the sacrificial ritual. Buddha being born in an age when the Upanishadic doctrines were having great influence upon people's minds was naturally influenced by the Upanishadic thought.

Probably this may be the reason for some of Buddhist doctrines owe their origins from the Upanishadic ideas. But this does not stop us to suggest that Buddism is a departure from the earlier Upanishadic tradition. Buddhism criticizes the Atmavada of the Upanishads and challenges the theories of the unchanging, eternal soul which lead to inaction. Early Buddhism shares many concepts with the Upanishads like, Karma, rebirth, liberation through insight, etc. Both are convinced of the transitory and therefore sorrowful character of individual existence in the world. Through renunciation and meditation they hope to attain a blissful and serene state.

The Upanishads suggest that suffering is due to desire and when desire ceases the mortal becomes immortal and obtains Brahman. 'The Upanishad maintains that the attainment of Brahman helps to transcend hunger, thirst, sorrow, old age and death. Renunciation according to the Upanishads is the means of overcoming sorrow and attaining Brahman. When a person dies his Karma controls his new existence.' Some of these ideas definitely influenced Buddhist doctrines. But the Buddha gave new interpretation of them. 'The Buddha also speaks of desire as the cause of sorrow, but uses the term 'trshna' [thirst] which carries a starker meaning of thirst, rather than the more ambiguous karma'.

In Buddhist doctrine the emphasis is on causality and this is linked with the concept of Karma. In the Upanishadic thought an Atman is the basis of everything, where as Buddhism maintains that 'everything in the empirical world is only a stream of passing Dharmas which therefore has to be characterized as *Anatta,* i.e. being without a persisting self.' In the Pali Canon the word *Atman* does not occur in the sense of 'universal soul'. Romila Thapar's observations on the Upanishadic and the Buddhist ideology: 'If the Upanishads mark a watershed between the ideologies of vedic brahmanism on the one hand and the 'heterodoxies' on the other and draw upon the concerns of certain categories of brahmans and *kshatriyas,* Buddhist ideology changes the paradigm to focus on the concerns of the *Gahapatis* and *Setthis.*

It abolishes the notion of a secret doctrine and universalizes its teaching.' By the seventh century A.D. having spread through out East Asia and South-east Asia, Buddhism probably had the largest religious following in the world. For centuries, Buddhism enjoyed patronage from the royal houses and merchants in India. However, Buddhism in India died out gradually after the seventh century, though it did not disappear completely. It is suggested that shifts in royal patronage from Buddhist to Hindu religious institutions, deviation from original teachings of the Buddha and adoption of popular religious forms from Hindu religious traditions, origin and development of new Hindu religious orders, etc. contributed to the gradual decline of Buddhism in India.

In this Unit we have explained the circumstances in which Buddhism developed in India. Then we have explained the important features of the Buddhist philosophy, followed by discussion on how in the absence of the Buddha Buddhism developed in India. We have tried to conclude by examining the relationship between the Upanishads and the Buddhist philosophy. Before listening to this teaching, first cultivate *bodhicitta*, thinking, "I want to receive enlightenment for the benefit of all mother sentient beings." In other words, before listening to teachings, it is necessary to think of, to remember, all mother sentient beings.

The subject today is *Lam-drön, A Lamp for the Path to Enlightenment*, which was written in Tibet by Atisha, who was also called Dipamkara Shrijnana, who was born the son of a Bengali king. Bengal is in northeast India. Buddhadharma had already been established in Tibet before Atisha's arrival there, but an evil king called Langdarma (Udumtsen), who was said to have horns growing from his head, hated the Dharma and cause it to degenerate in Tibet. But even though the teachings had been corrupted, they still existed, but not as purely as before. It took about sixty years to restore the teachings to their original purity in what became known as the later spreading of the Dharma in Tibet.

How that happened was that in western Tibet, in the kingdom of Gugé, there lived a Tibetan king, Lha Lama Yeshe

Ö, and his nephew, Jangchub Ö. They decided to invite a learned and realized teacher from the great Indian monastery of Vikramashila to spread Dharma in Tibet. When they investigated to see that was the most learned and realized person there, they discovered that Atisha would be by far the best one to invite. But before Lha Lama Yeshe Ö could request Atisha to come from Vikramashila to Tibet, he needed to find gold to make a proper offering, so went to a place called Garlog in search of it.

But the ruler of Garlog threw him in prison, where he died. In that way, Lha Lama Yeshe Ö he sacrificed his life to bring Atisha to Tibet. Then his nephew, Jangchub Ö, sent emissaries to India to invite Atisha to Tibet. When he finally met Atisha, he explained how the Dharma there had degenerated during Langdarma's rule and how correct teachings no longer existed in Tibet. He requested Atisha to write the precious teaching, A Lamp for the Path to Enlightenment, to give fundamental teachings to the Tibetan people because they were so ignorant.

He requested Atisha to explain about refuge, *bodhicitta* and so forth. Therefore, Atisha wrote the precious teaching, A Lamp for the Path to Enlightenment, the source of all the Gelug lam-rim texts, as well as those of the Sakya and the other schools of Tibetan Buddhism, who all practice the graduated path to enlightenment and quote the Lam-drön in their teachings. Furthermore, the Lam-drön is based on the Prajnaparamita teachings of Sakyamuni Buddha. After generating *bodhicitta*, our main task is to attain enlightenment.

Now, even though we might think that life in *samsara* is pleasant, it's not. There is no true pleasure in *samsara*. Enlightenment can be attained only through the practice of Dharma. Therefore, we should all practice Dharma. In terms of teachings in general, there are two types: Buddhadharma and the teachings of the mu-teg-pa (Skt: tirthika). The latter are teachings based on mistaken beliefs, an understanding opposite to that of Buddhadharma - teachings followed by outsiders. By following such non-Buddhist teachings, you can be born anywhere from the lower realms to the peak of *samsara*, the highest of the four formless realms, but can never escape *samsara*.

Within the Buddhadharma, there are also two divisions: Hinayana and Mahayana. By following Hinayana teachings, you can escape from *samsara* but cannot attain enlightenment. To attain enlightenment, you have to practice Mahayana teachings. Within the Mahayana, there are the teachings spoken by the Buddha himself and those recorded later by the learned followers of the Buddha, the great Indian pandits. Included in the latter are such teachings as those written by the six great pandits, the ornaments of the world. Then there are also the teachings written by learned Tibetan masters. The teaching we are discussing here is that written by the learned pandit Dipamkara Shrijnana.

What does the Lam-drön contain? It derives from the *Abhisamayalankara* and explains the three levels of teaching: the paths of the lower, intermediate and highest practitioner, especially that of the highest. The text opens with the title of this teaching in Sanskrit, which in Tibetan is Jang-chub lam-gyi drön-ma.

This is followed by homage to Manjushri. The first verse includes three things. First there is homage to the Triple Gem: the Buddhas of the three times, the oral teachings and realization of them, and the *Sangha*-those who have received the unshakable, or noble, path. Second, he mentions that his pure disciple, Jangchub Ö, requested him to give this teaching. Third, he makes the promise, or vow, to write this teaching, this lamp for the path to enlightenment, the Lam-drön. In the second verse, Atisha explains what he's going to write about: the graduated paths of the persons of least, intermediate and greatest capacity.

These are also the paths that Lama Tsong Khapa explains in his short, middle-length and great lam-rim teachings; in the various lam-rim teachings of Lama Tsong Khapa, he, too, explains the graduated paths of the persons of least, intermediate and greatest capacity. Of the three levels of follower, Atisha first explains the graduated path of those of least capacity. Such people think, "I don't care what suffering or happiness I experience in this life; I must avoid rebirth in the lower realms and attain an upper rebirth." With this in mind, beings of least capacity abstain from negative actions and practice virtue.

Persons of intermediate capacity develop aversion to not only the sufferings of the three lower realms but also to those of the upper realms; to the whole of *samsara*. Such practitioners abstain from negative actions in order to free themselves from *samsara*, without concern for other sentient beings. Who, then, are the beings of greatest capacity? They are those who, having understood their own suffering, take it as an example of the suffering that other beings are also experiencing and generate the great wish of wanting to put an end to the suffering of all sentient beings.

There are six preparatory practices. First, visualize the merit field and make offerings. Then kneel down with your hands in prostration and take refuge in the Triple Gem. After that, generate love for other sentient beings by thinking of the sufferings of death, old age, sickness and rebirth as well as the three sufferings and the general suffering of *samsara*. In that way, generate *bodhicitta*.

It is necessary to generate the aspiration to attain enlightenment, and the benefits of doing so have been explained in the sutra called Array of Trunks. Atisha also quotes three verses from another sutra, the Sutra Requested by Viradatta, to further explain the benefits of *bodhicitta*.

There are two types of *bodhicitta*, relative and absolute. Within the category of relative there are two further divisions, the *bodhicitta* of aspiration-wanting to receive enlightenment for the benefit of other sentient beings, thinking, "Without my receiving enlightenment, I cannot enlighten others"-and the *bodhicitta* of engagement, actually following the *bodhisattva*'s path by taking the *bodhisattva* precepts and engaging in the actions of a *bodhisattva*, thinking, "In order to engage in positive actions and avoid negative ones, I am going to practice the six perfections."

The teachings explain that in order to practice engaged *bodhicitta,* we should take the *bodhisattva* ordination, but in order to do so we should hold one of the seven levels of *pratimoksha* ordination, such as gelong, gelongma, getsul, getsulma and so forth. Ideally, then, we should hold one of these fundamental ordinations before taking the *bodhisattva* vow, but the learned ones say that in general, those who avoid negative karma and create virtuous actions can receive *bodhicitta,* even if they don't hold any pratimoksha precepts.

The *bodhicitta* of aspiration can be generated without dependence upon a lama, but engaged *bodhicitta* depends on a lama. To find a lama from whom we can take the *bodhisattva* vow, we have to know the qualifications of such a lama. First, the lama should know all about the ordination and how to bestow it. He should have compassion for the disciple and himself be living in the *bodhisattva* ordination. That's the kind of lama we need to find in order to take the ordination. But what if we can't find a perfect lama like that? Atisha then goes on to explain what we should do in that case.

The Ornament of Manjushri's Buddha Land Sutra explains how, long ago, Manjushri received *bodhicitta*. This is what we can do. Visualize the merit field and all the Buddhas and generate *bodhicitta,* the wish to receive enlightenment. Then promise, "I invite all sentient beings as my guest to the sublime happiness of liberation and enlightenment. I will not get angry or harbor avarice, covetousness, jealousy and so forth. I will not harm other sentient beings in any way. I will live in pure discipline by avoiding all negative actions, even worldly desires and sense objects of attachment, such as attractive sounds and beautiful forms and so forth. I shall give up such things.

As all the Buddhas have followed pure moral conduct, so shall I. "I will not try to receive enlightenment for myself alone. Even though it takes and endless amount of time to work for even one sentient being, I shall remain in *samsara.* I shall make pure the impure realms of sentient beings, places where there are thorns, rocks and ugly mountains. I shall also purify my three doors of body, speech and mind and keep them pure. I shall create no negative actions from now on."

The best way of keeping our three doors pure is by generating the *bodhicitta* of aspiration and engaging in *bodhicitta* and following the path to enlightenment. This depends on observing the three different levels of moral conduct. If we do this properly, we can complete the two collections of merit and transcendent wisdom. One thing that really helps us complete these two collections is the ability to foresee the future; therefore we should try to acquire clairvoyance. Without it, we are like a baby bird that has not yet grown feathers and whose wings are undeveloped, and remains stuck in its nest, unable to fly. Without clairvoyance, we cannot work for other sentient beings.

The person who has achieved the psychic power to foresee the future can create more merit in a day than a person who does not have this ability can create in a hundred years. Therefore, to complete the collections of merit and transcendent wisdom quickly, it is necessary to acquire the psychic power to see past, present and future. In order to do this, it is necessary to achieve samadhi-single-pointed concentration. For this, we must understand the details of the method of attaining samadhi, such as the nine stages, the six powers and the four mental engagements.

In order to practice samadhi meditation properly, we must ensure that the conditions are perfect. If they are not, then even though we try practicing it hard for even a thousand years, we'll never achieve it. Therefore, we should find a perfect environment, remain quiet and avoid having to do work such as healing the ill and making astrological predictions-any activity that keeps us busy. The way to meditate to attain single-pointed concentration is to focus our mind on a virtuous object, such as an image of the Buddha. Visualize such an image in front of us and simply concentrate on that.

As we focus our mind on the object again and again, we'll be able to hold it for increasingly greater periods of time, and through the continuity of such practice will eventually attain calm abiding (samatha) and single-pointed concentration. Thus we will gain ngön-she or, literally, higher seeing, the psychic power to see the future and so forth. But that is not the point. Next we have to practice lhag-tong, or vipasayana-penetrative insight. Without it, our samadhi cannot remove our delusions. In order to eradicate our two levels of obscuration-the obscurations of delusion (nyön-drib) and the obscurations to knowledge (she-drib) we must achieve the wisdom realizing the non-self-existence of I.

Doing so also depends upon achieving method, such as compassion and so forth. It's a mistake to practice only wisdom and not method. This can lead us to fall into individual liberation, the lower nirvana. Similarly, practicing only method and not wisdom is also a mistake and causes us to remain in *samsara*. The Buddha taught that of the six perfections, the last of the six is the path of wisdom and the first five-charity, morality, patience, effort and concentration-are the path of method, or skillful means (Tib: thab). First, we should meditate on method, then on wisdom, then on both together. By practicing both together, we can receive enlightenment; by practicing the wisdom of selflessness alone, we can't.

Realizing the five aggregates (Skt: *skandhas*), the twelve sources and the eighteen constituents as empty of self-existence is recognized as higher wisdom. There is existence and non-existence: there is no such thing as the production of the existent, nor is there such a thing as production of the non-existent. There is no such thing as production of both existent and non-existent, nor is there production of neither existent nor non-existent. That is one form of logic negating the production of both the existent and the non-existent.

There is also another form of logic negating production of a thing from self, other, both or neither-the four extremes. The main thing to discover here is non-self-existence. That can be found through the first line of logical reasoning, which negates production of the existent and the non-existent, and through the second, which negates production of the four extremes. It can also be discovered through a third line of reasoning that examines things to see whether they are one or many. These lines of reasoning are elaborated by Nagarjuna in his Seventy Stanzas on Emptiness and in other texts such as his Treatise on the Middle Way.

These things are explained in those texts, but here they are mentioned just for the purpose of practicing meditation. Meditating on the non-self-existence of I and the non-self-existence of all other phenomena is meditation on *Sunyata*, or emptiness. When the wisdom realizing emptiness analyzes the subject and the object, it cannot discover self-existence in either of those. Moreover, it cannot find self-existence in the wisdom of emptiness. Thus, we realize the emptiness of even the wisdom of emptiness itself. Since this world is created by superstition (Tib: nam-tog) [conceptuality], if we eradicate the creator, superstition, we can attain liberation.

The Buddha said that it is superstition that causes us to fall into the ocean of *samsara*. Therefore, that which is to be avoided is superstition, but the emptiness of superstition, which is like the sky, like empty space, is that which is to be practiced. By achieving this, we will be able to see the absolute nature of existence. Therefore, the *bodhisattva*s' practice is to avoid superstition and thus to achieve the non-superstitious mind. Through the various different means of logic-by realizing the emptiness of the produced and of inherent existence-we can avoid superstition and achieve the wisdom of *Sunyata*.

Then we can also attain the different levels of the path of preparation (Tib: jor-lam), the second of the five paths. We attain the four levels of this path and gradually the ten bhumis (Tib: sa), or *bodhisattva* grounds, as well. Finally, we attain the eleventh level, enlightenment itself. Having realized *Sunyata*, we can also gain the general realizations of tantra, such as the four powers of pacification, wrath, control and increase, and other attainments, such as accomplishing the "good pot." Accomplishing the good pot means doing a particular meditation in retreat for a long time, and if you are successful, just by putting your mouth to the opening of a pot and saying something like, "May I become the king of this country," your wish will be fulfilled-in this case, you will become king of that country. Or, we can gain the tantric power of "eye medicine."

By accomplishing this technique, if you apply this ointment to your eye, you can see such things as gold, jewels and other precious things even hundreds of miles beneath the surface of the earth; no matter how far away it is, you can see it. By practicing tantra, we can receive enlightenment without the need of much austere practice. The tantric was to enlightenment is through happiness, while other paths to enlightenment are through hard, austere practice. There are four different level of tantra, such as highest yoga tantra and so forth; four different aspects of the tantric teaching. So, first we have to receive initiation.

In order to do so, we have to make material offerings, such as gold or even members of your family; a spouse, or a sibling, requesting our guru for the initiation with great devotion. If our *guru* is pleased, he will then give us the initiation out of his compassion. Having taken an initiation, we also receive the great fortune of being able to receive enlightenment and all these high realizations that come with it. There are four different initiations: the vase, secret, transcendent wisdom and word initiations, the latter being where the guru imparts clarification, or proof, through verbal explanation.

However, the secret initiation should not be given to those living in ordination. If monks, for example, take the secret initiation, they have to leave the monastic order, because those who have taken the secret initiation are required to practice with a female consort. If they do these practices without first returning their ordination, they lose it, the consequence of which is rebirth in the hells. To receive tantric commentaries, you first have to receive initiation. Without initiation, you cannot receive tantric teachings. You also cannot perform pujas of burnt offering or give tantric teachings.

In the last verse, Atisha closes this text by describing himself as an elder (Tib: nä-tän), a full monk who, in the first twelve years after taking ordination, hasn't created any moral falls; a senior full monk. He states that he has briefly explained the teaching on the steps of path as requested by his noble follower, Jangchub Ö. Conclusion Every lam-rim teaching ever written refers back to this text, A Lamp for the Path, irrespective of the Tibetan Buddhist tradition; not only Gelug, but also Nyingma, Kagyu and Sakya. Where does the Lamp itself refer back to? That is to the prajnaparamita teachings. In terms of prajnaparamita texts, there are elaborate, intermediate and short, but the author of all of them is the Buddha.

Therefore, all lam-rim texts have their source in the teachings of the Buddha. If you want to understand the lam-rim well, you should study it as extensively as possible. When you understand the lam-rim well, you will understand the Lamp for the Path. Once you do, you should teach it all over the world. Even within the Mahayana tradition, the teaching has many aspects, but in general, it contains great knowledge. The main thing, however, the fundamental thing, is concern for others, working for others, benefiting others.

Followers of the Hinayana are concerned with only their own samsaric suffering; in order to escape it, they follow the path of the three higher trainings: higher conduct, higher concentration and higher wisdom. But there are many ways in which the Mahayana is different from and higher than the Hinayana, many ways in which this can be explained, but the main difference is that Mahayana practitioners are more concerned with working for the welfare of others than their own. People nowadays might think of helping other people, but Mahayana practitioners benefit not only other people but also suffering hell beings, pretas, animals and every other sentient being.

There is not one sentient being who has not been our mother; all sentient beings have been our mother numberless times, therefore, we should be concerned for their welfare, wanting them to become enlightened as quickly as possible. This, then, is the fundamental difference between the Hinayana and the Mahayana, this concern more for others than oneself, in particular, the wish to enlighten all sentient beings. That's what makes the difference. It is excellent that you are studying the vast and profound teachings of the Mahayana, thinking about them, analyzing them intently, and you should continue to do so.

In general, there are many religions and everyone thinks that the teaching of his or her own religion is the best. But just saying that one's own religion is the best doesn't prove it's the best; that doesn't mean anything. Therefore, simply saying that Buddhadharma is the best religion in the world doesn't make it so. However, there are many logical reasons you can use to prove that Buddhadharma is, in fact, the best. For example, even accepting and practicing *bodhicitta* is very different from not practicing *bodhicitta*. Even in this, there's a big difference between Buddhism and other religions; the fact of the presence of the practice of *bodhicitta* shows that Buddhism is higher than other religions, that Buddhism is the best.

Buddhism also talks about dependent origination and emptiness; it explains dependent origination as it exists, right there. So, not only in conduct but also in view, Buddhism is very different from other religions and therefore the best. There are many ways to prove this. However, Buddhadharma is something that the more and more you study it, the deeper and deeper it becomes, the more and more profound you find it to be. This is a quality unique to Buddhadharma. With other teachings, the more you study them, the lighter they become. If you have understood any of what I have taught here, keep it in mind and build upon it.

When you have understood more, keep that as your foundation and build further upon that. In this way, your knowledge will continually increase. Then, like the sun rising, spread Dharma in the West. There are many countries, such as Vietnam, where Buddhism existed for centuries, but none were like Tibet. In those countries, there existed only one aspect of the Buddhadharma, not all, but in Tibet, all the aspects of the teaching existed, Hinayana, Sutrayana and Vajrayana. In order to study all this, you should learn the Tibetan language, study its grammar, and follow your lama properly.

# 5

# Rejecting Emotions

While listening to the precious teachings of the Dharma, it is most important to express proper conduct of body, speech, and mind. One needs to present oneself with a sense of collectedness while receiving the teachings, especially with the genuine aspiration that all living beings without exception experience the awakened mind. We aspire to establish all beings in the state of Buddhahood. For this reason, one takes the special opportunity to receive the teachings, listens to them with devotion, and maintains an altruistic motivation.

The Buddhist teachings speak about *samsara,* conditioned existence, and nirvana, the state of enlightenment that is beyond *samsara*. The characteristics of *samsara* are suffering and pain. The characteristics of nirvana are happiness and well-being. Our relationship to *samsara* is to become liberated from suffering. Our relationship to nirvana is to experience freedom from suffering.

Lord Buddha's teachings distinguish *samsara* and nirvana. One's understanding of both is wrong, though. One doesn't experience benefits in *samsara* due to being deluded, thus one seeks liberation from *samsara* and strives to attain the peace of nirvana and one's notions of *samsara* as a state of suffering and nirvana, as a state beyond suffering imply running away from *samsara* and towards nirvana. Such ideas are illusory - they are dualistic fixations about *samsara* and nirvana and are an expression of confusion.

The 84,000 collections of teachings that Lord Buddha presented are contained in the two truths: the relative and ultimate truths. While gaining a gradual understanding of both, one differentiates relative and ultimate reality because of phenomena's display. The fundamental nature of all things presents no reason to separate the ultimate from the relative levels of being. The two truths are inseparable -this is the ultimate truth of the nature of relative existents. Discussing relative and ultimate levels of being misleads one to separate the relative truth as a world of confusion from the ultimate truth as a world beyond confusion. This separation itself is a misconception and an expression of confusion.

It is a split, and therefore one relates to the relative world of phenomena in and around from a state of confusion. For instance, there are so many religions in the world that have evolved from many individuals' wishes and attempt to become free of suffering and confusion, but confusion has developed around religions instead of being resolved. Many people see the world from a confused viewpoint, believing it was created by a self-created creator, by somebody who decided how it should be and fashioned it in that manner.

Many people believe in a universal architect, in somebody who manipulates the world and its inhabitants. On the other hand, some people believe that nobody had anything to do with the world's creation. How did it come about then? They shrug their shoulders and simply reply, "It just happened." Both notions, belief in a creator and belief in coincidence, are delusive. The desire to leave a spot of suffering and to reach a spot free of suffering is the fundamental mistake, and more confusion evolves as a result. The teachings I will present deal with what is and what is not. The above concerns what is not?

The theme *what is* includes everything that is fundamentally valid without mistaken cognition, i.e., free of confusion. Somebody who is confused nourishes beliefs about things that contradict the way things really are. Bewilderment is confusion and has far-reaching consequences. Confusion is a mental state in the absence of knowledge as to the way all things really are and the way they arise and appear. But confusion can be unravelled; a mistaken view can be understood and dispelled. One's approach is bewildered, though, as long as one's practical relationship with one's delusions make one shun confusion, which doesn't bring about freedom from confusion.

## CONFUSION AND ITS CAUSE

From the Buddhist point of view, it's necessary to understand the source of confusion. One needs to investigate and recognize the ground of confusion. During the times of Buddha Sakyamuni, his teachings were divided into three schools or *yanas*. Later, many great scholars studied how his vast body of teachings could be best presented and preserved for future generations.

Based upon their insight, four schools developed, two from the Hinayana and three from the Mahayana, 'the lesser and greater vehicles.' I will give a brief summary on how each school defines confusion. The two schools that developed from the Hinayana are the Vaibhashika and the Sautantrika. The three schools that developed from the Mahayana are the Yogachara or Chittamatra, the Madhyamaka, and Vajrayana. Each school approaches *samsara* and explains the source of confusion differently.

The two schools of thought that developed from the Hinayana tradition of Buddhism see the ultimate and relative truths differently. In general, however, they agree that the consciousness exists in a single moment. They teach that the tiniest fraction of time is a moment and the tiniest fraction of consciousness truly exists in that moment. They also claim that the smallest imaginable particle truly exists. Confusion about the consciousnesses and phenomena arises due to assuming that the many moments of consciousness and the tiniest particles compounding a whole are each a unique and substantial entity.

Hinayana followers argue that the basis for confusion is not seeing that an object consists of tiniest parts that truly exist and thus one mistakenly assumes that the collection of tiniest parts is a single entity. This mistake also applies to one's cognition. They teach that instead of seeing that a consciousness only exists in a tiniest fraction of a moment, one erroneously believes that the collections of moments of consciousness are a single entity. They say that failing to see the moment and mistakenly taking the collection of all parts to be a unique consciousness is the cause for confusion.

Followers of the Chittamatra, the 'Mind-only School' of Mahayana Buddhism, teach that the basis for confusion is the all-ground consciousness or that aspect of the mind that is the storehouse for all other consciousnesses. Whatever activities one engages in become habitual patterns that subside and are stored in the *alaya*, 'the all-ground consciousness.' When activated by a thought, confusion arises. The Madhyamika state that the cause for confusion is being ignorant of the true nature of existents, which arise due to interdependent origination.

Failing to see that everything that one apprehends exists in dependence on other things, one relates to things as though they exist through and of their own accord. Assuming that phenomena truly exist is taught to be the source of confusion in the Madhyamaka philosophy. One identifies and designates apprehended objects as if they exist of their own accord and clings to one's imputations as real. The Vajrayana tradition of Buddhism explains that the true nature of all phenomena is the inseparability of luminosity or clarity and emptiness.

Clarity is unimpeded manifestation, and emptiness is the non-existential ground for dependent manifestations to arise and appear when causes and conditions come together. The cause for confusion is failing to realize the true nature of phenomena. Not realizing that inner and outer phenomena are manifestations of luminous clarity, one assumes that apprehended objects exist in opposition to the apprehending self, calling them "self" in contrast to "other." Both instances are being divisive, which is explained in great detail as the source of confusion in the Vajrayana tradition.

One needs to know the source of all one's problems, which is confusion, in order to become free from suffering. One needs to know what confusion really is and shouldn't see it negatively. In Buddhism, being confused and deluded is not seen as final, as unmanageable, or as unchangeable. The source of confusion must be understood, though, so that one can eliminate it. One's thoughts about *samsara* are based upon confusion and therefore evolve in confusion. One thinks of confusion pertains to the external world, e.g., when coming to New York City, visitors certify their notions by screaming, "its big *samsara*!" But the world, as it expresses itself, is not deluded.

Confusion is the way one relates to the world. One can relate to the world delusively or with awareness. From the Buddhist point of view, whatever happens in New York City is not *samsara*; rather *samsara* is one's way of apprehending and judging. Certainly, one understands *samsara* based upon one's confusion, which is why I spoke about the different Buddhist interpretations of confusion. All Buddhist schools agree and teach that the source of confusion is ego-clinging or self-cherishing. Belief in a truly existing self gives rise to one's acceptance or denial that other things truly exist, no matter what "other" might be. Dualistic clinging is the major problem that brings on habitual patterns and the accumulation of karma.

The Madhyamaka philosophical school of thought explains in great detail that the fundamental nature of all existents is non-substantial emptiness, which is not a negation of the phenomenal world. Lord Buddha never negated the relative world; rather he spoke about the relative truth of conventional reality and the inseparability of the ultimate and relative truths. The great Mahasiddha Tilopa taught that we are not entangled in confusion on account of appearances rather due to clinging to inner and outer appearances as true existents.

## KARMA AND THE HABITUAL MENTAL PATTERNS

The source for confusion and delusiveness is dualistic clinging, not the world of appearances. One seeks the source of confusion outside oneself and struggles to vanquish it with outer means. Buddhism teaches students to look inwards and seek the source of confusion there by asking questions like, "Where does confusion abide?" By investigating, one slowly starts discovering that confusion is a state of dividedness and that the world only seems to be confused to the extent that one experiences it in that way. By investigating, one sees that one apprehends dualistically and thus experiences the world darkened by one's own confusion.

This means to say that due to clinging to duality, emotional patterns are born and increased in one's mind and thus one creates more and more karma. The Buddha did not teach that an architect or creator made the world or that things arise haphazardly. For a Buddhist practitioner, believing in such ideas means seeking an easy way out. When one investigates well, one discovers that such statements fall short of reasoning. Buddhist practitioners strive to understand the world based upon awareness. What is awareness? It is awakening to one's relationship to the world and to the way the world is. Awakening to the way the world is means awakening to emptiness; awakening to one's relationship to the world means awakening to loving kindness and compassion.

Appearances in the world are created by one's own karma. The truth of *karma,* 'cause and result,' is that one's wholesome activities give rise to positive experiences and one's unwholesome activities give rise to negative experiences. The result of karma need not be experienced immediately after or simultaneously with the cause nor need the result be an evident experience. One experiences the consequences of karma, one's actions, when it ripens.

One fabricates one's ideas about solidified existents outside oneself, believes they are real because one clings to a truly existing self, and acts accordingly. All experiences that develop from mind-made constructs become habits, which are stored as habitual patterns in one's all-ground consciousness and arise again as karmic results. As long as one clings to duality, one's ground consciousness will remain the storehouse of one's karmic imprints that ripen as results.

No matter how often one takes on a new birth, accumulated karma is never spent and cannot be washed away until it has ripened. Every individual creates his or her own karma, which can be experienced after many lifetimes due to the unerring force of karma. Nothing remains unaccounted for -the law of karma is infallible. Nobody can run away from karma nor deceive it. Karma is definite and can't be eliminated through wishful thinking.

## THE ANTIDOTE TO CONFUSION

As Buddhists, we have learned that it is possible to become free of habitual patterns by correctly purifying karmic imprints that are stored in one's ground consciousness. The most important point to remember while engaging in the purification practices is to regret one's past unwholesome negativities of body, speech, and mind. One can engage in wholesome activities, but the benefit of doing good depends upon feeling genuine regret for past bad deeds. The pure experience of regret is a deep experience that loosens one's clinging to oneself.

Heart-felt regret directly addresses ego-clinging and causes one not to want to repeat negative actions again. In fact, sincere regret is the primary means to correctly engage in purifying one's habitual patterns. One should not think that karma is something one borrowed and can simply return later. Such an illusion isn't the correct approach. Karma is the active cause created from clinging to duality, habits being the result. One needs to apply an antidote in order to untie the knots of karma. Lord Buddha's teachings elucidate how one accumulates negative karma due to the three main mind poisons, which are ignorance, attachment, and aversion.

These three mind poisons arise from clinging to duality. The method that discourages one from continuing to remain stuck in one's mind poisons is genuine regret. It is the most workable antidote to purify one's karma. One needs to be aware of the basic problem instead of entertaining concepts like guilt. Furthermore, working with karma does not mean one merely denies or covers it up. There is no cosmetic solution and thinking there is only intensifies its effects. For example, should a thief acknowledge and admit his misdeeds and have the sincere wish to give up that bad habit, he will readily accept a fair verdict.

Genuine regret stops one from engaging in further negative deeds and from thus accumulating more negative karma. Without regretting past bad actions, one's unwholesome activities will most likely increase. Sincere, heart-felt regret can be approached from a theistic or from the non-theistic viewpoint in Buddhism. It is an experience that arises from deeply realizing one's transgressions. Thinking a being outside oneself washes away all wrongs one has committed upon confession is not the Buddhist approach. Regret is a personal experience and doesn't mean one needs confirmation from someone else.

It is being honest with one and having the wish not to repeat misdeeds -it is an earnest resolution without any if's or but's. One needs to know that karmic habits increase and bring interest by becoming stronger and stronger. This is why one needs to develop sincere regret. I want you to understand that genuine regret is an antidote for negative karma and that one's unwholesome habits diminish if one sincerely gives rise to it. Again, the cause for confusion is clinging to duality. Due to dualistic clinging, habitual patterns and karma are born in one's mind. The world, i.e., all inner and outer phenomena, is created by karma.

Where do the phenomenal world and one's experiences come from? They come from karma. The Abhidharma instructions explain karma according to six causes, four conditions, and five results. I have explained that the world is seen differently due to various religious beliefs. Some religions teach that the world and phenomena are real. Buddhism teaches that the main misconception one can have about the world and appearances is thinking that phenomena really exist and that believing this is an illusion.

According to Buddhism, phenomena appear because of dualistic clinging -the twofold discursive fixations that a self and things other than the self truly exist and are separate. Based upon these erroneous concepts, emotional patterns evolve and give rise to karmic patterns. As a result, one experiences individual and collective karma. Lord Buddha showed that the world is only the appearance of collective and personal karma, that it is not a solid entity separate from the cognizing mind, and that it is not produced by anybody but oneself.

Lacking awakened awareness of how things are and how they arise, one imagines that the relative world of appearances and experiences is solid and real. The Vajrayana teachings state that one fails to experience the world and oneself correctly as long as one has not ascertained the inseparability of lucidity and emptiness. The problem is that one hasn't been able to see phenomena and experiences in the light of wisdom.

## KARMA ACCORDING TO THE ABHIDHARMA

The general definition of *karma* is 'the truth of cause and effect.' There are many coarse and subtle classifications of karma and it's very hard to fathom it in its entirety. Only a fully awakened Buddha is able to know the subtle workings of karma. The Abhidharma explains karma according to six causes, four conditions, and five results. The first cause of karma is *byed-pa'i-rgyu* in Tibetan, which means 'the cause of creating or developing.'

For instance, there is the visual sensory organ and a visual consciousness. There is no direct connection between a visual consciousness and a perceived object. But due to the specific faculty of the visual sensory organ - said to resemble a fresh flower that has a form, which is the essence of sight -one perceives forms. One has five sensory faculties on the one hand and the objects that can be perceived with a respective sensory faculty on the other hand. When these three components come into contact -a sensory form faculty that is associated with a sensory organ and the respective object -then a sensory perception takes place.

One sees a flower, for example, with one's visual sensory faculty that is associated with that specific sensory organ. One's sensory consciousness does not identify the flower, but the visual consciousness becomes involved with that specific perception and experiences the sensation of that sight. This is due to the law of cause and effect. Cause and effect do not coexist for an ordinary being, for which perception and the associated apprehension of a form, for example, arise successively. They are co-emergent for a fully enlightened being, though.

Back to the example: The eye faculty perceives a flower and the visual consciousness senses that it has apprehended an object that is other than the apprehending subject, which is the self. When an object, a sensory faculty, and the respective sense consciousness come together, cognition of a visual form, sound, smell, taste, or tactile object is established. The first classification of the cause of karma is that a sensory faculty perceives an object that is fit to be perceived with that faculty and is sensed by the respective sensory consciousness; then the mind consciousness apperceives and becomes involved with that specific consciousness.

By becoming involved, the mind consciousness gives rise to subtle mental activities, differentiating good, bad, or neutral sensations. These mental reactions are called *sems-byung* in Tibetan, 'mental factors or events,' or 'thought patterns' that are not the same as the object that was perceived. The second classification of the cause of karma is based upon an object of engagement, which means that the mind and mental events are simultaneous. The third classification is that a similar mind and mental event arise after having perceived an object, i.e., they arise in the same stream of consciousness. The fourth classification is that mental activities correspond to the concept one has of a perceived object.

The fifth classification is called "all-pervading cause," because a cause can give rise to various results. For instance, there are the five mind poisons of ignorance, attachment, aggression, jealousy, and pride. In this case, attachment needn't necessarily give rise to attachment, but can give rise to pride, jealousy, aggression, or any other mind poison. If this weren't the case, it wouldn't be all-pervading, rather an identical or similar cause and effect. Since the habitual patterns lead to effects, birth in any of the three lower realms of the desire, form, and formless realms takes place. Usually, desire and attachment only lead to birth in the desire realm, but the all-pervading cause leads to experience different realms.

The sixth cause is *rnam-smin-pa'i-rgyu* and means 'the fully ripened cause.' It refers to all living beings that have a body and mind. Virtuous activities lead to birth in the three higher realms of conditioned existence and non-virtuous activities lead to birth in the three lower realms of conditioned existence. Cyclic existence, *samsara*, continuously takes place. Why do beings experience *samsara*? Other than that one knows that it exists, one is lost for an answer. Yet one comes up with many assumptions why and how the world exists. One should know that the Buddhist texts cannot be understood that easily.

The instructions presented here are a brief outline of the paramount topic of Buddhism, which is the law of karma. Being aware of the fact that karma applies to one's life in many ways is already very beneficial. Dharma' is a Sanskrit word that has many meanings. One meaning is 'to adjust'; another is 'to redirect'. What is being redirected here? Our current state of mind is very wild. Having observed this, we can redirect awareness toward the true nature, awakening the beautiful qualities of the primordial reality of the mind. We have to turn the mind away from anger and negative emotions and tune into the ways of love and compassion.

This change of direction does not mean that we are trying to get love, compassion and wisdom from somewhere else. We already have these within us and only have to reveal them, to learn to appreciate them and so bring them forth. This is extremely important to understand. Who is going to redirect the mind? No one is going to do it from the outside. It is your responsibility, 100% of it, and you are fully capable. To redirect ourselves, we have to maintain a balance among the three states; the body, the speech and the mind. Work on keeping these in balance with courage and commitment, and joyfully redirect the wild mind and restless emotions towards the mind of love, compassion, and wisdom.

The moment we do that, we find that peace and happiness are already there. We don't have to search outside of ourselves. In developing true love, genuine compassion, and wisdom, the mind automatically becomes balanced with the speech and body. The freedom that we have been looking so hard for externally is actually experienced.

Buddha gave 84,000 different teachings. All of them are designed to bring more happiness and ease into our lives and then ultimately to reveal our Buddha-nature. That is the whole purpose of the Dharma. The 84,000 teachings do not merely repeat the same thing again and again, but offer an abundance of approaches to realizing the true nature. Because people have different ways of understanding, Buddha explained things in many different ways. To begin awakening all beings to the true nature of the mind, he presented the Dharma from all angles, offering us plenty of choices. It is not like Buddha has forced us to accept one single method of teaching or practice and left us no alternatives. That limitation is not here.

This is why Buddha is known as the gracious teacher. He offers us many possibilities, so that we can all begin to explore our primordial nature. All 84,000 teachings can be categorized into two vehicles; the Hinayana and the Mahayana. The Mahayana teachings are deeper than the Hinayana, and within the Mahayana, the Vajrayana is deeper than the sutra Mahayana. Deeper in that they reveal more of the true, primordial nature of the mind as it is. To bring balance to the body, speech and mind, and to reveal their nature, it is important to integrate all levels of these teachings.

In the Vajrayana and Dzogchen texts, it is repeatedly stated that the authentic ground, free from all obscurations, is the always already enlightened state, the primordial nature of the mind. They clearly and precisely explain that the original condition of mind is already awakeness. These are known as secret teachings and they are very special and important in revealing the ultimate state of the true nature. It is not enough to just read books. To actually follow this path and understand the meaning of the secret teachings, you should approach qualified teachers who can transmit pure lineage teachings.

Beyond that, it is not sufficient to simply hear or know about these things. We must practice to gain an experiential realization of the meaning. You might be inspired on the basis of hearing or knowing something about the teaching, and of course that will bring some benefit, but this is relatively superficial and does not sink deeply enough into your mind to bring about full awakening. Realization will not come merely by receiving teachings. Realization only comes by actually putting the instructions into practice through meditation. In order to practice and meditate and be able to absorb the Dharma within your heart, mind and body, you must have devotion and confidence.

That is really the only method. Enlightenment will not come through the intellect or external pursuits, but only by looking within, with joy, confidence and devotion. This attitude will merge the teaching with your body, speech and mind. It is always important to practice and meditate on the teachings you receive. Meditation and study are not separate from each other. Both can be done at the same time. When you hear a teaching or start contemplating a text, you are also beginning to practice meditation. In this way, you begin to actualize the teaching while you are studying and contemplating.

And meditation clarifies the meaning of the teaching, so in a way, it is like gathering knowledge, helping us gain insight into what the Buddha really meant. Understanding more and more, realization inevitably comes. When you study, don't just think, 'Oh, this was said by the Buddha or a great master, so it must be true.' Buddha Sakyamuni taught not to believe what he said is true simply because he said it. Your own discriminating wisdom must be applied to the teaching. You should analyze and think about it; you can reject it. Discuss it with others; freely investigate the truth and implications of all these statements. Do this as much as you'd like. Inquire and find out for yourself whether what is being said is true or not. But once you come to your own conclusions and find the true path, then you must follow it.

If you hesitate and vacillate about the truth of the path after that, this is an obstacle. It has become doubt. In the beginning, be sure to analyze and investigate, but once you develop certainty wisdom, do not retreat from it. To waver then is an obstruction that will weaken understanding and delay realization indefinitely. Doubt stops spiritual growth and destroys the foundation of effective practice. Once you have a good understanding and certainty wisdom arises, you should courageously follow through. Then full realization will inevitably come. But having already established yourself in the practice, to be stopped by thoughts is a fetter and will block realization.

It wastes all previous efforts. Problems like these may arise. In the course of practice you will experience the entire spectrum of emotions. Practice is not limited to things always working smoothly. Awakened states can shine through in many ways. Emotions reflect the condition of the winds in the channels and many different configurations are possible, but once we establish true confidence with courage and commitment, no matter what comes up, whether it is a good sign or a bad sign, - whatever, we should continue to hit the target and persevere in moving toward the realization and full revelation of love and compassion in our heart and mind. That is really the goal. Until then, don't falter but continue to press forward.

Devotion includes loving respect and appreciative understanding, but the ultimate form of devotion is characterized by deep confidence or faith. In practice, these three qualities tend to reinforce each other. First you investigate the teaching to contemplate what it really means. Once you develop certainty wisdom and become intimate with the meaning, you feel a sense of great appreciation. A wonderful feeling of closeness develops in relation to the teacher and the teaching and this leads to a clearer understanding and greater confidence. If you analyze this, as Buddha advised, you can see how closely all three are interconnected. For example, one of the Buddha's teachings is that every compounded thing is impermanent. If we have never heard this before, we might think, 'What does this really mean?'

All compounded things are impermanent. Is this the case or not? Think and analyze to see if this statement is true or false. Impermanent means changing. Each instant everything is changing. Time, the kinetics of mass-energy, and the flow of mental events, everything is continually changing states. If you consider this and can see for yourself that it is true, you will develop certainty wisdom and recognize the truth of impermanence. As you come to discover the truth through both your own wisdom and in the teaching, these two merge together so that it becomes unnecessary to backup and say,' Oh, that's not true.' Such is doubt and it is an obstacle.

All the Buddha's teachings reveal the true nature; therefore it is called the truth. Buddha never talked about anything outside of this. He said love and compassion are the ultimate state of realization, that the Buddha-nature is inherent in all sentient beings as love, compassion and wisdom. All these teachings point to the true nature, so once you connect with your own deeper intelligence, you should not back out or pull away as this will not bring any benefits to you or to others. Having developed certainty in relation to the dharma, joyful effort arises spontaneously. With good causes and conditions, the ultimate result will inevitably ripen.

This is a general explanation of the teachings. Now the one who shows the teaching is known as the teacher. There are many different classes of teachers, but as Buddha Sakyamuni said many times in both sutra and tantra, the teacher should be seen as kinder than all the Buddhas. The Buddhas left this world long ago and have since passed into history, but their liberating message continues to be carried and preserved in the world by qualified masters so that there remains direct contact and communication for those wanting to explore their natures, to learn the meaning of the dharmas and to develop their realizations.

The teachings are made available through the teacher so it is said that his kindness exceeds that of the Buddha himself. This expresses a great appreciation of the importance of a qualified master. Qualified teachers are also lineage holders. The lineage began with the Buddha and has continued into the present. This is known as the chain of wisdom. According to one system, there are two lineages; these are known as the oral transmission lineage, consisting of the actual words and explanations, and the chain of the powers of the wisdom blessing.

In the Vajrayana it is said that from Buddha Samantabhadra until now, qualified teachers have maintained both the oral and wisdom powers intact. The Nyingma School recognizes three lineages: the mind to mind transmission lineage, the symbolic transmission lineage and the oral transmission lineage. There are also many teachings which describe qualified students. The relationship between a teacher and a student depends on the strength of their spiritual bond, in sharing a warm feeling of closeness, discriminative appreciation, and true confidence.

These are the key elements, the heart of their connection. If these come together, great realization is forthcoming because awakening is based upon meeting the teacher, analyzing and investigating the teaching argument, and applying oneself to the practice with devotion. Devotion is the doorway to receive the light of the Dharma. It is said in the Buddha's teaching that devotion is like a channel to bring continuous blessings. If we aren't devoted, we have no to receive these blessings. Devotion is connected to your heart; it even penetrates your bones.

It deepens our inherence in the natural state and then begins to work on and redirect the body, speech and mind. So devotion is very important in making a close connection with the lineage and in bringing about full realization. Without it, we are not prepared to actualize the practice and teaching. As I said before, devotion is a combination of appreciation, closeness and confidence based in wisdom. If we don't have it, we are not ready.

In many of the biographies of the great masters of Tibetan Buddhism, it is said that your realization will correspond to your devotion. If your devotion allows you to see the master as a living Buddha, you will develop the realization of a Buddha yourself. If you see the lineage masters as just good lamas or nice people, then you also will have just a good or nice realization. If your devotion to the master is small, your realization will be small. If you have no devotion at all, you will have no realization at all. The degree of realization depends upon the quality of devotion.

Take for example, the very renowned Tibetan teacher Milarepa. He was not a scholar. He did not go through monastic training programs or have any academic education at all. However, the moment he met his teacher Marpa, he gained complete certainty wisdom and unfailing, unshakeable confidence. Milarepa saw Marpa as a true living Buddha. Even though Marpa put him through so much difficulty, Milarepa's confidence, courage, and commitment never wavered. If he didn't have this kind of commitment, if it was someone else, there would be no such realization.

Perhaps he would not have stayed around his teacher for more than a few weeks before he decided to go away and never come back. He might say 'How could I stay? Marpa is completely cuckoo!' However Milarepa's faith and commitment were never shaken throughout all those hardships, and soon afterward he became realized. The life of Milarepa is well known in Tibet and I am sure many of you have read the story. He is just one very good example of the power of devotion. If you have similar confidence, courage and commitment to the true teaching, you can observe the precepts and you will get the same realization. There is no question or doubt about any of this.

Marpa asked Milarepa to build a nine-story watchtower. Milarepa had finished the first level when Marpa's children came along playing and one of them helped him move a boulder. Marpa visited the site when the tower was almost half done. He watched for awhile and expressed his approval until he noticed this big rock in a lower wall. He asked Milarepa where he got it and Milarepa told him that one of his sons had helped him move it.

Marpa got very angry when he heard this. He said, 'How is this possible? You think you can use my children as your servants? I never said you could do that! Remove this stone immediately!' Then he left without waiting to hear any excuses. That was that. Milarepa had to break the tower down to the ground and return the boulder back to the space from where he'd dug it out. Marpa did this kind of thing to Milarepa many times. If Milarepa did not have devotion, he would think Marpa was crazy for making such a big fuss over that rock. But Milarepa never backed down from his original motivation, his initial feeling of love and devotion. He bravely persevered.

In the Vajrayana, the practice of devotion involves a lot more than just trying to be nice. Whatever Marpa asked, Milarepa considered part of the practice and purification designed to release and remove his negative karma and obscurations. He thought in this way and saw it was true. He did exactly as Marpa said and accepted it as his meditation and practice. When he finished these labors, Marpa gave him a few teachings and then directed him to go to the mountains and practice. He continued to do exactly as Marpa instructed by meditating in the wilderness and soon became enlightened.

With Marpa's help, Milarepa realized Buddhahood in one lifetime. All the hardship he went through became meaningful. It was all understood to be part of the teaching, purifying his karma and revealing his true nature. This type of understanding and realization is only possible through a continuity of deep devotion, confidence, courage and wise appreciation. In the Tantras, it is taught that everything is already in the condition of enlightenment; not only the teacher, but all beings, the elements and world systems they comprise abide as primordial purity. In studying the Vajrayana teachings, you must have heard many times that we are to see everything as the pure land, to see everyone in the already awakened state.

This is the essence of the Vajrayana vision. And it is based in truth. Everyone is really grounded in the enlightened state all the time and we can know this if we recognize their real condition. When we look into the ultimate reality of everyone's qualities, these are all enlightened states. Devotion is the door opening mind to the original purity of the true nature and in this way; it is a very special Vajrayana practice. If we just continue living with regimented attitudes and old habit patterns, clinging to our ideas and biases, we reify the regular, mundane, ordinary world view.

Carrying on like that, there is no way to reveal the other side of the true nature and we are not really mantra practitioners. Without devotion, we won't discover the secret aspects of existence. As long as our habit patterns are rooted in dualistic conceptions, there is really no way to discover our transcendent qualities. To refocus or redirect ourselves, devotion is extremely important. Devotion is the gateway between mundane conceptions and the non-conceptual. It is the bridge that connects habit patterns to the natural expression of primordial reality.

It allows conditional habits to dissolve and transform into wisdom qualities so that you can experience the unity of everything abiding in one inseparable, dynamic display of the true nature. To actually practice Dharma and redirect our energy, we must have devotion which manifests as love, a sense of closeness, appreciation and confidence. In exercising devotion, we are also practicing pure perception. The teacher may be very different or quite similar to us. Perhaps there is no difference at all in our realizations.

The teacher may be a little more advanced than the student but sometimes the student has more realization than the teacher. In any case, devotion is the way to develop pure perception. Pure perception is to appreciate the primordial qualities of the true nature. Start with the teacher and then begin to apply the same pure vision to all beings. Practice on the teacher first, and then gradually see everything in the state of primordial purity, just as you would observe the teacher. Echoing Buddha Sakyamuni, the great Nyingma master known as Patrul Rinpoche, said, 'You must see your teacher as kinder than Buddha, even though he may not have the realization of a first bhumi *bodhisattva*.

Why is that? Because regardless of his realization, he is carrying and preserving the true lineage teachings and his transmission can spark you into full enlightenment if you apply joyful effort, courage and commitment in living your response to that teaching. Because we can't be served by the historical Buddha in this way, the kindness of our teacher may be said to exceed that of the Buddha himself. Therefore we should see the teacher as even kinder than the Buddha. A Dzogchen tantra describes the nature of the connection between the teacher and the student and concludes that their relationship is one of true love, true compassion. Love is the bond.

True love awakens pure perception. You will recognize something precious and unique in the teacher. And not just there. True love allows us to see that everyone is special, even beautiful, not just the teacher. The quality and power of love will transform perception and deepen understanding. Throughout the teachings, from the Hinayana scriptures all the way to Dzogchen, the Buddha spoke again and again on the importance of love. Real love has nothing to do with attachment, dualistic habit patterns or neurotic grasping. True love is pure and beautiful with no trace of negative emotion, so it allows us to see everything in the state of beauty.

Genuine love for each other is the heart of the teacher-student relationship. With unconditional love or devotion as the foundation, we may begin to practice and meditate. That is the next step. Meditation practice must be done in three stages. Begin by arousing *bodhicitta*. *Bodhicitta* is the non-dual wisdom of love and compassion in relation to all living beings, including us. Also, cultivate a sense of appreciation for our opportunities and the good situation we have.

This circumstance has not just come about accidentally, but has many causes and conditions, beautifully detailing who you are and what you have. We should feel happy with all this. Think about it, wish for the good of all and hold a strong and courageous commitment to use this opportunity to gain a better insight into the ultimate meaning, to develop more love and compassion so as to realize greater benefits for both ourselves and all others. This is the initial stage of practice. On that basis, generate devotion and feel the presence of the teacher. Guru Padmasambhava is our real teacher.

See every qualified master as an emanation of Padmasambhava and understand Guru Padmasambhava as the supreme embodiment of all Buddhas and realized teachers. Feel his presence strongly and keep a heart connection with Guru Rinpoche. Many of you have *thangkas* and pictures of Guru Padmasambhava, so learn to visualize and feel him in a strong way, with joy, happiness and heartfelt appreciation. Make wishes such as, 'May I actualize my Buddha-nature instantly, so that I can benefit all beings. May everyone be realized?'

Arouse a strong aspiration and positive thoughts. These are very good and important foundations, opening the door to pure perception and transcendent understanding. Then maybe you can do the Seven Line Prayer three times or Calling the Lama from Afar. The third and main part of the practice is often referred to in the teaching as the non-grasping state. This non-dual freedom from grasping is the essential meditation and is divided into two; the developing and completion stage practices. When we are doing the visualization or the creation stage, we begin to see ourselves as Buddhas. This is also the practice of pure perception and inseparable from devotion. You will begin to see yourself as a true living Buddha; Guru Padmasambhava, Chenrezig, Vajrasattva, Tara, or whatever you practice.

You should totally merge with the deity when you are in that state. You are not just wearing a mask of the deity as if it was Halloween or a Broadway show, but you are really seeing things as they are. Without any doubt or hesitation you must seat yourself completely in that understanding. You are not trying to become something that you are not. Attachment to dualistic conceptions creates obstacles, so that we shrink from embodying reality qualities, but when we begin to break through that conceptual prison, collapsing and removing the wall, we are coming back to the original state. You must learn to abide as the deity in a Buddha field, without any hesitation. This is known as perfect visualization.

When you see yourself as a Buddha, you do not simply consider yourself as Buddha and the rest of the world as ordinary, but everything is transformed into that state, subject and object, the universe and all sentient beings, everyone is in that Buddha field together. This is known as true visualization. Many times in the teachings you will hear that all forms are the body of the Buddha. Whether in the shape of human beings, mountains, trees, water or furniture, all appearances are emanations of the body of the Buddha.

There is also Buddhas' speech. Every sound whether it originates with human beings, animals, natural phenomena, or even inaudible frequencies, such as the primordial sound, is all the speech of the Buddha. Not just mantra or human speech, but every vibration is a manifestation of the original purity of the Buddha's voice. This is the true understanding of the speech of the Buddha. Then there is the Buddha mind. Every mind, including your own, is no other than the Buddha mind. Not only individual sentient minds, but openness or space itself is a display of the mind of the Buddha. In Dzogchen, this is known as *kun-khyab rigpa,* pervasive awareness. What is pervasive awareness?

The state of openness is pervasive awareness. It is also called the unimpeded true nature, which indicates that Dzogchen realization or the Buddha mind is not just a limited, biased attitude or narrow understanding. The Buddha mind is the unbounded, expansive reality, which pervades the whole of space. Again, it is referred to as the fresh, naked state. It is always already fresh. It is completely naked. It is never deluded or mixed up. It is never second hand. It is the original purity, as it always is; pervasive, unimpeded, fresh, naked and original. All this terminology is used in order to awaken the perfect realization of this all-pervasive nature which is the primordial mind of the Buddhas.

Clearly comprehending these three dimensions of the Buddha while we meditate and recite mantra is known as perfect visualization, perfect recitation and perfect meditation. Now if we look at all of this, where does it come from? Where does it exist, where does it go? It is all beyond conception. Conceptions cannot comprehend this because concepts do not go beyond the surface. Limiting judgements accompany the arising of conceptual subject and objects. We begin to hallucinate, superimposing delusions over the true nature. The original state is beyond conception. It can only be perceived by the pervasive nature of the mind.

The *kun-khyab rigpa* alone can understand that realization which is beyond conception. When conceptions are informed by the true nature qualities, they are transcended in place. As Guru Padmasambhava said, all phenomena, all dualistic conceptions, disappear like clouds in the sky. Where do clouds come from? From space. Where do they exist? In space. Where do they go? Back into space. The whole of phenomenal existence arises, abides and dissolves within the primordial state. Nothing separates or moves away from the sphere of reality. Things are always in that condition. Similarly, all emotions, whether they are positive or negative, are part of the display of openness, the Buddha mind.

All phenomena appear, exist and dissolve within that context. If you aren't deluded, you will recognize the original purity flowing through the movement of the emotions. The real nature of emotions is not as you might think. What we call negative is just a superficial perception, another aspect of the beauty of the true nature. Therefore, it is said that the emotions are already liberated, already happening as a display of wisdom energy. Also, in the higher tantra or Dzogchen teachings, it is repeatedly stated that all emotions and conceptions are expressions of freedom and realization. To practice with this understanding is known as non-grasping, non-judgmental, non-dual meditation.

Continue to maintain this meditation without distraction. Without ego-clinging or grasping phenomena, is part of reality as it is? Applying that view to the whole of our life can really become a very special practice. At the end, dedicate the merit to all beings and make aspirational prayers on their behalf. In offering them the benefits of our practice, we again invoke the power of *Bodhicitta*. Having begun with the right motivation and then to practice in a non-grasping, non-judgmental way, is good, virtuous activity. To end a session, we should offer to share whatever energy or merit we may have generated through this practice with all beings.

The dedication and aspirational prayers are an important part of regenerating *Bodhicitta*. At the same time, understand that dedication practice defines a transition in the overall form of the meditation. But if we are devoted practitioners, we don't have to make any limiting divisions. When one form of practice ends, another begins. The end of formal meditation is the beginning of the post-meditation state. The great Master Patrul Rinpoche taught that there is no fundamental distinction between the states of meditation and post-meditation.

With a good understanding of the teachings, we transcend any differences. Both are aspects of one whole. In this way, the closing prayers do not indicate the end of our practice but signal the beginning of carrying the meditation experience into more externally active levels of participation. After the dedication and aspirational prayers, bring that same realization forward into the post-meditation state and begin to engage your daily activities. Sometimes it may be difficult to sustain a strong meditative continuity in the post-meditation state, but we must be brave and stay inspired. Think, 'I am going to take the essence of this practice back into the world.'

Once in a while throughout the day as you're working, reflect on the value of love, compassion, *bodhicitta*, courage and commitment. When strong emotions arise, don't hold on to them; simply notice to let them go and move forward. This is the way to begin practicing post-meditation awareness. Non-grasping meditation is the best kind. That means not clinging, not holding on to things. This doesn't mean that you give up everything indiscriminately, but you do not cling to emotions. Learning to let go brings patience and tolerance. Courage also comes quite easily then. If emotions come up, don't just immediately buy them. Check yourself with mindfulness and look within before you act. That will make the whole situation a little softer. It will be easier to handle the emotional energy and liberate it.

## THE THREE LEVELS OF VOWS I

Today's topic is the three vows. The common understanding of Tibetan Buddhism is that it is all Vajrayana. This is not the case. Guru Rinpoche said one's outer conduct should accord with the shravaka vehicle, inwardly one's motivation should accord with the *bodhisattva* vehicle and in secret one's mind should accord with the Vajrayana. One person can hold all three vows by avoiding the ten unvirtuous actions, by benefiting others one practices the *bodhisattva* vow, and by perceiving the world as a Buddha field and all beings as deities, which accords with the Vajrayana vow. But without *bodhicitta* you cannot be liberated by Vajrayana.

Even Hindu sadhakas practice Tantra. But liberation only comes from absolute and relative *bodhicitta*. Without *bodhicitta* Tantric practice leads to rebirth as a demon. So it is important to practice all three levels of vows. There is a Tibetan joke. It goes, "When I held my vows, I didn't know the Vinaya. When I learned the Vinaya, I no longer held my vows." So it is important to protect one's vows. But without knowing them you cannot protect them. In a monastery the discussion would focus on the vows of the ordained. But since most people here are lay practitioners, we will focus on the lay vows and the one day vow.

Shariputra asked Buddha why many monks are reborn in hell, but many lay persons are reborn in the deva realms.

Buddha replied, "Monks take their vow for their whole life, but don't keep them. Lay persons take their vows for a day and keep them." Many stories are told of the value of keeping the vows. One story says that one day a park ranger found a delicious apple beside a spring. He gave the apple to the palace guard, who gave it to the minister, who then gave it to the queen, who gave it to the king. The king thought it was the most delicious thing he had ever eaten.

He found out the park ranger had found it and told the ranger he had to bring him an apple every day. The ranger went back to the spring and cried. The naga of the lake appeared and told the ranger to tell the king that he would destroy the town unless he was offered a text with the eight one day precepts. This was at a time after Kasyapa Buddha's teaching had disappeared. The king asked his minister, who told him of a pillar that displayed miraculous activity. They looked inside and found the text. The king presented the text to the naga and the naga said that during the life of Kasyapa both of them had taken the one day vows.

The naga had broken the vow about eating after noon, and so was reborn as the naga. The king had kept the vows and so was reborn as a king. The first of the eight vows is not killing. All the vows have four aspects: basis, intention, endeavor, and completion. In the case of the first vow, the basis is the sentient being that is killed. The intention is the intention to kill. Even though the karma is lighter, it is still there if you kill unintentionally. For example, Nagarjuna killed a grasshopper when cutting grass in a previous life. And as a result he was able to be killed by a blade of grass when he was Nagarjuna.

You don't have to worry so much about keeping the vow of not killing. The next vow is sexual misconduct and you have to worry about that a little. But the vow you really have to watch is lying. Lying about your spiritual attainments is a very serious fault and causes a monk or nun to lose their vows. You shouldn't even joke about it. The fourth vow is stealing. If taking something is illegal, it becomes stealing. The fifth vow is drinking alcohol. Drinking creates all sorts of problem, as it relaxes your vigilance about your behavior. We can see that alcohol causes many problems in society.

In Buddhism it's said that if you ask someone to kill somebody, you get the same negative karma as if you kill them yourself. Some people say tantrikas can drink alcohol. But the Tantric texts say if you become drunk, you will be reborn in hell. Tantric practitioners have greater mental power, so they can indulge in activities and be unaffected. For example, Padmasambhava drank a thousand liters of beer and was unaffected. When you see a deity in union with a consort, they remain mindful and undisturbed by passion. But we are talking about Vinaya. In Vinaya the outer conduct is the most important. That is because your conduct is visible to all, but your mental attitude is not so outer behaviour is controlled.

The sixth vow is to avoid dancing and singing. The main problem is that they cause us to lose our mindfulness. Without keeping the vows you cannot be mindful. It's not that something is right or wrong because Buddha said so. If it is a cause of happiness, it is virtue. If it is cause of suffering, it is nonvirtue. Even though it may bring temporary suffering the end result of virtue is always joy. If you cultivate virtue you won't have to ask for the lama's help for problems.

The lama's help can only be a supporting cause for our happiness, not the principal cause. When the Buddha first taught there was no Vinaya. He merely taught one should practice virtue, avoid non-virtue, and tame the mind. By being mindful of body, speech, and mind, one upheld morality before the Vinaya was taught. JIgten Sumgon taught there was no distinction between actions that are naturally unvirtuous and those that break a vow. An action is nonvirtuous whether you hold a vow or not.

The seventh vow is not to use a high or expensive bed or throne. Using these is a cause of pride. Water will not remain on a hill, but will flow into the valley. So it is better to be humble. If you desire expensive things, you will work more to attain them and not have time to practice. Animals are smarter. When they've eaten enough, they go to sleep. Monks wear patchwork robes because the poor people of the time could only offer a scrap of cloth. The last vow is not to eat after noon. Anything that cannot pass through a cloth strainer cannot be consumed. The reason is that you wake refreshed and are able to meditate in the morning. So these are the eight one day vows.

Buddha bound Mara with a meditation belt. He freed Mara after he promised to take the refuge vows. When he did so, Buddha predicted Mara would attain enlightenment. Mara said, you are lying, because I didn't take the vow with a sincere motive. Buddha said, even so, you will still be enlightened. A lay person can just hold the vow not to kill. Or they can just take the two vows of not killing or stealing, or the three vows of not killing, stealing, and sexual misconduct. Or they can hold all five vows. Some lay person takes the additional vow of celibacy. Or a lay person can take the eight one day vows for their entire life.

Anyone who has gone for refuge holds the lay person vows. It's good to hold as many of the vows as you can. It's said it's more difficult to hold the vows during this degenerate time and as a result there is more merit. If you take the fully ordained vows, you cannot take the eight one day vows, as the fully ordained vows already contain them. The Moon Lamp Sutra says the the merit of holding the one day vows during a degenerate age is greater than making offerings to Buddhas and *Bodhisattvas* for as many aeons as grains of sand in the Ganges. And its said that holding the four root vows in a degenerate age is greater than upholding all the vows during the Buddha's lifetime.

It's better to take a vow and break it than not take it at all. If you take a vow, you will feel remorse when you commit nonvirtue and you will purify it as a result. If not, you will commit the action without paying attention to it until it becomes a habit. Buddha said nonvirtue only has one good quality; it can be purified through confession. Sometimes being careful is a kind of laziness. So taking vows is better than not taking them. There are two traditions of *bodhisattva* vows: the profound view lineage which comes from Nagarjuna to Shantideva and the vast conduct lineage which comes from Asanga to Serlingpa.

Our main tradition comes through Serlingpa. We uphold both traditions, so I will speak about both. In addition to these two lineages there is also the blessing lineage which comes from Milarepa. Gampopa unified these three into a single lineage. In the vast conduct lineage there are five root downfalls of a king, five of a minister, and eight of a common person. The first five mostly apply to a king, Stealing the wealth of the triple gem is the first downfall. This means stealing the wealth of a monastery. The second downfall is forbidding the practice of the dharma. This also includes rejecting the dharma.

For example, Mao forbade the practice of religion saying it was poison. The third downfall is seizing the robes, beating, or imprisoning a monk or nun or forcing them to give up their vows. Mao also did this. The fourth downfall is to command someone commit the five heinous faults of immediate consequence. These are killing your parents, killing an arhat, injuring a Buddha or dividing the *Sangha*. The fifth downfall is destroying a city or town. The five downfalls of a minister are the same as a king. The first two of the eight downfalls of a subject are: holding a wrong views and explaining the view of emptiness to beings that have not been trained. This means training in the four thoughts that turn the mind from *samsara*.

If one does not have a certainty about these, one can fall into a nihilistic view. The next downfall is to cause people who have entered the path of Buddhahood to abandon it. This means to persuade them to seek individual liberation. The next is to say that practicing the Mahayana means you don't need to keep the pratimoksha vows. The next is holding that the Hinayana path does not dispel the afflicting emotions or teach that to others. The next is proclaiming one's good qualities and disparaging the qualities of others. But this does not mean losing your self confidence.

The next is wrongly proclaiming you have realized the patience that is the fruit of enlightenment. The path of juncture is like feeling the warmth of a fire or smelling food and there is a kind of patience there. There is a greater patience on the path of seeing and when one reaches the eighth bhumi. The next downfall is to cause a practitioner to be falsely punished, to receive an offering intended for the three jewels, or accepting a bribe. The last downfall is disrupting someone's calm abiding meditation or taking offerings from a retreat practitioner and giving them to a person saying prayers. These all cause rebirth in hell.

In the tradition of Serlingpa there are four root downfalls and forty six subsidiary downfalls. The first is to praise you and disparage others for the sake of gain. But if you do so to correct others, that is not a downfall. The second is to withhold wealth from stinginess from those in poverty. The third is not to accept someone's apology, but to hold a grudge against them. The fourth root downfall is to pretend to be a practitioner after having abandoned the Mahayana. Depending on the seriousness of the downfall one must expiate it in different ways. If you commit these downfalls again and again and feel no shame in them, and see them as positive, you must retake the *bodhisattva* vow.

If you have regret and embarrassment, and someone corrects your action, you can confess them in front of three vow holders. If you feel embarrassment and remorse and no one needs to point it out for you, then you can confess it in front of one vow holder. If the violation one of the forty six subsidiary vows is motivated by an afflictive emotion, it must be confessed in front of one vow holder. Otherwise you can confess it mentally. If you can help a person through nonvirtue, it is a fault not to do so. An example would be a parent yelling at their child. It is wrong to accept an offering that was obtained fraudulently.

It's wrong to take pleasure in frivolous activities. It's wrong to seek to remain in *samsara*. Instead we should achieve enlightenment so that one can help others. It's wrong to not correct faults that others have pointed out to us. One should not retaliate when others hurt you verbally or physically. Atisha said the best teacher is the person who points out your hidden faults. But that doesn't mean you should respond in kind. You should not neglect those who are angry with you. You should accept the apologies of others. You should not hold onto anger.

You should not be lazy and oversleep. You should not scatter your attention in idle talk. You should make an effort to stabilize your mind and abandon the obstacles to stability. You should not be attached to the experiences that arise from meditation. These include bliss. If you attach to experiences, that will obstruct realization. You should not disparage the Hinayana, but you should not neglect the Mahayana. You should not criticize your teacher's teaching or be attached to the letters rather than the meaning. We should help others and repay their kindness. You should alleviate poverty according to your ability. But you should not neglect the needs of your family. You should praise the good qualities of others. But you should prevent the harmful actions of others.

# 6

# The Four Attentions

The three levels of Buddhist teaching are called 'vehicles' because they comprise the teachings and methods that will carry us to enlightenment, in much the same way that vehicles carry us to our destination in everyday life. Hinayana is the basic level of Buddhist teaching and practice that is common to all traditions, though it is often associated with the Theravada tradition.

It is called 'the lower vehicle', but it is not lower in the sense that it is of lesser value than the Mahayana or Vajrayana vehicles. Instead, it is the foundation level of Buddhism. Just as a house needs a solid foundation in order to be strong, so also do the other Buddhist vehicles or paths need the solid foundation that Hinayana provides.

## INDIVIDUAL LIBERATION

We start building this foundation by focusing on ourselves. Consequently, the Hinayana path is an individual journey of discovery and freedom. We face the confusion and difficulty in our lives, identify its causes and then seek to uproot them by practising the skilful means of the path, such as doing no harm, behaving in a wholesome manner and training the mind through meditation. As these aspects of the Hinayana are mastered, the Mahayana aspiration to guide all sentient beings to enlightenment becomes possible. Without first putting our own house in order, however, we will not be able truly to help others. We start putting our house in order by cultivating renunciation.

## RENUNCIATION

This is the heart of the Hinayana path. Renunciation means that we clearly look at how we are living our lives and what forces are driving it. The great insight of the Buddha was that normal life is pervaded by *dukkha* or suffering. His perception was that everything is in a state of perpetual change, that nothing lasts, and so holding onto things as if they are solid and permanent brings us nothing but dissatisfaction, unhappiness and pain. So what we renounce are our unhelpful and habitual ways of doing things because they cause suffering. Instead we try to live life in a more realistic and conscious way that will allow us to develop wisdom and compassion. We start this process by taking refuge.

## TAKING REFUGE

This is the way in which we formally become a Buddhist and it lays the foundation for all that follows on the Buddhist path. The notion of 'refuge' is one of seeking guidance and inspiration as we travel the path to enlightenment. It is a support for us as we purify our mind of its limiting patterns and cultivate wholesome qualities. We take refuge in three things: the Buddha, the Dharma and the *Sangha*. They are often referred to as the Three Jewels because they are seen as rare and precious gifts.

- *Refuge in the Buddha* - The first thing we take refuge in is the historical Buddha himself. Since he achieved enlightenment, he showed us that it *can* be achieved by ordinary people. So we look to him as a role model and inspiration to help us along our own path towards liberation from the cycle of birth and death and suffering.
- *Refuge in the Dharma* - The second thing we take refuge in is the Dharma, which is the Buddha's vast and profound body of teachings. Initially these teachings and methods are simply learnt and applied to our lives as best we can,

but as we practice them and integrate them into our daily experience, the Dharma becomes a vivid inner process of awakening.

- *Refuge in the Sangha* - The third thing we take refuge is the *Sangha,* which is the community of experienced and committed Buddhists who have helped preserve the Buddha's teachings throughout the ages right down to the present day. We seek refuge in them to provide support and guidance as we practice the Dharma. Of particular value to us are those dharma teachers, known as 'realised beings', who have attained unshakeable insight into the true nature of mind.

## ETHICAL CONDUCT

Once we have taken refuge we commit to living our lives according to certain ethical guidelines. In this respect, the Hinayana vehicle is also called 'the path of details' in that close attention is paid to cultivating discipline and ethical conduct. In building the foundation of a house we need to pay careful attention to the details of construction, otherwise the whole structure will be unstable. Therefore, once we have committed ourselves to the Buddhist path, we build this strong foundation by living our lives according to the principles of not harming any living beings and performing wholesome actions wherever possible. For lay practitioners these ethical guidelines are based on the Ten Virtues. They apply to our actions of body, speech and mind:

*Physical Actions:*

- Not intentionally killing any living beings. Instead saving and protecting life.
- Not taking things that do not belong to us. Instead being generous with our wealth and possessions.
- Not engaging in sexual activity that causes harm to us or others. Instead maintaining healthy sexual relationships.

*Speech:*

- Not lying. Instead speaking truthfully
- Not saying things that will provoke discord amongst other

people. Instead patching up quarrels caused by slander.

- Not speaking harshly and negatively to other people. Instead speaking in a kind and gentle manner.
- Not engaging in idle gossip and chatter. Instead talking in a meaningful way about worthwhile topics.

*Attitudes of Mind:*

- Not being envious of the property and possessions of others. Instead rejoicing in the good fortune of others.
- Not resenting others for their happiness and good fortune. Instead cultivating loving-kindness and thinking only of their benefit.
- Not holding incorrect views about the true nature of things, such as the law of karma, cause and effect. Nonetheless maintaining tolerance of other philosophies and religious traditions, while still adhering to one's own.

**FOUR NOBLE TRUTHS**

The central teaching of the Hinayana vehicle is the Four Noble Truths. This was the very first teaching that the Buddha gave after he attained enlightenment. It is also referred to as the "First Turning of the Wheel of Dharma" because it represents the first phase of the Buddha's teaching. It is called a "wheel" because it is a means for travelling the path to enlightenment in much the same way that a wheel enables a vehicle to move along a road. The Four Noble Truths are:

1. *Suffering exists* - This truth means that everything that exists is unstable and in a state of continual change. Nothing is truly satisfactory because nothing lasts. There are three aspects to this truth:
    - The actual experience of suffering, such as feeling pain and discomfort.
    - The suffering that comes from change and impermanence, such as not getting what one wants or losing what one cherishes.
    - The suffering that comes with being alive and embodied. It is the suffering of being limited and conditioned and can manifest in the feelings of

loneliness and alienation.

2. *Suffering has a cause* - This truth explains that the underlying cause of suffering is an attachment to a sense of 'me' - to the perception that we are an individual separate from everything else. This belief causes us to feel powerful desire, aversion and confusion. As a consequence, we grasp onto things and become identified with them, but because everything is impermanent and ever-changing, we inevitably suffer loss. Otherwise, we feel strong aversion towards something and try to push it away; but because everything is impermanent and ever-changing, at some point we are forced to confront what we dislike and this causes us suffering. This cycle of suffering and being bound to our patterns of aversion and attachment is called *samsara* or the "cycle of conditioned existence". Moment by moment and lifetime after lifetime, we perpetuate these patterns of grasping and aversion, always fiercely attached to who we think we are; and in so doing, we repeatedly experience dissatisfaction and sorrow.
3. *Suffering can end* - This is the "truth of nirvana". Nirvana is described by Sariputra, one of the Buddha's main disciples, as a "the extinction of desire, the extinction of hatred and the extinction of illusion." It is a state of profound peace unsullied by mental activity and attachment to a self.
4. *There is a path to the ending of suffering* - This is the truth of the Noble Eightfold Path.

## NOBLE EIGHTFOLD PATH

The Noble Eightfold Path is the essence of the Middle Way, the path between the extremes of self indulgence and denial. It contains eight interrelated aspects that make up the "skilful living" that the Buddha taught is necessary to uproot suffering and its causes, and to sever the cycle of conditioned existence.

The Noble Eightfold Path comprises the three essentials of Buddhist training: ethical conduct, mental development and wisdom. (Please note that 'right' in this instance means 'skilful and wise'.)

There are three components of ethical conduct:

1. Right Speech
2. Right Action
3. Right Livelihood

There are three components of mental development:

4. Right Effort
5. Right Mindfulness
6. Right Concentration

And finally, for a total of eight, there are two components of wisdom:

7. Right View
8. Right Intention

**NO SELF**

The root cause of suffering, according to the Four Noble Truths, is attachment to a fixed sense of self, while the liberating insight of the Buddha was that what we take to be 'me' is merely a label that we apply to our changing experience of body and mind. It is not who we really are. In essence 'me' is an illusion. This view of no-self or "anatta" is what distinguishes Buddhism from other major religions. We tend to see ourselves as being a single, permanent and independent personality, but if we examine our experience more closely we see that our thoughts and feelings are changing all the time. One moment we feel happy, then something happens and we feel sad.

Then someone distracts our attention and our mood shifts again. We are used to thinking of this constantly shifting process as 'me' - as a fixed entity to whom these things are happening. From the perspective of Buddhist philosophy, however, there is no fixed entity called 'I'. Instead 'I' is simply a label that we apply to this continuous flow of physical sensations and mental phenomena. It is not something separate that experiences it. The problem comes when we behave as if there is a single, permanent self, base our life around this assumption and become emotionally attached to our sense of self. We are then at odds with the way things are.

Everything that we identify with as 'I': my body, my feelings, my thoughts, my life - all of these things is composed of many physical and mental processes that are interconnected and changing moment by moment. So our assumption of 'me' being single, permanent and independent is simply not true. Everything is composite, changing and interdependent. This mistaken perception is the fundamental cause of suffering, called ignorance, from which all other forms of suffering spring.

**FIVE AGGREGATES**

The physical and mental processes that make up our ever-changing personality are classified into five groups called aggregates (or *skandhas* in Sanskrit).

The Five Aggregates are:

1. Form
2. Feeling
3. Perception
4. Mental formations
5. Consciousness

The first aggregate - form - comprises the material elements of our physical existence. This includes our sense faculties and their objects. Feelings of pleasure, pain or neutrality arise when a sense faculty makes contact with an object, such as hearing a beautiful birdsong and feeling happy. Perception is the recognition of the sound and naming it, as for example identifying what kind of bird is singing. Mental formations are the thoughts and emotions that arise in relation to one's feelings and perceptions, as for example thinking 'I would like to get up every morning and listen to that beautiful bird singing'.

Consciousness is what links the senses with their objects and enables us to have awareness of them. There are five consciousness pertaining to each of the five senses of sight, sound, smell, touch and taste; and a sixth consciousness pertaining to the mind and the consciousness co-ordinate with the input from the five senses and experiences thoughts and feelings. When the five aggregates are working together in combination, we develop the idea of 'me' as someone who is doing this seeing, feeling, thinking, etc, but this is merely a mental construct, much the same as we develop the idea of a 'stream' when we see drops of water aggregated together. It remains that this is just an idea - a mental formation - and what is really there are simply the five aggregates working together.

## KARMA

Although on an ultimate level self is an illusion, we experience 'self' at a relative or everyday level happens because of ignorance and karma. When we fixate on a sense of 'me', we then perceive everything else as 'other than me' and our way of relating to things is conditioned by this separation. This is the meaning of 'ignorance' in Buddhism.

This sense of separation causes us to develop feelings of attachment and aversion. We then act on these emotions, seeking to be nearer things that we like, pushing things away that we don't like and ignoring the rest. Like planting a seed, which bears fruit, these actions produce results. In Buddhism, this cycle of actions and results is called "karma". Furthermore, the Buddha taught that if we act in unskilful ways we experience suffering and if we act in skilful ways we experience happiness.

## TWELVE LINKS OF INTERDEPENDENT ORIGINATION

The Twelve Links describe in detail how the process of karma works. According to this teaching, the life that we are now living is not something that has just happened by itself, it is not a 'one off' experience. Instead, it is part of an on-going process of actions and results over many lifetimes. Our current life has been moulded in the way it has because of things that we did in former lives. In the same way, what we are doing now is shaping what our next life will be like. In Buddhism, this is called the process of interdependent origination, meaning that things originate from each other and depend upon each other.

This process is going on all the time and is unbroken. We are the way we are now due to how we acted in the past. Depending on how we act now, we shape the future. This circular, on-going process is often compared to a wheel in Buddhism. It is the famous analogy for *samsara*: a wheel that turns round and round and round. The process starts with ignorance because it is ignorance which causes the mistaken perception of reality that happens when the mind contracts around a sense of a 'me', thus separating 'me' from what is 'other' or 'not me'. Once ignorance is present, it starts the process of 'becoming', which is made up of the Twelve Links of Independent Origination. This process is the force which propels sentient beings through *samsara* and results in them taking birth in different realms of existence.

The Twelve Links of Interdependent Origination are called 'links' because each one is the cause of the next one. They don't happen independently. Instead, they behave like a row of dominoes lined up next to one another. If you push the first one over it knocks down the second one, which knocks over the third one and so on. In a similar way, when the first link occurs, it then causes the second link to happen and this in turn causes the third link to occur and so on. These links describe our moment by moment experience of the world, as well as the life cycle of an individual.

The Twelve Links are:

1. Ignorance produces
2. Karma (the law of cause and effect) produces
3. Consciousness produces
4. Form produces
5. Senses produce
6. Contact produces
7. Feeling produces
8. Craving produces
9. Grasping produces
10. Becoming produces
11. Birth produces
12. Aging and death

And death starts the cycle of existence over again by producing a state of unknowing or ignorance. The twelve *Nidânas*; character of the precepts; incitation to abstract meditation: gradations of perfection. At the time of Sâkyamuni's death the inhabitants of India were not yet so advanced in civilisation as to have a literature, and the claims of the Buddhist to scriptural documents of his law written down during his life (as the Nepalese believe), or immediately after his death (which is the opinion of the Chinese), are decidedly groundless.

New researches have made it very probable that the alphabets in which the earliest historical records we know, the inscriptions of king Asoka (about 250 B.C.), are written, were imitated from the Phœnician alphabet, communicated to the Indians by merchants of that nation as early perhaps as the fifth century B.C., at which period already Greek letters became known in the ancient districts of Gandhâra and Sindhu, the countries at the foot of the Himálaya drained by the Indus. We are now able to assert that the words and doctrines attributed to Sâkyamuni were transmitted orally down to the first century before the Christian era.

The scriptural record was undertaken by the southern and the northern Buddhists independently of each other. In Ceylon the priests wrote them down during the reign of king Vartagâmani, 88-76 B.C.; their northern brethern brought them into a written form at an assembly of the priests, or synod, arranged by the Turuschka king Kanishka, 10-40 A.D. The Singhalese chose the vernacular language, from which the books were translated into the sacred Pâli dialect at the beginning of the fifth century A.D.; the northern branch used the Sanskrit.

Up to these periods, the religion had been preserved orally, and although, according to Buddhist history, Sâkyamuni's words were brought into a well-defined and precise form already in the year of his death, yet it is very doubtful whether the natural changes to which oral tradition is subject allowed his original law to remain unaltered. Moreover, we have a positive proof that arbitrary alterations and additions have been purposely-made, especially with reference to the historical details given in the earlier compilations. Such changes soon became numerous and assumed an importance not properly belonging to them, owing to the claim set forth by each new sect, that its peculiar dogmas had been revealed by Sâkyamuni.

The orthodoxy of each new and dogmatic school is maintained on the supposition, that the word of the Buddha is to be taken in a double sense, as he had often been compelled, in consideration of the mental capabilities of his hearers to give explanations about certain subjects quite at variance with his real opinion, and the new sects do not base their existence upon the rejection of previous works as spurious, but claim to have discovered the true meaning. During the first century after Sâkyamuni's death there was no controversy about his laws, but after this period a numerous fraternity of monks (12,000 it is said) asserted the validity of ten indulgences.

Their doctrine was rejected by the assembled priests at the synod of Vaisâli, a place north of Pátna (Pâtaliputra), on the eastern bank of the Gándak River, and as they would not submit to the judgment, the first schism took place. At this new stage of Buddhism, in which the fundamental dogmas of Sâkyamuni began to be interpreted from various points of view, the ancient sects are called the Hînayâna system. The name means "little vehicle," and has originated with the later Buddhists.

The epithet was given because the adherents of this system restrict themselves to morality and to external observance only, without making use of such an abstruse, refined, and highly mystical theology, as did, at a later period, the Mahâyâna schools, or those of the "great vehicle." Yâna, vehicle, is a mystical expression, indicating, that man may escape the troubles attendant upon birth and death by practising the virtues inculcated by the Buddhas, and finally attain salvation.

The following details may be quoted as particularly characteristic of the Hînayâna system.'

I. It distinguishes itself from the Srâvakas in the mode of explaining the principle of Buddhism: that the world must be abandoned because it entails upon man existence, pain and death. The source of existence is no longer demonstrated from the four truths only, but also from the twelve *Nidânas* (in Tibetan Tenbrel chugnyi), which are based upon the four truths.

The *Nidânas*, the theory of the causal connection, or concatenation of the causes of existence, are formulated as follows: "On account of ignorance, merit and demerit are produced; on account of merit and demerit, consciousness; on account of consciousness, body and mind; on account of body and mind, the six organs of sense; on account of the six organs of sense, touch (or contact); on account of contact, desire; on account of desire, sensation (of pleasure or pain); on account of sensation, cleaving (or clinging) to existing objects; on account of clinging to existing objects, renewed existence (or reproduction after death); on account of reproduction of existence, birth; on account of birth, decay, death, sorrow, pain, disgust, and passionate discontent. Thus is produced the complete body of sorrow.

From the complete separation from and cessation of ignorance, is the cessation of merit and demerit; from the cessation of merit and demerit is the cessation of consciousness; from the cessation of consciousness is the cessation of (the existence of) body and mind; from the cessation of (the existence of) body and mind is the cessation of (the production of) the six organs; from the cessation of (the production of) the six organs is the cessation of touch; from the cessation of touch is the cessation of desire; from the cessation of desire is the cessation of (pleasurable or painful) sensation; from the cessation of sensation is the cessation of the cleaving to existing objects; from the cessation of cleaving to existing objects is the cessation of a reproduction of existence; from the cessation of a reproduction of existence is the cessation of birth; from the cessation of birth is the cessation of decay. Thus the whole body of sorrow ceases to exist."

II. In the books of discipline attached to this system we also meet with a vast accumulation of precepts and rules intended to release its followers from the ties binding them to the present and future states of existence, and to strengthen them in moral virtues. One curious feature predominating throughout is worthy of mention. The whole of the precepts (which are comprised in 250 articles) display a negative character; thus, charity is inculcated, not by the command "to give," but by the prohibition "to take," save when the gift be offered as alms.

Already this school had put forth the doctrine, that perfection in abstract meditation is indispensable for final salvation; this perfection guarantees an energy not to be derived from the more practice of simple virtues. Nevertheless the idea is not carried so far as to assign to mental speculation a higher value, than to virtues. Assiduity in undisturbed reflection was, however, found under any circumstances to be a most difficult task; certain preparatory exercises are, therefore, recommended, in order to finally lead the mind to abstraction from outward (worldly) objects; but here already we meet in Buddhism with decided extravagances in moral considerations.

The counting of inhalations and exhalations is named as an excellent means for obtaining tranquillity of mind. Detestation of the world is said to result from meditating upon the attributes of the body: if, therefore, one begins with regarding his body as an abscess, he will be convinced that the body contains nothing but misery and decay, and he will then easily cast off all affection for it, and will even end by considering food also as a mass of putridity, with which he will become disgusted.

III. As regards the degree of perfection which man has attained in virtues and science, this system acknowledges several gradations, which are based upon the following philosophical considerations. The comprehension of the doctrines as taught by Sâkyamuni is different with different men. There are several degrees of comprehension. Those who have succeeded in arriving at the highest degree are superior to those of a lower one. There are four paths to comprehension, and in order to arrive at final emancipation from re-birth, at Nirvâna, it is indispensable to have entered one of them at least. Emancipation takes place either instantaneously, on account of the merit accumulated in previous existences, or by assiduous attention to the various exercises prescribed.

To each of the four paths to comprehension are assigned particular faculties arising from its pursuit. Those who have not yet entered any of the paths, are designated in the sacred books by the name of "unwisemen," or those who live in the meshes of the cleaving to existence, of evil desire, ignorance, and impurity. These unwise men have not availed themselves of the means revealed by the Buddha to obtain freedom from metempsychosis; "their minds are still obscure, slow, and incapable of clear comprehension; such beings are not in the path securing final liberation, which is only accorded to one of the paths of wisdom."

The gradually increasing importance of the four paths is defined by the Buddhists as follows:-

*First path* - This is attained by the Srôtâpatti, or "the man who have entered the stream" leading to Nirvâna, and have thus advanced one step towards salvation. Nirvâna is reached by rejecting the error which teaches "I am," or "this is mine," by not doubting the real existence of the Buddhas, and by perceiving that the practises and exercises ordained by them must be carefully attended to. From the time of entering this path up to the attainment of Nirvâna itself, there remain only seven more births, but none can take place in any of the four hells; such a saint constantly wanders about, and according to Chinese notions, his migrations last 80,000 kalpas, or periods of a mundane revolution.

*Second path* - The graduate is here called Sakridâgâmin, "he who will receive birth once more." Such a graduate's mind is enlightened upon the subject of the three doctrines understood by the Srôtâpatti, and is, moreover, freed from the desire of cleaving to sensuous objects, and of wishing evil to others. He may either enter this path in the world of men and afterwards be born in a world appropriated to gods, or he may enter it in a world of gods, and afterwards be born in the world of men. He has still to wait 60,000 kalpas, before he arrives at Nirvâna.

*Third path* - Here the graduate, Anâgâmin, "he who will not be born again," is free from the five errors already cast off by the Sakridâgâmin, and also from evil desire, ignorance, doubt of the precepts of the sceptics, and hatred. He may enter, by the apparitional birth, a world of gods, and from that world attain Nirvâna, for which, however, he has still to wait 40,000 kalpas.

*Fourth path* - This, the highest path to perfection, is attained by the Arhats, Arhants, or Archats, a title meaning that they deserve to become members of the assembly of the faithfuls (samgha). In the earliest period of Buddhism the name Arhat was given to every one who had arrived at the comprehension of the four truths. But such a steadiness of the mind, the Hînayâna followers say, can only be attained by those who have renounced the world, viz. by the priests; and these alone consequently enjoy the advantages of entering the fourth path, which consists in nothing less than the emancipation from re-birth, and the possession of five supernatural faculties, or the *Abhijnâs*. To allege of any one that he has "seen Nirvâna," is the same as saying, that he has become Arhat. The restriction of Nirvâna to the clergy cannot be imputed to Sâkyamuni, who, on the contrary, admits all his followers to the full blessings of his law.

At the early period of the Hînayâna system the list of the different gradations must have been closed with the Arhats, the Buddha even not being originally called by another name; but in the progressive developement of this system the Arhat was superseded by the *Pratyêka Buddhas*, the *Bôdhisattvas*, and the most perfect Buddhas.,

*Pratyêka Buddhas* are those men who, though attaining by their own unaided exertions the *Bôdhi* of the supreme Buddhas, remain limited in their powers as well as their intellects. They are unable to release any one from the repetition of existence, as they only care for their own salvation, without contributing in the least towards that of other men. *Pratyêka Buddhas* are accordingly never said in the legends to have accomplished miraculous works similar to those of the supreme Buddhas, and are further considered never to appear when a real Buddha is living upon earth.

Bôdhisattvas are the candidates for the Buddhaship, or those men who, by assiduity in the practice of virtues and meditation, have finally arrived at the intelligence, or Bôdhi, of the supreme Buddha. Whoever Strives to attain this sublime rank, has to pass through countless phases of existence, during which he gradually accumulates a greater degree of merit; he gains thereby the favour of a Buddha of contemporaneous existence on earth, and by his assistance he rises to one of the celestial regions above the earth, where he awaits his next birth as Saviour. Such candidates are not enumerated in the sacred Hînayâna books amongst the companions of the Buddha Sâkyamuni, with whom indeed no Bôdhisattva could be contemporaneous; nor are they believed to take an active part in the general welfare of man. The title simply denotes the condition of those who shall attain the Buddhaship at their following birth.

The most perfect Buddhas (whose plurality has been promulgated by the Santrântika-Hînayâna) are those Bôdhisattvas who, at their last birth, have arrived at the sublime wisdom which enables them to direct man to the path leading to the cessation of existence. From the moment of departure from earth they have left behind them every kind of personality and form, and all connection with the world; they interfere with nothing and leave it to man to seek salvation by his energy. This dogma was still further enlarged by some of the Hînayâna sects, the Mahâsâmghika School even going so far as to discuss the infinity, eternity, and omnipotence of the Buddha.

The reason for rebirth in *samsara* is ego-clinging. All emotions arising from ego-clinging will not be virtuous and with such self-centred ego, there is no way to perform virtues.

All the karmic activities will not be virtuous and each of these bad karmic causes will lead to rebirth in lower realms for ten thousands of times. If you can contemplate on this fact, then you will be able to realize how precious the human body is. In the innumerable times of rebirths, the chance of being reborn in the human realm is one to ten millions.

Therefore, now that you possess the precious human body, please do not waste it. You must make use of this precious human body to practice. Unless you are already enlightened or else there is no way to be completely liberated. The above is the first requirement of the basic practice. Next, to be a Vajrayana practitioner the second requirement is to be equipped with great compassion. That is to say, in order to practice Vajrayana, one must be a Bodhisattve. *Bodhisattva* means a person with *bodhicitta* and compassion.

*Bodhicitta* is the seed for Buddhahood and a *Bodhisattva* must have *Bodhicitta* and Compassion towards all sentient beings, without the slightest selfishness. Once you have generated *bodhicitta,* any merits performed will be transformed limitlessly and can lead to liberation and Buddhahood. Contrary to this, if you do not generate *bodhicitta,* all merits performed will be limited. Only merits done with *bodhicitta* can guarantee enlightenment or Buddhahood.

Besides practicing the *Bodhisattva* path, Vajrayana practitioners also use certain special skillful means in their practice, such as visualization of deites, etc. In the Vajrayana tradition, the Kalacakra is said to be the highest tantric practice. Kalacakra has a profound meaning and the characteristics of the Kalacakra deity are also very special. It has many faces, many hands and many legs and these represent many meanings of the practice. Another example is the four arms Chenrezig with its white body which symbolizes purity and compassion, lotus flower and crystal rosary held in the hands symbolize compassion and wisdom, and the ornaments worn on the body represent the various qualities of realization.

The deity or yidam can manifest in the form of *Sambhogakaya* or *Nirmanakaya*. These manifestations stem from the primordial awareness that is *Dharmakaya*. For example whether Chenrezig is perceived as manifestation in the form of a *Sambhogakaya* or *Nirmanakaya* depends on the level of practice and capacity of the practitioner. When you are doing the *yidam* practice, do not think that you are inviting the deity to you. For example in the practice of Chenrezig, it is not really that Chenrezig will appear in front of you. Certain people think that *yidam* practice is to invite the deity to come forth or to enter their bodies.

These are wrong views. Further, to clear ego-clinging, we must focus our attention on another thing beside the 3 posions, i.e., visualizing a seed syllable. For instance the syllable "HRIH" contains the blessing of the *samadhi* of Chenrezig which can transform into the image of Chenrezig. Now with our ordinary bodies we visualize this seed syllable and through this seed syllable, we transform into Chenrezig. This will clear our thoughts and habitual tendencies. From this we will know that yidam practice has a lot of benefits.

- Firstly, it contains samatha meditation because you have to do a lot of visualizations.
- Secondly, *yidam* practice can clear bad karma and habitual tendencies
- Thirdly we can attain the *Dharmakaya* or *Sambhogakaya* state.

The heart mantra of Chenrezig - Om Ma Ni Pad Me Hung arises from the *samadhi* of Chenrezig and by reciting this mantra can help us to increase our concentration and eliminate bad karma of speech. Also, visualization of the deity is not in solid form. Its nature is emptiness, *Dharmakaya* and its manifestation is the *Nirmanakaya*.

In the completion stage of yidam practice, we have to visualize Chenrezig dissolving into light and enter into the nature of our mind. At this moment, the power of our meditation dissolves into the natural state of mind. In the sutra, this is called *Prajna Paramita*.

The visualization of the seed syllable "HRIH" is to clear our habitual tendencies. Usually, when beings are reborn into human realm, the consciousness will first cling to a body and then enter the womb. Of course with the present technology it is not able to detect the conception of consciousness in the womb. What we can see is only the gradual process of growing. The conception of consciousness is caused by greed and attachment and these are very hard to get rid of. It needs the natural transformation of the mind. Therefore, we visualize our mind and dissolves into "HIRI", which will transform the bodies of sentient beings into the bodies of Chenrezig.

The concept of yidam dissolving into light entering emptiness can change the habitual tendency of death. Usually when sentient beings die, they must enter the bardo stage. By this practice and visualization, it can clear the tendency and enter the state of *Dharmakaya*. These are the practices of Vajrayana but most importantly, they require meditation as the basic. The methods of meditation are mostly found in esoteric sutras. If you are practicing Vajrayana and lack of this basic, whatever you practice will go wrong. You will be unable to visualize the empty state of a yidam and you will visualize the yidam's body as a solid form. When you recite the mantra, you will neglect its essence. Therefore, without the basic of esoteric teachings, all practices serve no purpose.

To be a practitioner of Vajrayana, we need to have a thorough understanding of its practice and also the complete *bodhisattva* vows. Vajrayana should not be taught openly to people who have not taken the *bodhisattva* vows as it is the teachings of the *bodhisattva*s. Therefore, only *bodhisattva*s are eligible to pracitice. However, the practice of Chenrezig consists of exceptionally great compassion and can be taught openly.

## NIKAYA BUDDHISM

The term Nikaya Buddhism was invented by Mahayanist scholars, in order to find a more acceptable (less derogatory) term than Hinayana to refer to the Early Buddhist schools. The Early Buddhist schools are those schools of Buddhism which accept only the scriptures which correspond to the Suttapitaka,

Vinayapitaka and (possibly) an Abhidhammapitaka. These schools of Buddhism do not recognize or accept the Mahayana Sutras as the word of Buddha. Examples of these schools are pre-sectarian Buddhism, the early Buddhist schools, and any possible other schools or views in which the historical Tipitaka represents the scripture with the highest authority. Some scholars use the term as excluding pre-sectarian Buddhism.

The most famous example of these historical Tipitaka texts is the Pali Canon. Other scriptures which correspond to these are the agamas and some of the Gandharan Buddhist Texts. Hinayana or Nikaya Buddhism is distinguished from the Buddhism of the various Mahayana and Vajrayana schools, which accept the authenticity of a range of other scriptures as spoken by Buddha (mainly the Mahayana Sutras). Many of the sutras corresponding to those of the Pali Canon are accepted by every school. Historically, there were many 'Nikaya schools', but only one still exists today in (close to) its original form: the Theravada. Mahayana and Vajrayana Buddhism use the ordination lineages of these schools. There were once at least eighteen Nikaya schools.

Many commentors on Buddhism have used the term Hinayana to refer to Nikaya Buddhism. However, that term is now generally seen as flawed:

- Hinayana, (literally "inferior vehicle"), is often regarded as an offensive or pejorative term.
- Hinayana was coined by the Mahayana, and has never been used by Nikaya Buddhists to refer to them.
- Hinayana as a technical term indicated the vehicles of both the *Savaka* Buddha and the *Pratyeka-Buddha*, whereas as a division of Buddhism, it refers solely to the individuals who follow the former vehicle, towards the achievement of *Savaka* Buddhahood, while the Mahayana in the sense of the *Bodhisattva* path existed within the early schools already.
- It is sensible to use a terms for a division of population which is ideally used by themselves, and failing that, at least not offensive to them.

According to Robert Thurman, the term "Nikaya Buddhism" was coined by Professor Masatoshi Nagatomi of Harvard University, as a way to avoid the usage of the term Hinayana. "Nikaya Buddhism" is thus an attempt to find a more neutral way of referring to Buddhists who follow one of the early Buddhist schools, and their practice. The term sravakayana (literally, "hearer vehicle" or "disciples' vehicle") is also sometimes used for the same purpose.

Other terms that have been used in similar senses include sectarian Buddhism, conservative Buddhism and mainstream Buddhism (this last might be considered derogatory by Mahayanists, as implying that they are fringe). Note that *Nikaya* is also a term used in Theravada Buddhism to refer to a subschool or subsect within Theravada.

Like the term Hinayana Buddhism, the term Nikaya Buddhism focuses on the presumed commonality between the schools, and not on the actual schools themselves. This commonality is thought to be found in a certain attitude. The difference is that in 'Hinayana Buddhism' the common attitude was stated to be a certain 'selfishness', while the term 'Nikaya Buddhism' tries to shift the attention to the more neutral issue of attitude concerning the authenticity of scriptures.

**Disadvantages of the term Nikaya Buddhism**

Some disadvantages of the term Nikaya Buddhism are:

- The term is not well known.
- The term Nikaya Buddhism isn't very clear: it's not obvious from the term what is meant by it.
- Neither possible literal interpretation fits the coverage of the term "Hinayana":
    - If the term refers to the nikayas into which the Buddhist *Sangha* divided, it excludes the period before these divisions (pre-sectarian Buddhism).
    - If it refers to the scriptures known as nikayas or agamas, it has just the opposite effect, excluding the schools that use Abhidhamma: such as the Theravada, Sarvastivada, Dharmaguptaka, etcetera.

- When used, it is used by scholars only, and hasn't found adoption by any of the existing schools of Buddhism.
- The term 'Nikaya Buddhism' is just a replacement of the term Hinayana, which keeps in place the tendency to regard the separate early schools (and their differing ideologies) as one form or type of Buddhism. The early Buddhist schools themselves never used a term to refer to all the early schools together as one type of Buddhism.
- Conflating all the early schools as one 'type of Buddhism' originated with some proponents of Mahayana, who introduced the name "Hinayana" to distinguish their concept of the Dharma from the already existing schools. So, in some ways, the usage of the term 'Nikaya Buddhism', although neutral in import, points to a Mahayana (or Vajrayana) view of Buddhism.
- If Nikaya is used in its proper sense of monastic grouping, then Chinese and Tibetan Buddhism are included in it, belonging to the Dharmaguptaka and Mula-Sarvastivada Nikayas respectively.

## THREE-YANA MEDITATIONS

We will give here a simplified account of the whole Three-in-One system showing how through purification of the gross poisons affected by the Five Meditations in the Hinayana, these passions, now subtle, may be sublimated in the voidness meditations of the Mahayana and then finally transmuted into the functions of Buddhahood in the Vajrayana. So one by one we will take each of the five Hinayana Meditations and show the gradual processing of the poisons in the different Yanas.

### FIRST MEDITATION

This is on the Impurity of the Body. Everyone is born a layman, born from the craving for a body of flesh. Craving this physical body, one has impure lusts and passions. So the first thing necessary to bring about a cessation of pain (*duhkha*) experienced because of the action of the passions is quite simple: renunciation. If one does not renounce the objects both mental and physical upon which the passions arise, how will one get rid of either these cravings and desires or their accompanying sufferings?

Following renunciation comes purification which is threefold: of the body of flesh, considered as a whole; of the 36 inward parts composing it; and most inwardly of one volition toward the body. The first is purified by meditations on the decay of the body, the Cemetery contemplations, and the second by contemplating all the messy bits and pieces which compose it; and the third by the purification of the Sharp Driver of "own-body-view" through seeing the body voidness.

All this process is contained in the Hinayana where renunciation and purification are very much stressed. It is important to understand that none of these body meditations aim at "mortifying the flesh". All of them are skillful means which aim at purification of the body so that one may progress to higher stages of the Path. The body, which is neither to be attached to, nor to be "mortified" (which is a kind of self-hatred), but should be used as the vehicle to Full Enlightenment.

To gain this, meditations of the Hinayana are not sufficient hey only remove the sorrow of lusto that one finds that the practices of the Mahayana are necessary. These affect a sublimation of the body from being a human body of flesh to becoming the Buddha-entity body.

While the nature of the void (*Sunyata*) is the source of the *Dharmakaya* (the ultimate truth considered as an unmanifest body of the Buddhas), the conditions of *Sunyata* are the source of the Rupakaya (the variously manifested bodies of the Buddha). The aspirant has to labor many long ages while acquiring slowly all the necessary *Sunyata*-conditions before he can actually realize his aim (Full Enlightenment, Buddhahood, the *Dharmakaya*). It is like cooking food: The water boils and all becomes steam, but here we are not satisfied with that steam, which after all still contains the smell of the food, nor can we wait so long for the meal to be ready.

For this reason we take up the Vajrayana where we are at once initiated in the actual position of consequence of

Buddhahood. To obtain the Glorious Body of Buddhahood (*Sambhogakaya*, in which the Buddhas preach to the Holy *Bodhisattvas*) it is necessary to use one of the many methods found in the tantras. One should not think that the highest body among these three, the *Dharmakaya*, is something dead because it is inert and unmanifest. No, indeed! For the *Dharmakaya* must manifest as the other two Buddha-bodies, as the *Sambhogakaya* and the *Nirmanakaya* (appearance-body is seen by men and animals, as the Buddha-forms on this earth). All the functions from these two latter forms are the complete salvation found only in the Vajrayana.

## SECOND MEDITATION

The Great Compassion and the Four Kinds of Boundless Mind in the Hinayana teachings can cure the sorrow of Anger. The methods used in this *Yana* to control hatred is by the observation of the Moral precepts (and by the Vinaya for Bhikshus), which is indeed only an outward suppression, together with these Boundless Mind meditations which will only subdue this sorrow. As there is but little wisdom of *Sunyata* taught in the Hinayana so this process cannot be finished there.

So once again we see that there are three steps of which the meditations above constitute the first. Why must we go in? Hinayana *Sunyata* teaching is not thorough-going enough to pull up completely all the roots of anger. Some subtle fragments of this sorrow still remain which will surely sprout again as soon as the conditions are favorable. Thus we come to the Mahayana meditations of *Sunyata*, where inwardly one gets rid of this notion of a personal self and outwardly abandons ideas of selfhood in phenomena. When both these types of no-self have been realized, then it is easy to get rid of this sorrow.

This is a kind of negative approach. The real question is: How can anger be transformed into mercy? The same four Boundless Minds are practiced in Mahayana conjoined with *Sunyata* and then become truly boundless. When they are truly boundless then real Compassion emerges. How is this? Great

Compassion comes from the cultivation of the *Bodhicitta* and this in turn derives from *Sunyata*. In *Sunyata* there is no self and no others, so neither of these can be distinguished in the *Sunyata* of the *Dharmakaya*.

Most people do not recognize this and make some division into "I and mine" and "You and yours" and from this false discrimination, anger is produced. But the Great Compassion of the Same Entity arises in the opposite way when one knows the void nature of all persons and events and the impossibility in reality of distinguishing any "self" or "thing." Still something remains to be done for one should not be content to do good to sentient beings by one compassionate will alone; one must give them some actual benefits. This is possible in the Vajrayana where there are many methods in the position of Consequence. Here it is practicable to benefit beings by the functions of salvation of Buddhahood. To save them all from the woes of *samsara* is surely at once the highest good and the most complete transmutation of the poison of anger.

**THIRD MEDITATION**

The samapatti on causation in the Hinayana is to cure the sorrows of self bound up with ignorance. The twelve factors of Dependent Origination (*pratitya-samutpada*) are very much stressed as the system which explains the conditional production of ignorance (*avidya*). It is negative since it lists all those factors which lead to our continuous living and therefore suffering in the world of birth-and-death. This doctrine shows clearly how one action contains within it the possibility of certain results and is thus a guide for the purification of deeds by mind, speech and body.

The power of meditation must reverse the usual order of the twelve factors so that a stopping of one of these factors automatically leads to the inhibition of the following one. In this way, these factors all depending on ignorance and craving (*trisna*) are destroyed one after another. This system of causation corresponds to the Four Noble Truths taught by the Buddha but it is not deep enough to reveal Thatness (*Tathata*) which is the Lord Causation teaching in the Mahayana.

In the Great Vehicle, all sorrows are sublimated in *Sunyata*. From the *Sunyata* arises knowledge of the causation by Tathata. This is not merely a stopping but a discovery of the merits of Buddhahood from realization. At that time it is not only easy to attain Arhatship but more than this, to become a prince of the Buddhas, a *Bodhisattva*. But according to the holy salvation of Buddhahood, all holy causation has some correspondence with all sentient beings which are to be saved in this life. This cannot be done in the Mahayana.

The six perfections (*paramitas*) can only be regarded as skillful means for those who wish to follow the Buddha as *Bodhisattva*. Even to reach up to the first stage of *Bodhisattva* is very difficult, taking immense time, because so many things have to be done for innumerable beings. *Bodhisattva*s find it impossible to make much headway with their meditation in *Sunyata* as they are too much pre-occupied with doing things. For this reason they may even pass many lives totaling a kalpa of years but still fail to develop a deep samatha of *Sunyata*; and not having this they can make little progress towards Buddhahood.

We see from our examination that neither the causation of Dharmas and human beings (in Hinayana) nor the Mahayana causation of no causation are easily realized in the causations of a *Bodhisattva* life. Indeed, the *Bodhisattva* who wants to experience quickly the functions of salvation must use the Vajra Vehicle. The methods there in the position of Consequence of Buddhahood make the ultimate salvation of all beings possible. A Buddha, even while sitting down, can cause many things to happen for he can do everything for beings in the whole Dharmadhatu through his Vajrayana meditations.

## FOURTH MEDITATION

This is on the Discrimination of Elements and in the Hinayana it is the way to cure the sorrow of pride. Through its practice one comes to know that the whole of one personality is just five heaps, the first of which is form or materiality which is in turn composed of the five elements, while the other four heaps (of feelings, perceptions, mental tendencies and consciousness) are the mental components. Pride of self may definitely be purified through this meditation yet still one cannot positively use the six elements. So one must pass on to Mahayana teachings. On the other hand, concerning the mental heaps, one may keep one mind in the silence of *Sunyata* to convert them into the *Dharmakaya*.

On the other hand, the materiality of five elements may be sublimated and produce the mystic power to save all sentient beings. Such methods are not to be found in the Hinayana-they are only obtainable in the Great Vehicle. This is still not enough, for even if one gains some magical power over the elements, for instance by pointing at iron and turning it into gold to be given away to those in need, still this merciful act is a worldly action of a *Bodhisattva* and certainly not the way to bring beings to ultimate salvation.

If one wants to do this, then not only must the mind be changed into Truth, but the flesh must be transmuted into Light and the techniques for accomplishing the latter are known only in the Vajrayana. In this Diamond Vehicle there are many methods using the Five Elements and converting them into the Five Wisdoms. An instance of this is the Torga doctrine found in connection with the Great Perfection.

**FIFTH MEDITATION**

In the Hinayana the breath is just used to quiet the disturbed mind and to subdue the various doubts arising from the accumulated delusions. The sorrow of doubts is cured by meditation on the breath but if we make a fair comparison of the use of the breath in other yanas, then we see that Hinayana instructions are incomplete in this respect. It is true, though, that this forms a good basis for breath meditations in the Mahayana. Mahayana breath meditation is also used to make the mind quiet but this is in the samatha of *Sunyata* and does not concentrate on physical breath but becomes the breathing of a Buddha through *Sunyata*. The basic methods, however, are all taken from the foundation laid in the Hinayana.

When the mind is *Sunyata*, then the breathing is *Sunyata*. There are many methods to settle mind and breathe through meditation. Breath has not the same meaning in Mahayana as it does in Hinayana for in the former practice, breath is *Sunyata* transformed into wisdom-energy, though Mahayana has no specific practices taking advantage of this fact. The Arhat of the Hinayana may gain purification through breathing meditations though this is not a Buddha breath. The latter occurs when the mind is identified with the *Dharmakaya* so that the breath is similarly identified.

The Vajrayana, however, contains many breathing techniques quite distinct from the instructions in the other two yanas. It is because the *Bodhisattva*s of the Mahayana have no access to such meditations that their way through *samsara* is so very long. Not only do the Vajrayana methods aim at transforming the practitioner breath into that of a Buddha but also they take advantage of the use of a yogic partner (either physical or visualized) to bring about a combination of energy to form a complete Heruka breathing.

There is no gross breathing in the Consequence position of Buddhahood, all of it having been transmuted into light. This applies to the *Sambhogakaya* where the breath, both in and out, is of light. In the *Dharmakaya*, the Holy Light includes everything. But in the Buddha-body seen by most men, the *Nirmanakaya*, there is both gross and subtle breathing. When the flesh is transmuted into rainbow light, then all actions are produced by light and not in the ordinary way by breath. In Buddhahood, there is talking and working but this is all by means of light.

There cannot be Hinayana without Mahayana, nor the latter separate from Vajrayana. Why? Because these contain the three processes in the unified system of Buddhist Meditation. We have talked many times already about these processes. They are, of course: Purification, Sublimation, and Function and each of them can be compared to one of the three stages of the silkworm. When it is a caterpillar, it slips off its skin four times (Purification). When it makes up a cocoon it extrudes many strands of silk, which together form a continuous thread.

During this process it moves its head right, right is space, left, left is space, up and down it moves its head in all directions in space. The cocoon it makes is thus shown to be void in every part. Each condition of *Sunyata* is the combined, though different strands of silk, the many strands forming the cocoon (*Sunyata* nature); so *Sunyata* is the causation, causation is *Sunyata*- this way the caterpillar is sublimated to become a chrysalis (Sublimation). After this, the complete moth breaks out of its chrysalis and goes to find a partner and so produce eggs (Function in Vajryana).

Readers should pay great attention to these three stages of our whole system of meditation, and then it will be easy to see the most important point of our book. It is my own opinion and one never talked about by the ancient Sages, either that of Tibet or from China. So all who read this book must not only recognize the unity of the Buddhist tradition of meditation and wisdom but practice accordingly, and moreover, practice thoroughly. As regards the time which should be spent over these various yanas; Hinayana meditations should be given three years continuous practice and the same amount of time should be allowed for the realization of *Sunyata* in the Mahayana; then at least six years should be devoted to the Vajrayana for the attainment of Buddhahood.

Altogether this makes up a twelve year meditation course for hermits and yogis who are really serious about their practice. From such concentrated attention to meditation, one will surely get enlightenment in this life. It may happen that one is so fortunate to meet a Vajrayana guru well-learned and experienced in the disciplines of all three vehicles. If so, he may guide one through the whole system and one may be saved the trouble of finding first Hinayana teachers, then going to others for Mahayana teachings and finally gurus for the tantras. Time is also saved in this way as it is not then necessary first to visit Hinayana lands and then those where the other yanas are also taught.

## THE GOOD WISHES

In Chinese we have a proverb: "Try to learn the highest and you will gain at least the middle one, but try only for middling attainments then you will gain only the lowest and the highest remains beyond you." Therefore, we hope that readers will decide to win the highest, that is, Buddhahood in this life. We hope that to aid them in this noble endeavor the tantric doctrine will spread to the West and become firmly established there. Buddhism is well-founded in any country where all three yanas are combined harmoniously in the whole system of Buddhist teachings. May this be the case in Western lands?

Also, may the reading and practice of the doctrines contained in this book lead to the long life of all its readers? May this book be a guide for their practice through many years? May they all quickly gain Full Enlightenment! Again, we hope that all learned and studious persons may pick up this book and by reading its contents come to know the whole system of meditation in the Three-Yanas-in-One and then decide to practice what they have learned in theory.

Finally, the entire world may turn away from the path of materialism which is blindness, towards the glorious bliss-bestowing Teachings of the Buddha: May his Noble Teaching spread everywhere throughout the world. And may this Dharma of Enlightenment preached by the Enlightened One remain in this world for a very, very long time!

Whenever we listen to teachings, we should abandon the three faults of the vessel and cultivate the six attitudes (or six recognitions). Before we begin the lesson proper, we usually spend five to ten minutes meditating. During this time, it is useful to check whether we are able to abandon those three faults and cultivate the six recognitions. This doesn't simply mean being able to mentally list them out, but, rather, we should actively do something to abandon those faults and cultivate those attitudes. When we apply the art of listening in this way, it will make the session fruitful and worthwhile.

Buddha said, "Listen well, listen thoroughly and retain it in mind." So whenever we listen to the teachings, we first need to pay attention and focus on what is being said with our minds and with a pure motivation. We should not forget whatever understanding we may have gained in the session. So the point is not simply to be able to list out the three faults and the six attitudes. It is important to check whether those three faults and six attitudes are in our minds or not.

When the Buddha taught the *Perfection of Wisdom* sutras, the explicit subject matter was emptiness. The implicit hidden meaning of those sutras was the levels of clear realisations which are clarified in Maitreya's *Ornament for Clear Realisations* and summarised in the eight clear realisations. We will not be going through the eight realisations in detail. In order to know what the eight realisations are, we need to know their names so that we can understand their meaning. Therefore we have to pay attention to the words to try to understand what they do mean.

Once we have a rough understanding of these eight realisations, it will help us when we read a commentary on the *Ornament for Clear Realisations* in the future, our interest will be aroused, giving us the motivation to carry on reading the commentary. Otherwise, when we pick up a commentary on this text, we won't understand anything at all and without any prior understanding, it is unlikely that we will continue reading it.

This text, *Ornament for Clear Realisations* is challenging and is a profound treatise. Nevertheless, we can place some positive imprints in our minds and we can definitely understand some parts of it. We had started to look at the eight categories that make up the *Ornament for Clear Realisations,* covering the exalted knower of all aspects and the knower of paths:

- The exalted knower of all aspects refers to the path (or consciousness) in the continuum of the Buddha Superior.
- The knower of paths is basically the path (or knower) in the continuum of the Mahayana superior. (The *path* in the mental continuum of the Mahayana superior is the knower of paths. The *knower* in the mental continuum of the Mahayana superior is the knower of path. They both mean the same thing.)

The knower of paths can be divided into three:-

1. The knower of paths that knows hearers' paths
2. The knower of paths that knows solitary realisers' paths
3. The knower of paths that knows Mahayana paths

An illustration of the knower of paths that knows hearers' paths is the wisdom directly perceiving the selflessness of persons in the continuum of a Mahayana superior.

Generally speaking:

1. An exalted knower (or wisdom) that directly perceives the selflessness of person is a hearers' path.
2. An exalted knower that realises the emptiness of subject and object being different substantial entities is a solitary realisers' path.
3. An exalted knower that directly realises emptiness is a Mahayana path.

If it is a hearers' path, it is not necessarily included only in the continua of the hearers and if it is a solitary realisers' path, it is not necessarily included only in the continua of the solitary realisers. But when it is a Mahayana path, it can only be found in the continuum of a Mahayanist. The wisdom directly perceiving the selflessness of person in the continuum of a Mahayana superior is a hearers' path and also a Mahayana path. These two are not contradictory.

The wisdom that realises the emptiness of subject and object being different substantial entities in the continuum of a Mahayana superior is a solitary realiser's path and is also a Mahayana path. Boundary for the knower of paths: It exists from the Mahayana path of seeing through to the Buddha ground. This means the knower of paths does not exist prior to the path of seeing.

A path is necessarily a consciousness and not a view. There are five Mahayana paths -the path of accumulation, the path of preparation, the path of seeing, the path of meditation and the path of no-more-learning. Keep in mind that the *Ornament for Clear Realisations* is presented mainly from the perspective of the Yogic Autonomy Middle Way School.

In the Autonomy Middle Way School, the selflessness of persons and selflessness of phenomena are differentiated according to their objects of negation and not according to their bases of emptiness. According to the Consequence Middle Way School, however, the selflessness of persons and selflessness of phenomena are not differentiated according to their objects of negation but according to their different bases.

**KNOWER OF BASES**

The knower of bases is defined as an exalted wisdom conjoined with a wisdom directly realising selflessness in the continuum of the person who possesses it in his continuum that abides in a Hinayana class of realisations. An illustration of a knower of bases is the wisdom directly perceiving the selflessness of person in the continuum of a Mahayana superior. This wisdom is a knower of paths and is also a knower of bases.

A Hinayana path is either a path that exists in the mental continuum of a Hinayanist or it is something that abides in the Hinayana class of realisations. For example, the wisdom directly realising the selflessness of person in the continuum of a Mahayana superior is a Hinayana path not because it is included in the mental continuum of a Hinayanist but because that wisdom abides in the Hinayana class of realisations.

What is the meaning of "abide in a Hinayana class of realisations"? It means that that wisdom directly perceiving the selflessness of person in the continuum of a Mahayana superior has a similar observed object and aspect of it as the main object of cultivation of a Hinayana learner. In the last lesson, I had reviewed the objects of abandonment and the objects of practice according to the Yogic Autonomy Middle Way School, the perspective from which this text is presented. According to that tenet system, they posit three vehicles primarily because of their assertions regarding the objects of abandonment and practice, focussing on the self of phenomena and the self of person.

Is the wisdom that directly perceives the selflessness of a person in the continuum of a Mahayana superior a hearers' path? Yes. Is the wisdom that realises the emptiness of subject and object being different substantial entities in the continuum of a Mahayana superior a solitary realisers' path? Yes. Is the wisdom that realises the emptiness of subject and object being different substantial entities in the continuum of a Buddha superior a solitary realisers' path? Yes.

Buddha mentioned in many sutras that *bodhisattva* superiors need to know the hearers' paths and on the basis of that knowledge, generate them. With that scriptural authority, it is asserted that in the mental continua of *bodhisattva* superiors, there exist hearers' paths. They do meditate on hearers' path and generate them. Why do the *bodhisattva* superiors have to do this?

This is because *bodhisattva* superiors have to take care of disciples who are predisposed towards that lineage. In order to do that, they have to know the paths and generate them, experiencing the realisations themselves before they can teach them to such disciples. Similarly, in order for the *bodhisattva* superiors to take care of those inclined towards the solitary realisers' paths, they have to able to show the path. That is why the *bodhisattva* superiors need to meditate on and generate both the hearers' and solitary realisers' paths.

The knower of bases is mutually inclusive or synonymous with an exalted knower in a superior's continuum abiding in a Hinayana class of realizations. (It is insufficient to simply say that the knower of bases is mutually inclusive with an exalted knower in a superior's continuum).

The knower of bases has four divisions:-

1. The knower of bases that is close to the resultant mother
2. The knower of bases that is distant from the resultant mother
3. The knower of bases of the discordant class
4. The knower of bases of the antidotal class

(The knower of bases that is distant from the resultant mother and knower of bases of the discordant class mean the same thing).

Boundary for the knower of bases: It exists in the continua of all superiors. This means that the hearer superior, solitary realiser superior, *bodhisattva* superior and Buddha superior have the knower of bases.

The knower of bases that is distant from the resultant mother is separated from great compassion and is bound by grasping at true existence. An illustration would be the wisdom directly realising selflessness of person in the continuum of a hearer superior that has not yet realised emptiness (and is therefore bound by grasping at true existence). As long as one is bound by grasping at true existence, this means that one has not realised emptiness and is therefore further away from attaining enlightenment.

The knower of bases that is close to the resultant mother is an exalted knower in the continuum of a Mahayana superior abiding in the Hinayana class of realisations that is conjoined with great compassion and the wisdom realising emptiness. The wisdom directly realising the emptiness of subject and object as separate entities in the continuum of a Buddha Superior - is that a knower of bases? Yes, because that realisation abides in the Hinayana class of realisations.

# 7

# The Myth of Hinayana

What meaning can an ancient mythology or story have for persons in our alienated, absurd world? This is the question that must be explored in terms of the relevance and meaning of religious faith, as well as for secularized, scientific, modern men and women. This issue pertains also to Shinran's thought, as well as all contemporary religious thoughts. Shinran was an exponent of the Pure Land thought and way of salvation. The foundation of his thought was based on the three sutras that are known as the Three Pure Land Sutras. As with all sutras, all the traditional stories that begin "Thus have I heard," (nyozegamon) are reputedly the vehicle for relating the teaching of Gautama Buddha.

This phrase presumed to confer authority on the subsequent content as being in accord with the words of Buddha historically and with the truth itself. The term nyo, or nyoze - "Thus" has important meaning because it relates to such Buddhist philosophical principles as shinnyo - "true suchness" - and nyorai - the "Tathagata" (The Thus Come Thus Gone). The idea of nyo, or Thusness, signifies the essential truth of things and reality. In effect, it is an assertion of the truth of Buddhism.

The nature of Buddhist truth, however, presents modern people with a variety of problems in their attempt to determine the historical accuracy of the sutras and the truth of religion. In traditionalist faith everything could be spelled out by merely quoting honored authorities. Nothing had to be proved. It was all assumed. In modern times, however, people question the meaning of truth of such assertions and expect reasonable answers to their problems. The quest for truth, which was at the root of all traditions, re-emerges as a focus of importance for truth-seekers in this modern era.

Ancient man always attempted to see his life against the backdrop of eternity. Human beings, the only creature whom we believe to be aware that he must die, have always had to reflect on life and its meaning. They could never bring themselves to believe that the powerful forces which sustain their lives could simply end when they died of illness, old age, or some tragedy. In all traditions there were myths which depicted human destiny after life in this world. Salvation religions not only focused on the continuation of life itself, but correlated the quality of that future life with the quality of one's present life. To inspire religious devotion, there developed both positive and negative pictures of the afterlife. One might go to heaven, or one might end up in hell.

The heart of the story of these Pure Land Sutras is the endeavor of the *Bodhisattva* Dharmakara (Hozo Bosatsu) to acquire sufficient merit through his sincere practice to be able to secure the way to the Pure Land for all being everywhere in an infinite future. Once having achieved this, the Pure Land (described as being in the West or the Western Paradise) and the Buddha Amitabha (Amida, the Buddha of Infinite Life and Light) await those who avail themselves of the means of rebirth provided by the *Bodhisattva*. The "Larger Pure Land Sutra" tells the story, while the smaller "Amida Sutra" describes the Pure Land itself. The "Meditation Sutra" offers a variety of meditations whereby birth in the Pure Land may be achieved, but it also presents a system of meditation whose goal is to visualize the Buddha and attain union with him.

On the basis of these sutras, the various teachers in the popular Pure Land tradition began to spell out the implications and meaning of their contents for faith and practice. In China, there were teachers such as Hui Yuan who emphasized the system of meditation, while Tan Luan and succeeding teachers like Tao-cho and Shan-tao developed a popular teaching focusing on the practice of recitation of the Nembutsu (name of Amida Buddha), a practice that changed in meaning and emphasis as the Pure Land tradition evolved in China, and later, in the Kamakura period in Japan. Tao-cho and Shan-tao in their contribution to this evolution brought the teaching into relationship with the theory of degeneration, or Mappo, maintaining that the simple recitation was an appropriate practice for common people in the last age of the disappearance of the Dharma (Mappo).

When we review the story of the Sakyamuni Buddha and his progress towards enlightenment, we would not expect the development of myths and stories dealing with future destiny and its possibilities since, fundamentally, Buddhism are non-mythological. Buddha himself was a human being who developed his human potential to the fullest and gained insight into the true nature of existence. In his teachings, the gods were displaced, and deprived of any serious role in a person's attainment of enlightenment or Nirvana. Early Buddhist art did not represent the Buddha figure because, having broken through the bonds of existence, he must be regarded as inconceivable.

It could likewise be assumed that Buddhism would develop as a religion without myth as well as without image, and yet, from those earliest times, the devotion of his disciples and followers gave rise to legends about the Buddha, and of course, in time, to impressions that could be visually conceived and represented. Over the centuries there evolved a biography replete with mythic and legendary features such as stories of the Buddha's birth, and of his attainment of enlightenment. In comparison to ordinary men, we might say that the Buddha virtually became a divine being in terms of Buddhist mythology and art. At the same time, however, Buddhism constantly held to the firm tradition that he was not divine, but as "the supremely awakened one" he was the highest human being.

With the development of Mahayana Buddhism, the myth-making tendency became even more pronounced. The figure of Buddha expanded from a historical person to a cosmic reality - all embracing and indwelling. The multiplicity of Buddhas who filled the infinite worlds of the universe all became manifestations of the Cosmic Buddha. In the "Lotus Sutra" we see that the Buddha (Sakyamuni), who taught 40 years and went into Nirvana, was really only one manifestation of the eternal Buddha who has never gone into Nirvana but continually strives for the salvation of all beings. With the advent of Pure Land thought, this eternal Buddha Amida symbolized the infinite time and space.

In the "Larger Pure Land Sutra," the story of Dharmakara's attainment of Buddhahood offers an eloquent testimony to the depth of compassion which Mahayana Buddhists perceived in the Buddha reality and which they felt impelled to express in the constant refrain of the *Bodhisattva*: unless and until all other beings can achieve the same goal, he would refuse enlightenment. The focus of this Sutra on the central characteristic of the Buddha being compassion is intensified also in the first of the four *Bodhisattva* Vows (shiguzeigan):

"However innumerable sentient beings are, I vow to save them ..."

Or, as another version states:

"I will save those who are yet to be saved; I will make those who are frightened feel secure; I will help enlighten those who are yet to attain enlightenment; I will cause those who are not in nirvana to be in nirvana."

In this spirit of the ideal of compassion, there developed an emphasis on *dana*, or "giving," the first of the six perfections to be practiced by *Bodhisattva*s: *dana*, giving; *sila*, morality; *ksanti*, endurance; *virya*, energy; *dhyana*, meditation; and *prajna*, wisdom. In his "Outline of the Triple Sutra of Shin Buddhism," Prof. Fujimoto eloquently translates the application of these six perfections of the compassionate idea expressed in the Pure Land sutras:

"Each of the *Bodhisattva*s manages to become a friend of swarming sentient beings though not asked; takes upon his shoulders the people's heavy burden; by preserving the inexhaustible stock of the Tathagata's profoundest Dharma, protects and develops their seed of Buddhahood so it will not be destroyed; commiserates with them out of his ever-rising compassion; shuts the door of the three evil worlds, unlocking that of goodness; preaches the Dharma to the swarming people before being asked, just as a pious son loves and pays respect to his parents; takes care of sentient beings as well as he does of himself, thus carrying them to the Other Shore by means of the supreme root of goodness."

Religion and religious endeavors must be the realization of deepest compassion through identification with all beings whatever their state. Through all the intricacies and details of the myth, this is its central burden, the confirmation that the heart of reality is activated by compassion. It is a profound statement of the faith that ancient Buddhists had in the worthwhileness of life and in its inclusive universal meaning.

The ideal of infinite compassion also sets an example of mission for those who would believe in this myth. It dramatizes for us that from the heart of compassion new worlds of infinite potentiality are created and thus, this ideal shines as a message of hope in a contemporary world that does not seem much moved by creative efforts, a world of technological values where altruism often seems ineffective and valueless. The composers of the ancient Buddhist sutras remain anonymous, since they ascribed everything they wrote to having heard the teachings directly from Sakyamuni Buddha or from someone who had heard it repeated by one he had directly experienced hearing them.

The chain of distance from the source expanded with the passing centuries, and composition continued, but the authority of that "Thus have I heard" was retained. It stirs the imagination to contemplate the depth of concern of those anonymous composers of the Pure Land sutras. Suffering humanity was their focus, and their path was not easy for often they were accused of distorting and perverting the original message of Buddha. However, they believed deeply in their mission and their commitment took them to the point of being willing to sacrifice their lives, as is illustrated in the "Exhortation to Hold Firm," Chapter XIII of the "Lotus Sutra."

Undoubtedly, the description in the sutra of the Buddha arising from contemplation with glowing countenance, followed by the inquiry of the disciples as to the reason for his exaltation and ecstasy, suggests the type of situation which must have produced the first versions of such sutras. They were, perhaps, inspired by concentration on the meaning of compassion. As this aspect of Buddha was probed, its comprehensiveness had to be given concrete expression over against the traditional goal of Nirvana. The Pure Land of Bliss and Peace can be considered an expansion of qualities sometimes associated with Nirvana (as is the interpretation of Ryukyo Fujimoto in his "Triple Sutras" I, 19, and 21). The Pure Land is not a place of isolation and simply individual enlightenment, but a place where fellowship and communion with Buddha and the *Bodhisattva*s is realized. Pure Land thought reflects the sociality of the Mahayana ideal of attaining Buddhahood together. The grandeur of their view was inspired by their deep human concern, a concern which emanates from and undergirded the symbolic structure of Shinran's thought.

Despite the idealism embodied in Buddhist and other myths, the form in which they are cast, their role in religious tradition have created problems as to what kind of authority and credibility these myths may have for contemporary culture. Modern people have come to believe that he is emancipated from myth. They criticize myth as "merely myth," by which they mean that the myth is an empty story. In western culture, from the time of Plato onward, myth has tended to have a negative meaning. In modern times Auguste Comte, a French sociologist, argued that with the development of civilization and science, society progresses from myth to metaphysic to science.

The intellectual evolution of humanity has come to be accepted in the west as being an evolution from religion to philosophy to science. Many modern anthropologists have tended to view myth as evidence of a pre-logical mentality, and as representative of the childhood of humanity. It appeared that ancient people and contemporary primitive people live controlled by their myths, while presumably civilized people are guided by reason and science. In Christian tradition there developed opposition between myth and history. Basic concepts were then brought into question. Is the Incarnation myth or history? Is the Resurrection myth or history? Buddhism developed outside the framework of these problems, but it did not long remain uninfluenced by the approach to their solutions once extensive contact with the West and western modes of thought began.

In Japan, such contact initiated similar questions to be faced by the traditional Mahayana Buddhist schools. Were the many Mahayana Sutras which claim to be taught by Sakyamuni (who is an historical person) really taught by him? Scholars began to discuss what is termed Daijo hibusetsuron, which is the theory that Sakyamuni Buddha did not teach the Mahayana sutras as had been traditionally assumed in the use of the opening phrase, "Thus have I heard . . ." (nyozegamon). A problem rose from this discussion. If Sakyamuni Buddha did not teach them, what authority do these sutras have in establishing particular practices as the way to enlightenment over against the way of the Four Noble Truths, the Eightfold Path, etc. which Sakyamuni declares as the way in the earliest days of Buddhism. The issue in this, and the impact of western people's modern scientific preoccupation, was perhaps most clearly stated in the Meiji Era work, "The Historical Buddha and The Eternal Buddha," by Masaharu Anesaki:

" . . . The eternal truth of Buddha cannot result from visionary speculation; ... it must be found in actual history."

Another scholar, Murakami Sensho, in his text, "The Unity of Buddhism," also criticized traditional Buddhism in this vein and wanted all sects to unite with a unified doctrine, while at the same time maintaining a basic Mahayana outlook. Stimulated by the quest for "basic Buddhism," 19th- and early 20th- century Japanese Buddhist scholarship advanced to the level of western studies in their assault on myth and application of historical research. The change in Japanese scholarship, in terms of this quest, did not occur in traditional Buddhist organizations in Japan, nor alter their views and practice to any significant degree.

The practical issue facing Buddhist tradition in this period in Japan was not the same as that occupying the scholars. Rather, traditional Buddhist teachers were concerned with the confrontation with Christianity and Christian missions that political and social westernization patterns brought to Japan after an absence of three hundred years. This confrontation left traditional Buddhist groups generally defensive, and reluctant to change in their views of their own history and doctrines. Among the attempts made to resolve the Japanese Buddhist dilemma between scholarship and faith referred to above was that of Murakami Sensho who declared "The criticism of Mahayana Buddhism is a problem of history, not of doctrine. From the doctrinal point of view, no one should doubt the Mahayana interpretation."

In straddling the fence of his sect connection and his scholarly approach, he concludes that the teachings of Mahayana, while not directly given by the Buddha, were a brilliant development of Buddhist thought. Another scholar, Maeda Eun in his work "An Interpretation of Mahayana History," claimed that the seeds of Mahayana did indeed lay in the teaching of Buddha during his lifetime. Kimura Taiken resolved the apparent conflict by regarding Mahayana as an effort to "revitalize primitive Buddhism from a deeper point of view." Against the background of this problem for Japanese Buddhists during the past century, we can understand Prof. Fujimoto's attempt to depict the basis for the origin of Mahayana Sutras:

"The Mahayana Tripitaka, we might say, is a kind of revised edition of the Hinayana one, for the former can be designated as the fruit of a revival movement rising among the direct disciples of Sakyamuni as well as later ones. It was in primitive Buddhism that the *Sangha* tended to be more stagnant in spite of the transient circumstances, becoming monastic in paying little attention to the lay people, and formalized in clinging to the time worn precepts or ritual."

Dr. D.T. Suzuki, in his essay "The Development of the Pure Land Doctrine in Buddhism," begins by taking note of this:

"If we believe, as we must from the modern critical point of view, that the history of any religious system consists partly, in the exfoliation of the unessential elements, but, chiefly, in the revelation and the constant growth of the most vital spiritual elements which lie hidden in the words of the founder or in his personality, the following question naturally comes up for solution in our investigation of the history of Buddhist dogmatics: 'How much of the Pure Land idea is deducible from the teaching of primitive Buddhism so-called, or from the personality of Sakyamuni Buddha himself?'"

From this perspective, Suzuki attempts to develop a philosophy of religious experience which would lead to such a formulation. After summarizing basic concepts and features of the Pure Land sutras, he concludes:

"Incidentally, let us note here that the idea of scriptural authority in whatever form is no more tenable and therefore that whatever ideas have proved vital, inspiring, and uplifting in the history of religion must find another way of establishing themselves as the ultimate facts of the religious consciousness. Scriptures, Christian and Buddhist, are divine revelations inasmuch as they tally with the deeper experiences of the soul and really help humanity break through the fetters of finitude and open up a vista full of life and light. In other words, authority must come from within and not from without ... This being our standpoint, the Pure Land teaching is to be interpreted, as I said before, in terms of religious consciousness, and not, as is done usually by its orthodox followers, in terms of scriptural authority or special revelation."

These reflections bring us back to the original problem of what stimulates the production of myth, and what established its grasp on religious consciousness as a normative guide or authority over against other similar or competing claims. The focal issue which must be considered is the nature of religious consciousness, and whether it contains sufficient principle within itself to determine religious truth without either analytical reasoning or metaphysical or philosophical reflection.

The structure of the sutras, which presents them as authentic words of Buddha, tends to suggest that there was once an objective basis for regarding the sutras, for although scholars might make qualifications; on the popular level they were given unquestioning reverence. Religion as a control instrument in society required that the ordinary person be encouraged in his belief in the truth of the religion, which in this case meant that Pure Land Buddhists be encouraged to rely on the authority and validity of these three sutras, and their expression of the myth of Amida's Vow.

The impact of the exposure of Japanese scholars to the western analytical viewpoint, and the western tendency to discredit myth and assess everything in terms of verifiable historic research made the views of Suzuki and others who shared his insight into the validity of religious consciousness increasingly significant for our times. Is indeed, religious consciousness merely an illusion as Freud asserts? Is religion itself simply an opiate for the masses as Marx insisted? Both Freud and Marx have become themselves archaic in their views as the twentieth century nears an end.

To the contemporary mind, being religious and being a thinker are sometimes considered contradictory, but if religion is not to be oppressive and exploitive of people, or if it is not merely to be a control mechanism for society, then its foundations in thought and experience must be frankly faced. This is particularly essential if we are to continue to pursue the tradition that Buddhism is a serious quest for truth, and if Shinran's critical attitude and search for truth is to be realized in us. A myth arises from the interaction of a consciousness and the world in such a way that the disparate and multitudinous elements of the world are given some degree of coherency and meaning.

Myths direct themselves to the crucial problems of human existence - value and destiny, tragedy, good and evil. Myths arise from the awareness of human limitations and the apprehension of mystery or uncontrollable power in the world. While myths may not have factual reality as accepted in the day-to-day world, nevertheless they have a reality by virtue of pointing to aspects of human existence which give them more compelling power over the mind than have things in the concrete world. People will die for their pictures or myths of reality more readily than they will die for particular possession of things.

While myths are, on the one hand, products of consciousness and so are never apart from the mind, they point to something beyond the mind and consciousness which is the basis for that mind and consciousness. In the case of Amida and the Pure Land, this myth may have been the product of a consciousness moved by its aspirations and hopes for a higher existence, whereupon the myth asserts the reality of the higher life. This myth is not knowingly a product of its own consciousness. The author did not believe he made it up, but rather that he was the vehicle through which this higher reality was expressed.

In effect, myth leads not only to psychology but to metaphysics or philosophy in order to discover what basis there is in reality for the particular myths which have grasped the consciousness. For Buddhists, and perhaps mainly Pure Land Buddhists who center their religious existence about the symbols of that tradition, there is a necessity to explore more deeply the philosophical implications of the symbol system. It will not be sufficient to invoke the concepts of hoben (expedient means), *Sunyata* (the doctrine of void) or to assess the claim that Amida or the Pure Land exist only in our minds. All these side step of the issue as to why that particular myth should be an authority controlling religious life and action.

At the same time, there is necessity that the Pure Land myth preserves fundamental Buddhist affirmations concerning non-duality and objectivity. If Shinshu is to meet the challenge of the modern world, all these issues must be taken seriously, and particularly the issue of myth and the symbolic structure of shinjin, or the faith that completely entrusts in the true, real and indescribable that the myth reveals. Earlier, we stated that modern man once believed he was emancipated from myth, but recent events have shown that this is not so. We have discovered in our times that people are moved by racial and economic myths (Nazis, KKK, capitalism, and communism), national myths (flag), and myths of science. Humans are myth-making animals and in their myths they enshrine (as in advertising) the values and meanings that integrate their lives.

Myths which ground a culture are rooted in the common experience of that culture. Myths are absorbed by the individual as norms for attitude and action. They have social enforcement in that there are penalties for opposing or otherwise rejecting the group myth. In a sense, in any and every culture, and at any and every time, including our own and perhaps even in most particular our own, one is born to these myths. However, religious myth (apart from those religious myths which are part of the folk culture or have been absorbed into folk culture) has a different relationship, since it is the realization of the truth of the religious myth by the individual which brings the particular group into existence. Religious myth gains its importance from the fact that it expresses what is ultimate for life.

It reveals to the person the unconditional element of existence which places a demand on the person's existence that he take that element upon himself as his ultimate concern. Profound myth calls upon the person to make a commitment, to take a risk in faith. There is an element of judgment and critique in myth which strengthens the inner man, who is thus committed against the forces such as society and culture which would deny his true, concrete existence by merely subordinating him to some larger whole and depriving him of any real or significant possibilities of action. Profound religious myth is therefore liberating, liberating the individual from all forms of subjugating bondage so that, in effect, religious myth enables the person to discover his true self.

In Buddhist history in China, the Confucianists recognized the implications of Buddhist egalitarianism and myths depicting an ideal world. They repeatedly worked for the restraining of Buddhist activity among the masses. The Pure Land persecutions in Japan likewise were based on the realization of so-called "anti-social" aspects of the teaching - such as disrespect and neglect of the gods of the land - which meant to undermine the Kyodotai-communality-social solidarity of that era. The history of religions indicates that myth is ambiguous.

The myth that frees may also subjugate. I think this is what lies behind I-hsuan's statement that the terms Buddha and patriarch are terms of reverence but also bondage. When faith turns into belief, and experience transforms to doctrine and theory, religion becomes the taskmaster and tyrant over the human spirit. Hui-neng in the Platform Sutra remarks that if one practices with the mind, one turns the Lotus, but if one does not practice, the Lotus turns him. The impact of ultimacy in the Buddhist myths of Pure Land has been limited largely because the teaching was regarded simply as a secondary and lesser alternative for reaching enlightenment. It was only a partial way.

The history of the tradition reaching to Shinran was an evolution culminating in his awareness of greater depth and ultimacy in the teaching. Shinshu means that Shinran's Pure Land teaching is not merely one among many alternatives, but must in itself express the greatest depth of meaning and reality; else it could not be "true" in the full sense. The myth of Amida and the Pure Land is thus an essential element in the consideration of Shinran's religious philosophy. It provides the pattern of compassion which is to suffuse our personal existence. It thus requires careful religious and philosophical study, and reflection, as the basis for the symbol structure of Shinshu and as a religious myth whose expression of awareness of one's absolute bondage to the human condition is the very expression that at the same time yields the absolute spiritual freedom that modern man so desperately seeks.

In the centuries around the birth of Christ there was a radical development going on in Buddhism. A new school was born, and its adherents called it Mahayana. How this new school differed from the earlier schools can be found in any history of Buddhism. Here we will concentrate on one of the results of this schism: the term Hinayana. The adherents of the older schools criticized the Mahayanists, especially for creating new sutras, forging the word of the Buddha.

The Mahayanists on the other side reacted to that critique by accusing their opponents of not understanding the teaching of the Buddha at all and for beeing narrowminded egoists. The debate got heated, and accusations flowed from both sides. Then some brilliant person at the Mahayana side of the debate created the word pair Mahayana/Hinayana, and it stuck. They called their opponents Hinayana, and this word worked excellently as an insult - with simplicity and parallellity to Mahayana that any fool could grasp.

Hinayana, or, more correctly, *hina*yana, is a highly derogatory term. It does not simply mean "Lesser vehicle" as one often can see stated. The second element of *hina*-yana -that is yana -means vehicle. But *hina* very seldom has the simple meaning of "lesser" or "small". If that had been the case, the Pali (or Sanskrit) texts would have used it in other connections as an opposite of maha -big. But they don't. The opposite of maha is cuu.la, so this is the normal word for "small". The term Hinayana is an echo of a debate long dead -or rather a debate where the one party is dead and the other one is shouting to the winds.

Who were the opponents who were labeled Hinayana? Theravada? Probably not. At the time when Mahayana was born, Theravada had mainly "immigrated" to Sri Lanka, and could hardly be counted among the dominating schools on the Indian mainland -where the Mahayana/Hinayana debate took place. Theravadins are only sporadically mentioned in Mahayana works. In *Karmasiddhiprakarana* Vasubandhu respectfully calls them "the honorable Tamraparniyas" (Tamraparni was a name for Sri Lanka), and he does not call them "Hinayana". The most influential of the old schools at that time, was Sarvastivada, so they were the most probable -but hardly the only -target for the "Hinayana"-invectives.

Now the Sarvastivada and the other early schools of India at that time are long dead, except Theravada, but the debate and the arguments found their way into the Mahayana sutras, as for instance is apparent from the anti-Hinayana propaganda in the Lotus sutra -and keep echoing in the Mahayana and Vajrayana teaching. Today there is confusion, for the Mahayanists/Vajrayanists use the term Hinayana in three different ways:

1. In the historical sense: Pre-Mahayanist schools are called Hinayana.
2. Modern Theravada is confused with Hinayana.
3. The term Hinayana is used for an internal part of the Mahayana/Vajrayana teaching.

Let's have a closer look on these three usages.

1. Some assert that the word Hinayana as a term for the earlier schools is a usage that belongs to the distant past only. This is not correct. It can be found in several modern reference works, and in more specialist literature it can for instance be found in H.V. Guenther, *Buddhist Philosophy in Theory and Practice,* citing Tibetan works from the 18th and the 20th century.
2. As an example of confusing Hinayana with Theravada, I will quote from the Bibliography of Jane Hope (Jane Hope studied with Chogyam Trungpa Rinpoche.), *Buddha for beginners,* printed in 1995 (I only have the Norwegian version available, so I hope my retranslation back into English will not be too inaccurate): "Hinayana Buddhism. A good introduction to the traditional Hinayana Buddhism is *What the Buddha Taught,* Walpola Rahula ... From a present point of view and written by two Westerners trained in the Theravada tradition, is ... *Seeking the Heart of Wisdom,* by Joseph Goldstein & Jack Kornfield ..."
3. Now for a persistent confusion that has its basis in Tibetan Buddhism. Some say that Hinayana and Mahayana from very early on are two terms used to describe two

different spiritual attitudes, and quote from the 7th chapter ("Loving Kindness and Compassion") of the Tibetan classic *The Jewel Ornament of Liberation* written in the 10th century, where the author, Jé Gampopa refers to Hinayana as "lower capacity" ("theg pa dman pa").

The paragraph reads as follows: "'Clinging to the well-being of mere peace' signifies the lower capacity attitude wherein the longing to transcend suffering is focused on oneself alone. This precludes the cherishing of others and hence there is little development of altruism. When loving kindness and compassion become part of one, there is so much care for other conscious beings that one could not bear to liberate oneself alone. Master Manjushriikiirti has said: 'A Mahayana follower should not be without loving kindness and compassion for even a single moment', and 'It is not anger and hatred but loving kindness and compassion that vouchsafe the welfare of others'."

The footnotes to this passage read as follows: (1) The Tibetan zhi.ba means "peace". It is translated as "mere peace" in this section of the book, since it is used by Gampopa to denote the relatively compassionless peace that results from developing only concentration meditation. (2) Hinayana: "lesser capacity" often translated as "lesser vehicle". The term implies the ability to carry a burden. In this case the burden is oneself since one's commitment is to bring oneself to liberation, not everyone (as is the case in the Mahayana, the "greater capacity").

The problem and confusion here is of course that this analysis does not refer directly to the Pali/Sanskrit word *hinayana,* but to its Tibetan translation "theg pa dman pa". This is a key issue, as will be shown below. The word Hinayana is not Tibetan; it is not Chinese, English or Bantu. It is Pali and Sanskrit. Therefore, the only sensible approach for finding the meaning of the word is to study how the word *hina*yana is used in the Pali and Sanskrit texts.

The second element *Yana* means vehicle. There is no dissent about this. How then "*hina*" is used in the canonical Pali texts? Every Buddhist knows the first recorded sermon of the Buddha, the Dhammacakkappavattanasutta spoken to the five ascets who became the first five bhikkhus. There the Buddha says: "These two extremes, monks, are not to be practised by one who has gone forth from the world. What are the two? That conjoined with the passions and luxury, low (*hina*), coarse, vulgar, ignoble and harmful ..."

Knowing that the sutta style often use strings of synonyms this way, so that they strengthen and define each other, one can regard "coarse, vulgar, ignoble and harmful" as auxiliary definitions of "*hina*" in this case. Here the Buddha clearly denotes the path not to be practised, as *hina*. In other Pali texts and commentaries *hina* often occurs in the combination *hina*-majjhima-paniita, that is: bad - medium - good. In the context of *hina* - majjhima - paniita (or sometimes only *hina* - paniita) the word *hina* is always used as a term for undesirable qualities, like for instance hatred, greed and ignorance. It obviously means "low, undesirable, despicable" -and not "small" or "lesser".

The commentary *Mahaniddesa-Atthakatha*, one of the texts where this triad occurs, defines the word thus: *hina*ttike *hina*ti lamaka (In the *hina*-triad "*hina*" is "lamaka"). Now lamaka is defined by the PTS Dictionary in this way: "insignificant, poor, inferior, bad, sinful. The usual synonym is papa". And *papa* means "bad, evil". So it seems the definitions go from bad to worse here. The commentary then gives examples, and explains that desires that cause rebirth in *niraya* (hell, purgatory) are *hina*.

In *Lalitavistara* we find a version of the Dhammacakka-ppavattanasutta, where the word "*hina*" is used exactly as in the above citation from the Pali-version of that sutta. In *Mahayanasutralankara* by Asanga, which is a very representativ Mahayana text, we find something of interest for our quest. Asanga says: "There are three groups of people: *hina*-madhyama-vishishta ... (bad -medium -excellent)." This expression is parallell to the Pali: *hina*-majjhima-paniita, and goes to show that the Mahayanists who coined the therm "*hina*yana", regarded "*hina*" as a derogatory term, with the same meaning as in the Pali texts.

A very interesting text is an edition of the *Catushparishatsutra* where the text is presented in four parallell columns: Sanskrit, Pali (Mahavagga), Tibetan and a German translation from a

Chinese version. Here, again, we find the Dhammacakkappavattanasutta. We have already looked into the Sanskrit and Pali. The German version from the Chinese says: "Erstens: Gefallen zu finden an und anzunehmen die niedrigen und üblen Sitten der gewöhnliche Personen ..." It is a little unclear wether it here is "niedrigen" (despicable) or "üblen" (evil, bad) that corresponds to "*hina*". But it at least is clear that the strongly negative connotation of "*hina*" was carried over into the Chinese translation. So far nothing had changed from the Pali and Sanskrit meanings.

In the the Tibetan column, we find that the Tibetan word "dman-pa" takes the place corresponding to the Sanskrit "*hina*", matching the above quote from Jé Gampopa. And here we have the cause of later confusions and misunderstandings of the term *Hinayana*. Let us see what Tibetan-English dictionaries say about "dman-pa": Sarat Chandra Das' Dictionary says: "dman-pa: low, in reference to quantity or quality, little". Jäschke's Dictionary is even more enlightening: "dman-pa: low, in reference to quantity, little in reference to quality: indifferent, inferior (Ssk: *hina*)."

It thus seems that the Sanskrit word *hina*, which without any reasonable doubt means "of low quality", came to be translated by the Tibetan word dman-pa, which has the double meaning "low quality" and "low quantity". And the above quote from Jé Gampopa seems to indicate that many Tibetans henceforth read only the latter of those two meanings into it, as "lesser capacity", "lower capacity", so that the meaning was distorted from "low quality" to "low quantity". Thus we see that the confusion arose from the fact that dman-pa has two meanings in Tibetan.

Hinayana originally meaning "vehicle of despicable quality" - thus acquired the new meaning "vehicle of lower capacity". But this is a result of a wrong method. It is of course wrong to project the new Tibetan meaning back onto the Sanskrit/Pali word, and say that "this is the meaning of Hinayana, because this is how the Tibetan masters explain it." What the Tibetan masters explain, is the Tibetan word dman-pa, not the Sanskrit word *hina*?

Therefore it is clear that one can not assert that Hinayana has the "mild" meaning that the Tibetan tradition has given it, via the Tibetan word dman-pa. Hinayana is not Tibetan, it is Sanskrit/Pali, and its harsh, derogatory meaning is unchanged by any attempts of mitigation. What then, is Hinayana? Is it Theravada Buddhism? No, that is both insulting and probably also historically wrong. Is it a spiritual attitude inside the Mahayana and Vajrayana system?

No, that is the Tibetan "theg pa dman pa", the lower capacity attitude, and not the Sanskrit Hinayana, "the inferior vehicle". Therefore, there is no Hinayana. Hinayana is nothing but a myth, although a confused and disruptive one and wise Buddhists ought to lay that word at rest on the shelves of the Museum of Schisms, where it rightly belongs, and find other words to denote those spiritual attitudes that they wish to define.

## THE SIX PLUS TWO

The fifth *skandha*, consciousness, has as its characteristics clarity and knowing. Consciousness is divided into six types corresponding to the six sense faculties. Thus there is eye consciousness, nose consciousness, ear consciousness, tongue consciousness, body consciousness, and mind consciousness. Here we conceive of the mind as a sense faculty because it can recall past events and perceive various mental objects. Through all six types of consciousness, one can know distinctly the nature and characteristics of phenomena. We have the eight consciousnesses: the five sensory consciousnesses of sight, hearing, smelling, tasting, and body sensation; the sixth mental consciousness, the seventh afflicted consciousness, and the eighth *alaya* consciousness. We do not "rest in the consciousnesses" because the consciousnesses are externally oriented.

We don't rest in the sixth mental consciousness, which is thinking mind, engaged in thoughts of the past, present, and future. These six consciousnesses are sometimes present and sometimes not. For example, our eye consciousness will not be present or function when our eyes are closed or it is completely dark. Does this mean that when the consciousnesses are not present, we die or turn into a stone? No, because there is an ongoing sense of the present and a lucid knowing quality of mind. This knowing, or awareness, is the eighth alaya or all-ground consciousness.

Even though the wisdom quality of the eighth consciousness is ongoing and unimpeded, we may not be aware of the emptiness of phenomena. Not realizing this characteristic of phenomena is called the consciousness or namshe aspect of the alaya. This ignorance forms the foundation for the other consciousnesses. However, with meditative training we see that even though there is no entity there, (i.e., when we look for this consciousness, nothing is there), present at the same time is this conscious wakefulness, the wisdom aspect of the eighth consciousness. Our task as a practitioner is not only to rest in the nature of this alaya, but also to be aware of its nature.

Consciousness consists of emotions and irregular thought patterns, all of which taken together form the different fantasy worlds with which we occupy ourselves. These fantasy worlds are referred to in the scriptures as the "six realms." The emotions are the highlights of ego, the generals of ego's army; subconscious thought, daydreams and other thoughts connect one highlight to another. So thoughts form ego's army and are constantly in motion, constantly busy. Our thoughts are neurotic in the sense that they are irregular, changing direction all the time and overlapping one another. We continually jump from one thought to the next, from spiritual thoughts to sexual fantasies to money matters to domestic thoughts and so on.

The whole development of the five *skandhas*-ignorance/form, feeling, impulse/perception, concept and consciousness is an attempt on our part to shield ourselves from the truth of our insubstantiality. The practice of meditation is to see the transparency of this shield. But we cannot immediately start dealing with the basic ignorance itself; that would be like trying to push a wall down all at once. If we want to take this wall down, we must take it down brick by brick; we start with immediately available material, a stepping stone. So the practice of meditation starts with the emotions and thoughts, particularly with the thought process.

## THE SIX REALMS

Those who suffer are the beings of the six realms, which are the six possible ways of experiencing *samsara* (the cycle of rebirth, existence unliberated from suffering). Beings experiencing the hell realms suffer from intense and unremitting heat or cold, and beings experiencing the hungry ghost realm are constantly deprived of food and drink; these beings of the most unfortunate realms must endure their extreme torment for unimaginable lengths of time without actually dying, until the negative karma that brought about such existences is exhausted. In the animal realm, beings suffer particularly from ignorance or stupidity and are unable to relate their suffering to others. Beings existing in the human realm experience a mixture of happiness and sorrow as a result of having accumulated both positive and negative karma.

The sufferings of human beings include: birth, sickness, old age, and death; the suffering of being separated from that which one loves, and of not being separated from that which one hates; and the suffering of not getting what one wants and of getting what one does not want. Beings of the demigod realm are more fortunate, but they suffer because of quarrelling, fighting, and warfare. The most pleasant existence is that of the gods, who do not experience suffering until the last seven days of their lives. Then they see signs that the end of their life of ease is approaching; they are abandoned by their attendants, their magnificent bodies deteriorate and their beautiful complexions fade.

Finally, they foresee the pain of their next rebirth in the lower realms, which they are bound to experience because their positive karma has been used up. Thus, there is no existence in the cycle of *samsara* that is free from suffering. There are six realms because there are six poisons, or defilements of the mind that are the seeds or causes of the experience of the various realms. There are no more than six realms because there are no more than six poisons to act as seeds.

The six poisons are: hatred, or anger, which creates the experience of the hell realm; greed, or miserliness, which creates the hungry ghost realm; ignorance of how to act virtuously is the cause of rebirth in the animal realm; attachment (virtuous action performed with attachment to the meritorious results) is the cause of human rebirth; jealousy (virtuous action sullied by jealousy) causes rebirth in the demigod realm; and pride, or egotism (virtuous action performed with pride) causes a godly rebirth.

The defilements lead to unskillful actions, which generate karma, the infallible operation of cause and effect in the mental continuum of each individual. The negative karma caused by the defilements is the origin of the sufferings of the six realms. The only way to eliminate suffering is to practice the path, method or remedy that will remove the defilements and the negative karma that they produce.

## THE METAPHYSICAL STRUCTURE OF SHINSHU

In interpreting Shinran's thought thus far, we have emphasized his religious experience and its apparent intensity and decisiveness. We have tried to follow its consequences in his altered style of life and transformed religious thought, together with its implications for our own approach to life and daily affairs. We have been theological and abstract in tracing the configurations of his thought, but at the same time we have tried to keep constantly in mind that Shinran's thoughts are eminently practical and can provide a life orientation.

As yet, however, we have said little of the philosophical foundations in Buddhist tradition from which Shinran drew. We did not mean to neglect that aspect. Rather, by placing it at this point in our exploration of Shin Buddhism and the nature and validity of the religious quest in our Mappo era, we wanted to suggest that Shinran had an experience which then sought philosophical understanding. Shinran's religious experience loses intensity and drama when it is considered only as arising from contact with Buddhist teachings for example, from the reading of a sutra or text.

To the contrary, his thought gains in universal importance because it arose from a sensitized awareness of the true nature of man. Shinran did not merely contemplate ideas. Rather, he confronted himself and as a consequence, had to seek a new path. Naturally, all aspects of his involvement in the Buddhism of his day stimulated him and ultimately shaped his understanding. The "Jinenhonisho" to which we will presently refer came from the latest period of his life.

This suggests that his thought constantly took shape in the light of his continuing experience and problems. It is clear from the historical materials we possess that Shinran was not simply a religious pragmatist, unaware of the nature of the ideas that he proposed. His thought evidences a philosophical perspective, and he is particularly rooted in the nondual-voidness philosophy of Buddhism from which he developed an understanding of the concept of Reality that is of great significance both in theory and practice.

In emphasizing the philosophical quality of Shinran's thought we should understand in our day of social and cultural upheaval that unless people develop a philosophical perspective on existence, they will only be buffeted by the forces surging about them, unable to understand or effectively participate. Americans are not a notably philosophical people - they are more pragmatic and interested only in results. They care less for the wider grounds of thought in religion than for the good feeling or consolation that may be gained from it.

In order to catch the flavor of Shinran's philosophical insight and perspective, I would like to focus briefly on the "Jinenhonisho" which he wrote in his 86th or 88th year. Though it is very brief, it is his most philosophical expression. Incisive with understanding, it came from long years of religious reflection. "When we speak of 'Nature' (Jinen), the character Ji means 'naturally' by itself (Onozukara). It is not (the result of) an intention (self assertion or Hakarai) of the devotee.

Nen is a word which means to 'cause to come about' (shikarashimu). *Shikarashimu* (also signifies that it) is not (due to any) effort (Hakarai) of the devotee. Since it is (the result of) the Vow of the Tathagata, we call it Honi i.e., truth. We say of Honi that it 'causes to come about' because it is the Vow of the Tathagata. Since the truth is the Vow of the Tathagata, we say generally that it is not (the result of) the effort of the devotee, and therefore, the power (virtue) of this Dharma is that it 'causes to be'. For the first time, there is nothing to be done by man. This is what we should understand as 'the reason which is beyond reason' (Mugi-no-Gi).

Originally Jinen was a word meaning 'to cause to be.' We say Jinen when the devotee does not consider his goodness or evil, in accordance with the fact that Amida has vowed originally (that salvation was to be attained) not by the efforts of the devotee, but by being embraced and caused to rely on the Namu Amida Butsu (his name). In the Vow which we hear, it is vowed that he will cause us (to attain) the highest Buddhahood. 'Highest Buddhahood' signifies to abide in formlessness. Because we are without form, we say *Jinen* (Nature). When we indicate that there is a form, we do not speak of the highest Nirvana.

We heard and learned for the first time that the one who makes known formlessness is called Amida. Amida is the means by which we are caused to know formlessness. After we understand this principle, we should not constantly discuss Jinen (Nature). If we constantly discuss it, the principle that 'what is beyond reason is reason' is made (to conform to) reason. This is the mystery of Buddha-wisdom." Although scholars have written much about the concept of jinenhoni and have analyzed the text written by Shinran in various ways, there has been little attempt to apply the concept concretely to contemporary life.

As a Buddhist term, the idea was not original with Shinran, but he did open up some new possibilities in interpreting it that are relevant to our present considerations. In terms of the broader context, Shinran defines Nature (Jinen), emphasizing its dynamic aspect in the word shikarashimu, "to cause to be of itself." The term suggests an organic view of Nature as a living reality in contrast to a purely mechanical system as represented either in the system of cause-effect of Buddhism or in the modern scientific system.

Nature, as presented here, brings things into being spontaneously þ that is, of itself þ without intention or cause. It is the ultimate order, because it is not worked upon or affected by anything outside itself. This understanding of Nature contrasts somewhat with the nuance in the traditional Buddhist concept of Tathata, or "suchness." Tathata is more static when it is defined as purity and tranquility. The idea of Nature as the context, basis, and dynamic of man's life in Shinran's thought is supported in modern thought by studies in quantum mechanics and the newly awakened concern with ecology, which deals with the relations of humanity and its total environment.

No small part of this interest arises from the problems of pollution and conservation that civilized people, in their self-assertion against reality, have themselves created. In the ecological relation, human beings are an integral part of the reality of Nature, and all Nature is integral to the life of sentient beings. The spiritual significance of this relationship is to develop an ethic in which people do not impose their will on the balance required to maintain life for all. We must survive, supporting our own existence, but not at the expense of everything else.

The generally objective scheme of Macro-Nature as presented by science assumes a system of cause and effect. In Shinran's thought, the philosophical understanding of Nature is the basis of religious existence. So far as we are a part of that system, we have a fate. When Nature is viewed as external to us, over and against us, it is Nature in its alienated state. In this context, we may feel oppressed by Nature. We may have to struggle against it, and may live with fear and anxiety in reaction to its irrational and erratic activities. Or (and this appears as the modern alternative) we may learn to manipulate it and subordinate it to human purposes, in which case it is we who become alienated.

The Nature that appears in Shinran's thought is the process within which we live and which gives us life. When we subjectively become aware of Nature in its spiritual dimension, we find harmony for our existence and emancipation from the anxieties of finitude in a non-alienated Nature whose being is our being. Though we are not unaware of the erratic and dangerous aspects of Nature, spiritual meaning is drawn from its life-supporting and life-enhancing features. Shinran did not simply consider the process of Nature in and for itself. Rather, we see in the text that he moves to a consideration of the activity of truth, Honi.

He sees a parallel between the spontaneous activity of Nature and the process of deliverance in the Vow of Amida. By relating the process of Nature to Amida's vows, Shinran established the certainty of faith on a firm basis. The working of Amida's Vow, in Shinran's thought, is a mythical statement of the process of Nature. This fundamental insight manifested by Shinran was not derived simply from sacred texts and traditions, but was, perhaps, grounded in tradition in the contemplation of Nature itself and the influence of the doctrine of Primordial Enlightenment of the Tendai sect.

The doctrine of Primordial Enlightenment is without beginning or end. It is based on chapter 16 of the Lotus Sutra, the basic scripture of the Tendai sect which contrasts the Eternal Sakyamuni with the historical Sakyamuni who lived only 80 years. However, the truth cannot be limited to 80 years. The truth must be eternal. Shinran, having studied Tendai thought, reinterpreted the teaching to apply to Amida Buddha whose name means Eternal Life or Infinite Light. In consequence, for Shinran, Amida Buddha became the ground of reality and the source of deliverance. Amida Buddha is also the symbolization of the all-encompassing process of interdependence which sustains our lives. Shinran's understanding of the concepts of self-power and other power in Pure Land teaching has also been shaped by the perspective of Primordial Enlightenment.

As a consequence of the cosmic understanding of Amida, Shinran revealed the unreality of self-power attitudes and transcended the dichotomy of self-power versus Other-power. An implication of his insight is the fact that our very existence in the world becomes itself a testimony to Other-power. Whatever activities we may carry out in the world, are not done solely through ourselves, but there is an order of things that supports and, in a sense, works through us. The dichotomy of self-power and Other-power is a delusion, since our act is our act and is, at the same time, not our act.

Self-power is the expression of alienated being. It is self-contradictory since it proposes to do away with delusion through a delusion. A consequence, then, of Shinran's view of nature is to provide a pervasive deep awareness of cosmic process as the foundation of religious faith. It is most likely that Shinran focused his attention on this term, Jinen-Nature, as a result of his deepened understanding of human nature. He observed that because of his passions and the ignorance and delusion they create, human beings cannot on their own, overcome the fundamental alienation that separates them from reality. This being the case, the source of deliverance must be other than beings as such.

The more sharply Shinran felt this alienation, the more he became aware of the power of reality that strives to overcome the alienation. Here we see dialectic between the perception of imperfection and the perception of absolute compassion and purity to counter that imperfection. Only in knowing ourselves as we truly are can we truly become aware that there is a power in the depth of reality that seeks to liberate us from our ego bondage and delusions. Penetrating that reality, Shinran came to realize that we are in reality, and reality is in us. Deliverance can only be achieved on the basis of an identity between human beings and Buddha.

The reason for this is that perfection could only be achieved by perfection. For beings to be able to become pure, they must have the potential of purity within them. This potential does not reside in the passion and ignorance that constitute experienced human existence. Beyond this there is a dialectic in which our passions and delusion make us think of Buddha as other than and outside ourselves, when in reality he is the ground and essence of our existence. The deliverance of Pure Land Buddhism is in coming to experience this non-duality. Here Shinran took very seriously, as the basis of his theory of salvation, the central Mahayana belief that all beings possess Buddha nature which is realized through faith. As a result of this view, Shinran overcame the tendency to a dualistic approach to Pure Land thought on the popular level.

The Buddhistic understanding of the fundamental identity between beings and Buddha, (ki-ho-ittai) the perception of which is enlightenment or deliverance reveals a keen insight into the problem of alienation. Alienation implies a separation, an estrangement of being. If one assumes the finality of dualism as the basic structure of being in the sense of a chasm between God and humanity as in Christianity then alienation cannot be truly overcome since there is alienation built into reality. It is noticeable in Christian theology, which maintains a discontinuity between God and humanity, that somewhere in the system it is necessary to posit some identity.

Hence, God incarnates; he joins himself to humanity. Paul Tillich attempted to deal with this problem and spoke of God as the ground of being. Thus alienation is not ultimate and is overcome by a return to the prior and primal union with the source of our own being. It was Shinran's heightened self-awareness which led him to perceive the unity necessary to deliverance more deeply - more intensely - so that within the "Jinenhonisho" there is the constant reminder that nothing comes about through man's hakarai, i.e., through his intention, calculation, assertion, or design. Neither Nature nor deliverance depends on us.

This is an important idea since it indicates for Shinran that religion is beyond the legalism of good and evil or human manipulation. Deliverance does not depend on living up to an imposed system of prescribed acts. Also, religion is not to be manipulated for human ambition and desire. Pride, anxiety of imperfection, and self-aggrandizement are all rejected.

Religion is not a tool. Not only does deliverance not depend on human capacities or the lack of them, it does not depend on a person's steadiness or wavering. Amida's Vow achieves its goal without obstruction.

By rooting deliverance in the process of reality itself, Shinran signifies that truth is beyond the mere opinion or constructions of men. Faith is not merely a person's view of things as a belief, but is itself reality, in which the symbol of Amida opens us to the vision of the Real itself. Shinran's emphasis on the transcendental aspects of the process of Nature, which brings things about of itself, reflects the unconditioned aspect of Nature. Unconditional Nature limits man's addiction to theory and words, which lead to disputes. The process is a mystery. When it is once glimpsed, one should not press his words to try to analyze or describe it.

We would suggest also that in "Jinenhonisho," Shinran is showing that faith above all has to do with truth with reality in its deepest dimensions. Since that is its essence, the knowledge and realization of truth brings deliverance. However, one should seek truth before deliverance. Shinran was willing to risk himself in his perception of truth when he indicated that he did not know as a matter of intellectual certainty whether the Nembutsu was the seed for birth in the Pure Land or in Hell. But as Yuienbo tells us in "Tannisho," having grasped a truth that illuminated his life, Shinran would stand by it.

There are many in our day who regards religion simply as a means of becoming happy or satisfied, or of getting peace of mind. Satisfaction, happiness, peace of mind may well result from religion, and Shinran also speaks of joy and peace and tranquility; nevertheless, these results come about only because one believes that one has perceived the truth. If religion is not first and foremost a search for truth and its realization in life, then it is a vain, self-seeking activity. Hence Shinran titles the "Kyogyoshinsho" in its full name "Kenjodoshinjitsu kyogyo shomonrui" (An Anthology which manifests the True Teaching and Practice of the Pure Land [tradition].)

Some interpreters suggest that the view of Nature and deliverance that Shinran sets forth enables the individual to have joy and peace within tragedy and suffering. We may attain an inward freedom in the recognition that what confronts us is itself reality. With faith in the compassionate essence of reality, we may endure with a quiet peace the troubles and turmoil of life and is enabled to take life as it comes and to respond to events positively. If we do not have truth about reality, about man there is no way to establish value and dignity. If human life is understood only within the scheme of life established through modern secular studies and science, there is no indication of the value of human personality and life.

Science has not tended to make us more respectful and aware of the value of existence. Science claims to make no value judgments. The conception of reality offered by Shinran establishes the value of the person, as of all life, in seeing that person as the object of the compassionate aspiration of reality itself. While this view is not itself scientifically demonstrable, nevertheless, it is evidenced as Shinran perceived, through the very way in which Nature supports our life and courses through our being. The meaning of life in this context is that our own being, despite our evils and, indeed, even because of our passion is itself the expression of that compassionate aspiration.

Therefore, in everyday life, in our relations to other beings and persons, we should become for them the realization of that compassionate aspiration. Shinran's religious thought and experience provide basic elements for the construction of a philosophy of existence that is applicable to contemporary problems. Despite the fact that he lived centuries ago, his human experience transcends time and focuses upon the universal problem of man. From within the broad perspective of Buddhist tradition, he offers insight into the fundamental nature of existence and the basis for human action and life in the world upon which all may draw.

# Bibliography

Anacker, Stefan, *Seven Works of Vasubandhu*. Delhi: Motilal Banarsidass, 1984.

Basham, A.L., ed. *Papers of the Date of Kaniska*. Leiden: E.J. Brill, 1968.

Dutt, Nalinaksha, *Aspects of Mahayana Buddhism*. London: Luzac, 1930.

Kalupahana, David, *The Principles of Buddhist Psychology*. Albany: SUNY Press, 1987.

Cleary, Thomas, trans., *The Flower Ornament Scripture*. Boston: Shambala, 1983.

Conze, Edward, *Buddhist Wisdom Books*. London: George Allen & Unwin, 1958 (also New York: Harper & Row, 1972). Contains Diamond-Cutter Sutra and Heart Sutra; translation with commentary.

Eckel, Malcolm David, *To See the Buddha: A Philosopher's Quest for the Meaning of Emptiness*. Princeton: Princeton University Press, 1992.

Garfield, Jay L., *The Fundamental Wisdom of the Middle Way: Nagarjuna's Mulamadhyamakakarika*. New York: Oxford University Press, 1995. Both the translation and the author's notes follow the Gelug interpretation of the text.

Harris, I.C. *The Continuity of Madhyamaka and Yogacara in Indian Mahayana Buddhism*. Leiden: E.J. Brill, 1991.

Huntington, C. W., Jr., *The Emptiness of Emptiness: An Introduction to Early Indian Madhyamika*. Honolulu: University of Hawaii Press, 1989.

Inada, Kenneth K., *Nagarjuna. A Translation of His Mularmadhyamaka- karika with an Introductory Essay.* Tokyo: Hokuseido Press, 1970.

Kalupahana, David J., *Nagarjuna: The Philosophy of the Middle Way.* Albany: SUNY Press, 1986.

Lindtner, Christian, *Master of Wisdom.* Berkeley: Dharma Publishing, 1986.

Kiyota, Minoru, ed., *Mahayana Buddhist Meditation: Theory and Practice.* Honolulu: University Press of Hawaii, 1978 [M].

Pye, Michael. *Skilful Means: A concept in Mahayana Buddhism.* London: Duckworth, 1978.

Nagao, Gadjin, *Madhyamika and Yogacara: A Study of Mahayana Philosophies.* Albany: SUNY Press, 1991.

Napper, Elizabeth, *Dependent-Arising and Emptiness.* Boston: Wisdom Publications, 1989.

Powers, John, trans., *Wisdom of Buddha: The Samdhinirmocana Sutra.* Berkeley: Dharma Publishing, 1994.

Ramanan, K. V., *Nagarjuna's Philosophy as Presented in Maha-Prajnaparamita-Sastra.* Tokyo, 1966; Delhi: Motilal Banarsidass, 1978.

Robinson, Richard H., *Early Madhyamika in India and China.* Madison: University of Wisconsin Press, 1967. Read pp. 21-70.

Ruegg, D.S., and L. Schmithausen, eds. *Earliest Buddhism. Madhyamaka.* Leiden: E.J. Brill, 1990.

Sprung, Mervyn, trans., *Lucid Exposition of the Middle Way.* Boulder, Colo.: Great Eastern, 1980.

Sprung, Mervyn, ed., *The Problem of Two Truths in Buddhism and Vedanta.* Boston: Reidel, 1973.

Stcherbatsky, Theodore, *The Conception of Buddhist Nirvana.* Leningrad: Office of the Academy of Sciences of the U.S.S.R.,1927.

Streng, Frederick J., *Emptiness: A Study in Religious*

*Meaning*. Nashville, Tenn.: Abingdon Press, 1967.

Suzuki, D. T., trans., *Lankavatara Sutra.* London: Kegan Paul, 1932 and 1956.

Williams, Paul, *Mahayana Buddhism: The Doctrinal Foundations.* Routledge & Kegan Paul, 1989.

Williams, Paul. *Altruism and Reality: Studies in the Philosophy of the Bodhicaryavatara.* London: Curzon, 1998.

# Index

## G



## H



## I



## K



## L



## M



## N



## O



## P



## R